IMAGES
of America

LOUISVILLE'S BUTCHERTOWN

I0809003

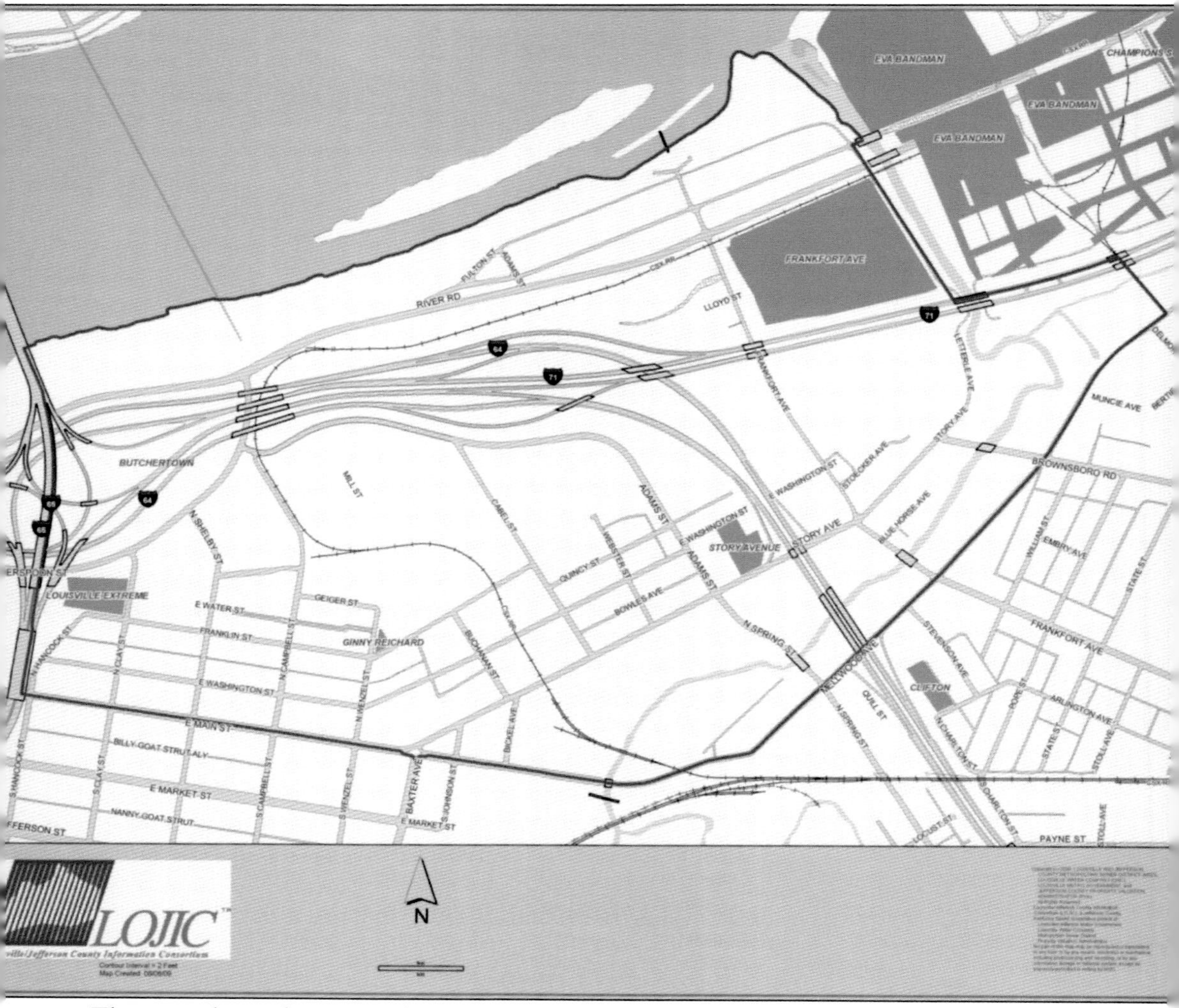

This map shows the current boundaries of the Butchertown neighborhood, with Interstate 65 to the west, Main Street to the south, Mellwood Avenue and Beargrass Creek to the east, and the Ohio River to the north. The area covered by Interstate 71 and parks, formerly the Point neighborhood, was wiped out by flooding in 1937 and 1945. (Courtesy of the Louisville/Jefferson County Information Consortium.)

On the Cover: This picture from the early 1900s shows the Stitzel Distillery located at 1033 Story Avenue, with trucks and wagons hauling slop for animal feed and fertilizer. Frederick Stitzel patented a system of racks to store whiskey barrels on top of one another, which eliminated the pressure that caused them to leak and improved air circulation. This was previously the location of the Union Stockyards, a competitor of the Bourbon House in the 1830s. (Courtesy the University of Louisville Photographic Archives.)

IMAGES *of America*

LOUISVILLE'S BUTCHERTOWN

Edna Kubala

ARCADIA PUBLISHING

ISBN 978-0-7385-6665-8

Published by Arcadia Publishing
Charleston, South Carolina

Printed in the United States of America

Library of Congress Control Number: 2009932221

For all general information contact Arcadia Publishing at:
Telephone 843-853-2070
Fax 843-853-0044
E-mail sales@arcadiapublishing.com
For customer service and orders:
Toll-Free 1-888-313-2665

Visit us on the Internet at www.arcadiapublishing.com

To my husband, Jeremy, and our families

Contents

Foreword

Louisville's Butchertown neighborhood—along the mighty Ohio River just upstream from downtown—has been a key intersection of diverse cultural forces for over 150 years. Early on, farmers driving livestock from the rural hinterlands on a key turnpike met livestock traders, slaughterhouse operators, and farm supply merchants near legendary Story Avenue. Those enterprises were soon supplemented by ancillary industries, like leather processors, brush makers, and candle and tallow works, as well as distilleries, breweries, iron fabricators, and a woolen mill.

German immigrants came to Butchertown attracted by the fact that city and farm met where a major creek provided an open sewer for their slaughterhouses and meat processing plants, while Irish newcomers, joined by African Americans, found work nearby or a short walking distance to a rail yard or maritime operation along the Ohio River. The poorest of the lot picked refuse off adjacent private and city dumps. Some of the homes of that diverse lot survive as handsomely restored Victorians, shotgun bungalows, or apartments above mom-and-pop grocers.

Over many years, rail lines, superhighways, and an earthen levee and concrete floodwall—on Quincy Street the barrier literally runs down the street—have carved up elegantly resilient Butchertown. Today the grande dame wrestles with the odors that continue from a thriving meatpacking operation, feels the abandonment of industrial intrusion that now is underutilized, and ponders a future filled with promise. The renaissance riverbank, waterfront residential, and park space development has quickened the old neighborhood's step, and residents are determined to maintain the integrity of the community.

—Dr. Tom Owen
Archivist and Louisville historian
University of Louisville

Acknowledgments

I would like to thank Carl Lutes, Conrad Selle, Leslie Tichenor, Dale McCall, the Collett brothers, the Kimpflein Family, Ethel Stoke, the Eye Care Institute, Jeannette Barnett, Connie Pratt, Mac and Catherine Willett, Eddie Mattern, Louis Moseson, Mary Sailor, Denise Wizor, Pohl Ironworks, Al Whiter, John Beckman, Rosemary Gatson, Kati Parrish, Vendome Copper and Brass Works, the Jefferson County School System Archives, Third Lutheran Church, Grace Immanuel United Church of Christ, St. Joseph's Catholic Church, and the University of Louisville Photographic Archives. Special thanks to Carl Lutes, Jim Segrest, and Tom Owen for taking the time to look through my rough draft, and to my husband Jeremy for reading over it again and again and again.

Images identified with the following: Name—NRHP (National Register of Historic Places) signify pictures made for the Butchertown Historic District application, a joint effort by the Louisville Landmarks Commission and Kentucky Heritage Council. A special thanks to Martin Perry at the Kentucky Heritage Council for letting us stay a little late scanning images on a Friday afternoon.

Introduction

Named for the butchers who developed their trade along the banks of Beargrass Creek, the area now known as Butchertown was settled by predominately German immigrants in the early 1800s and was eventually annexed by the City of Louisville in 1827.

Although a relatively large city for its time, Louisville was home to just 12 butchers in 1832; only two were located east of Main Street. With butchering banned in the city center and an increase in experienced butchers emigrating from Germany, the trade was predominately established to the east to take advantage of three features of the area: first pick of livestock arriving along the Shelbyville Turnpike; Beargrass Creek as a convenient backyard waste disposal; and, nearby, eager buyers awaiting a fresh final product in the city. While deriving its namesake from butchers, other industries, such as cooperages, Louisville's largest woolen mill, breweries, inns, tanneries, candle makers, and soap-making factories began to emerge to support the rapid growth brought about by the burgeoning meat business and the end of Civil War.

Due to the popularity of butchering, one of Butchertown's largest and most famous landmarks is the Bourbon Stockyards. Located on Story Avenue, an extension of Louisville's Main Street, the Bourbon House was built in 1834 to house farmers and drovers when they came into town. The enclosed pens in the rear became the site of informal buying and selling. With the completion of the Louisville, Cincinnati and Lexington Railway in 1851, driving livestock along turnpikes from the bluegrass was rendered obsolete, and so the construction of the Bourbon Stockyards occurred in close proximity to the railroad. In 1869, the large Bourbon Stockyards were completed.

With its mix of industries, Butchertown thrived on diversity until the dawn of the 20th century. When cars quickly replaced horse-drawn carriages, harness and wagon shops, blacksmiths, and feed merchants were no longer needed. The many local butchers who operated small shops gave way to a few large meatpacking establishments. The small family grocery and hardware stores could no longer compete with bigger stores, and the many corner stores of Butchertown disappeared.

Most of the streets in Butchertown were named for former property owners and prominent members of society during the early 1800s. The main thoroughfare of Butchertown, Story Avenue, was named after John Story, a resident since 1874 and carpenter and builder of stockyards; Washington Street was named after the first U.S. president, George Washington; Quincy and Adams Streets were named after the sixth U.S. president, John Quincy Adams; Buchanan Street first appears on a deed in 1844 and is attributed to property owner George Buchanan; River Road was originally named Van Buren Street after the eighth U.S. president, Martin Van Buren; Cabel Street is presumed to have been named for Senator Cabel, who introduced an act in December 1776 that created the county of Kentucky; Franklin Street was named after the eminent statesmen Benjamin Franklin; Campbell Street was named after local property owner John Campbell; Mellwood Avenue was formerly known as Reservoir Avenue because it ran to the first reservoir of the Louisville Water Company, now the site of the Veterans Hospital, but by 1907, it was renamed Mellwood Avenue in honor of the Mellwood Distillery; Shelbyville Turnpike was renamed Frankfort Avenue in honor of the new state capital; Ohio Street was previously known as Pork House Alley but renamed in honor of the Ohio River; Pocahontas Street might have been a Native American footpath and thus named in honor of John Smith's heroine; Maiden Lane, supposedly named after Maiden Lane in New York and now a portion of East Washington Street, ran between Adams Street and Ohio Street and was the entrance to slaughterhouses behind residences on the north side of Story Avenue.

Butchertown is not known for its architecturally opulent homes but for the integrity of building methods and neighborhood fabric. From the very beginning, Butchertown was a mixed-use neighborhood. Not only did residences and businesses coexist, but there were widely varying socioeconomic conditions as well. Wealthy business owners lived and worked next to families of limited means. Until the 1890s, people of different races and various citizenships lived in the same neighborhood.

While the majority of homes in Butchertown are plain structures, through the years, owners have added architectural details, increasing the character of their homes. Many homes have limestone lintels over windows and doors or Italianate window hoods that add distinction to facades.

Any book on Butchertown would be remiss not to mention devastating floods and the Point neighborhood. Because of its low-lying location close to the river, Butchertown and the Point have always been prone to flooding. Major flooding occurred in 1884, 1907, 1913, 1937, 1945, 1963, 1965, and 1997.

The Point neighborhood was the name given to the strip of land between the old mouth of Beargrass Creek near Third Street and the Ohio River, and it stuck even after the creek was rerouted. In the early 1800s, wealthy families built mansions on Fulton Street—known as "Frenchman's Row" for the many New Orleans families residing there—to escape the confines of the city. John James Audubon attended a Fourth of July celebration on the Point in 1809. Within a few years, the city had expanded around this formerly secluded area, and shotgun homes were built to house laborers of nearby sawmills and industries. Some residents of the Point were called river rats because they lived in shanty boats.

The Point neighborhood was largely swept away by flooding in 1937 and 1945. The City of Louisville bought the land to redevelop it into a city park, and portions of it were used for Interstates 71 and 64. Work is underway to make the Big Four Bridge into a pedestrian and cycling route across the Ohio River to Indiana. Of the grand homes on Fulton Street facing the river, only one—the Paget House—remains. It is one of the oldest homes in Louisville and has been almost completely submerged in several floods.

By the 1960s, about 50 percent of the housing in Butchertown was replaced by industrial and commercial use or demolished. The construction of the flood wall and Interstates 64, 65, and 71 also impacted the neighborhood, particularly Interstate 64, as it split the neighborhood in two.

One

BUTCHERTOWN

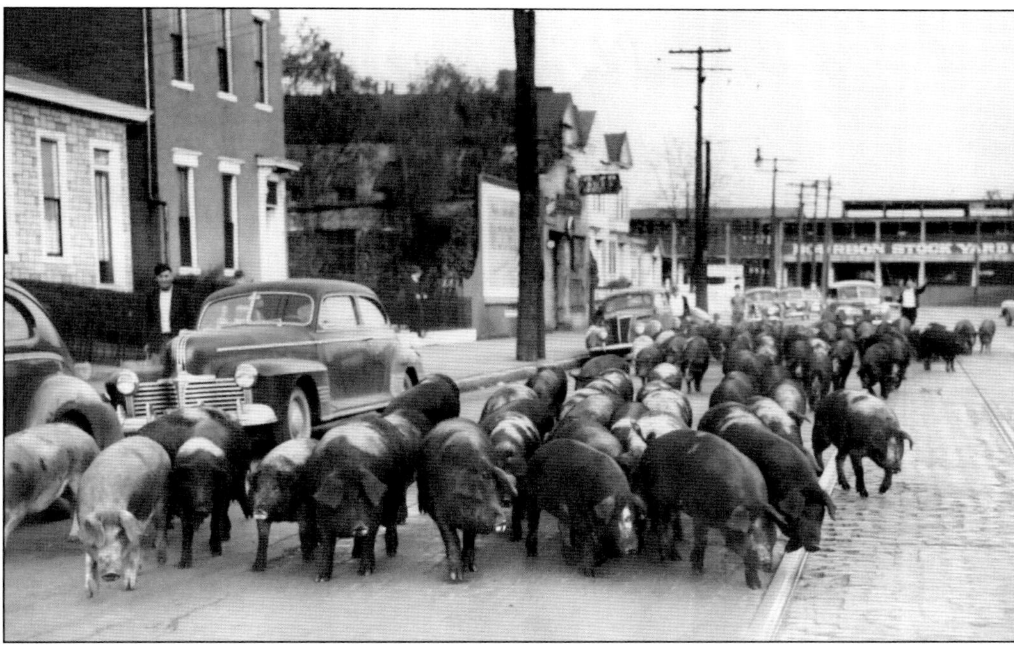

Hogs driven through the streets of Butchertown to the Bourbon Stockyards used to be a normal sight, and the iron fences along the street served as a barrier to keep any unwanted bovine guests out of residents' yards. Notice the trolley tracks in the bricked streets and the many homes along Market Street. The Bourbon Stockyards held its last auction in 1999 and was replaced by the Home of the Innocents campus. (Courtesy of the *Courier-Journal*.)

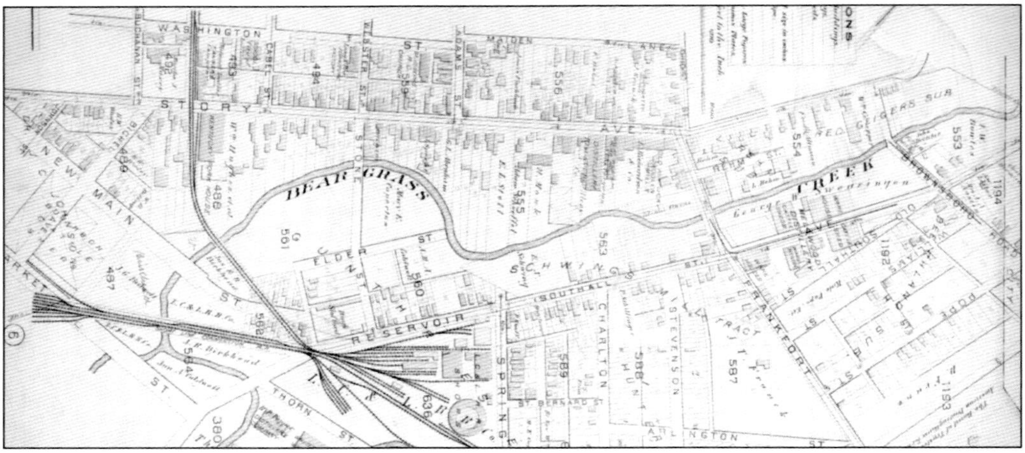

The so-called "boss butchers" built brick homes along Story Avenue and operated slaughterhouses in back along Beargrass Creek, disposing waste in the waterway. Possibly as a result of the waste ending up in downtown Louisville near Third Street (the old mouth of Beargrass Creek), the creek was rerouted in 1854 to empty farther east. Stagnant water in the disused waterway gave it the name Black Creek for the putrid odor and mosquitoes until it was eventually filled in. In 1881, railroad tracks were laid on the filled-in channel, crossing at Pocahontas Street on Washington Street. (Courtesy of the University of Louisville Archives.)

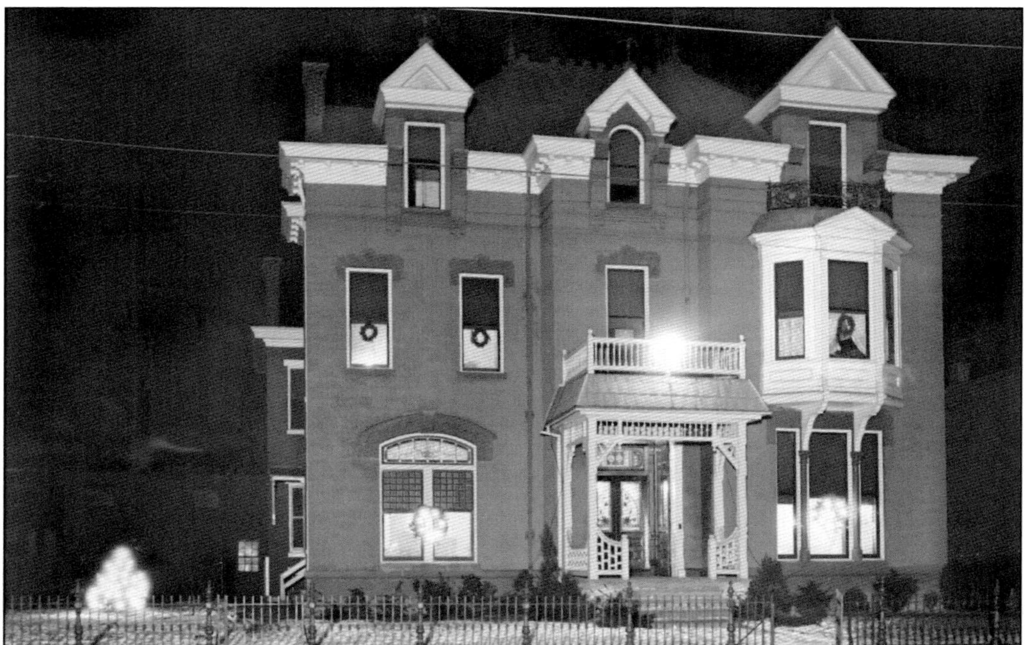

This mansion was built by Gottlieb Layer in 1889 and was located at 1516 Story Avenue. Layer was a meatpacker in the 1860s and later became one of the first park commissioners in the city of Louisville. This brick structure was reputed to have beautiful woodcarvings throughout and mirrors with flower and bird etchings above the fireplaces. In the rear was the Layer butchering and meatpacking business. This building was torn down in 1965. (Courtesy of the University of Louisville Photographic Archives.)

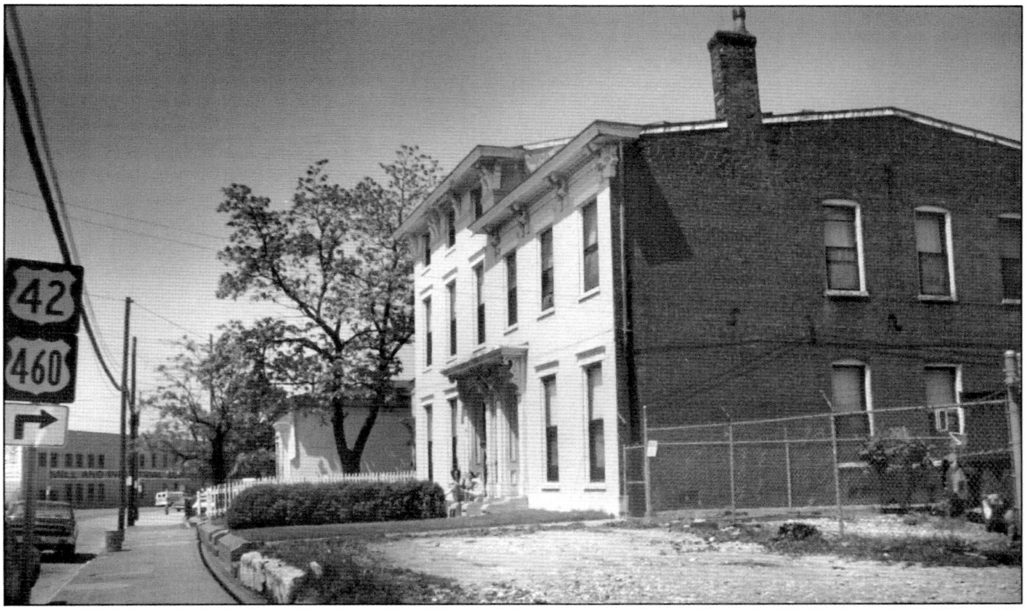

Nicknamed Cattle Baron Road for the livestock driven down the Frankfort and Shelbyville Turnpikes, Story Avenue was the main eastern entrance to the city of Louisville. The home of John Story, for whom Story Avenue was named, was built in the 1000 block of Story Avenue. He was an early resident of the neighborhood and a carpenter and builder of pork houses. (Courtesy of Mark Thompson, NRHP.)

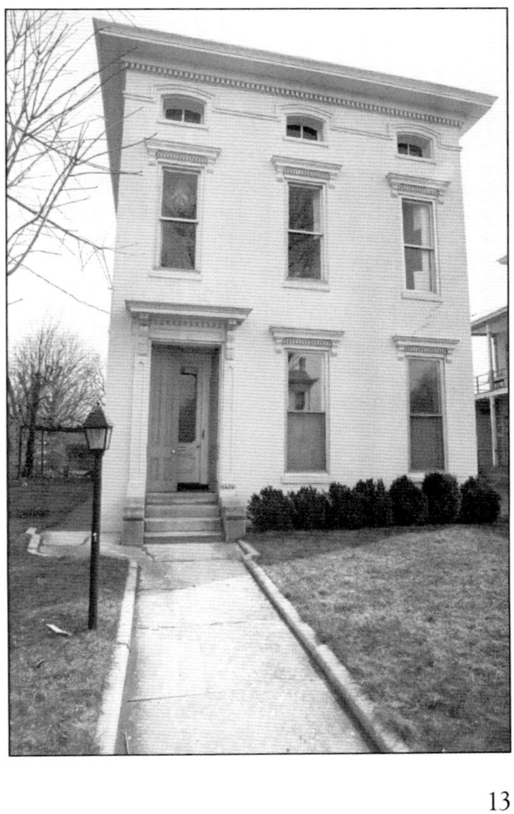

Formerly the home of butcher G. P. Conrad, this stately house at 1638 Story Avenue was the home of George and Mary Alice Hadley in the 1950s. While not the most romantic of professions, being a butcher did have its benefits. In a letter to John Cullinane in 1976, Louis Hebel wrote, "I was told by my grandmother that the reason that Butchertown did not suffer during the Bloody Monday Riots in 1855, as did sections of Louisville, was that the slaughterhouse butchers went out armed with their knives to meet the mob. The rioters wisely desisted and did not force the issue." (Courtesy of John Beckman.)

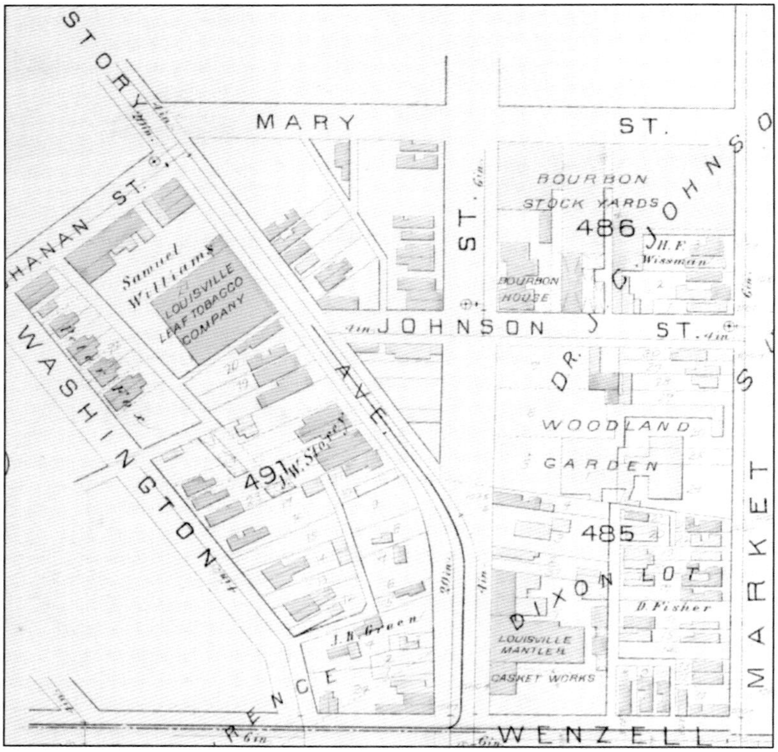

This 1884 map shows the Bourbon Stockyards at 1048 East Main Street and Woodland Gardens between East Main Street and Market Street. Woodland Gardens was a well-known recreation area, with trees, music, and beer gardens for the families of Butchertown. Related beer drinking—including on Sundays—was a popular pastime of German immigrants but drew the ire of many churchgoers. (Courtesy of the University of Louisville Archives.)

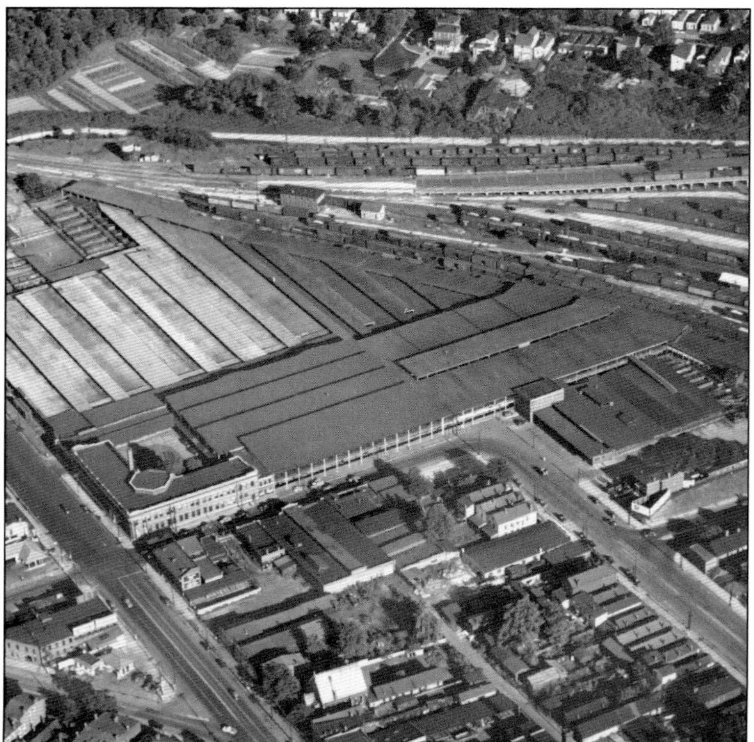

An aerial image from about 1960 of the sprawling Bourbon Stockyards shows the many cattle sheds hidden behind the main entrance. The rail lines that transported feed and livestock can be seen in the rear of the grounds. The Stock Yards Bank and Trust Company was established across from the stockyards in 1904 to serve farmers selling their livestock. (Courtesy of the University of Louisville Photographic Archives.)

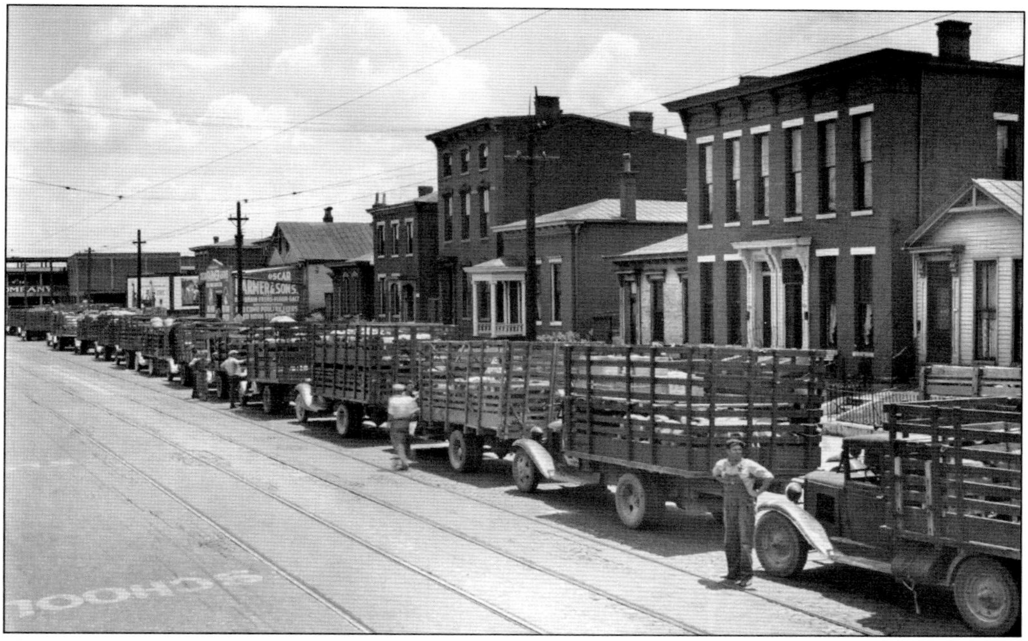

Shown is an early morning on Market Street, with farmers preparing to sell livestock at the nearby stockyards, a common sight until it closed in 1999. The Bourbon Stockyards Exchange building was designed by D. X. Murphy in 1914 and is one of a handful of Louisville buildings that feature Beaux-Arts details in terra-cotta. (Courtesy of the University of Louisville Photographic Archives.)

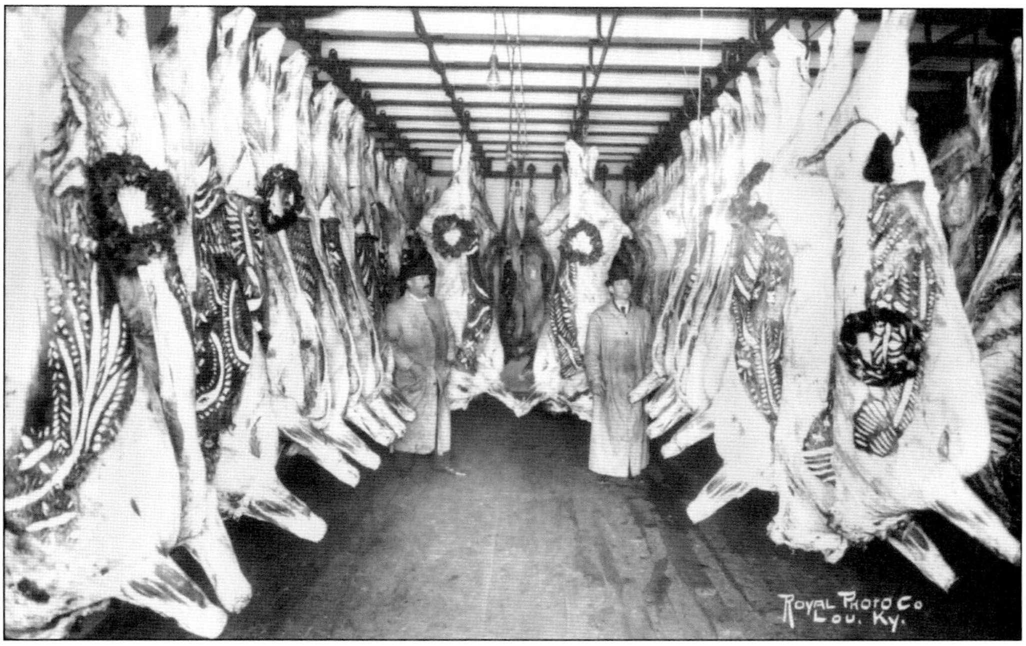

Workers in the Louis Bornwasser plant, located at 921–929 Geiger Street, stand among cattle carcasses in the freezer section before processing. The longest strike in Kentucky labor history was from 1912 to 1924, when Local 227 led a strike against the Bornwasser Meatpacking Plant. (Courtesy of the University of Louisville Photographic Archives.)

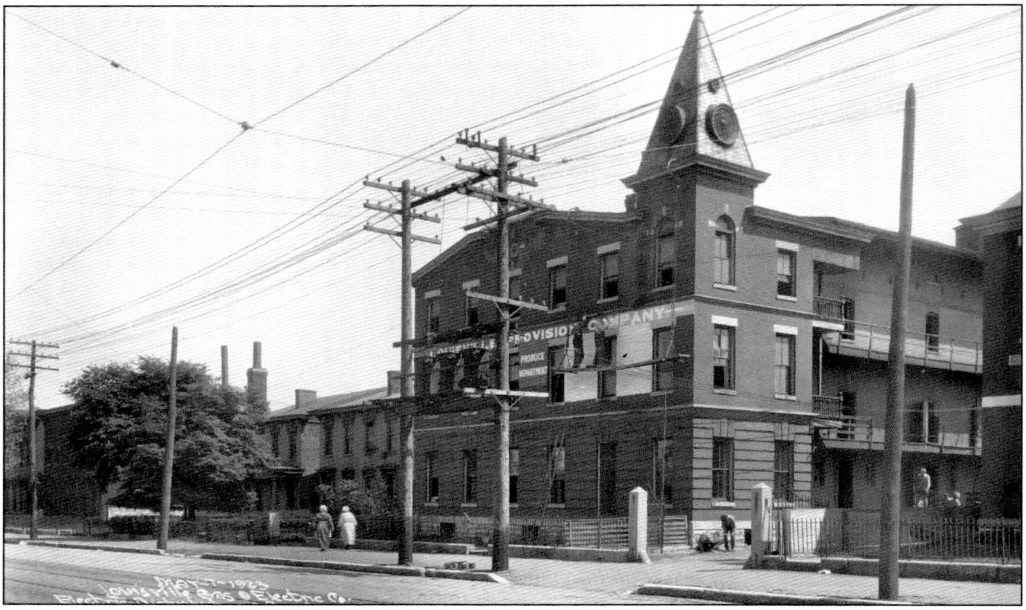

Louisville Provision Company, located on Main Street between Campbell and Wenzel Streets, is seen here in 1923. It was one of many large meatpacking operations that employed residents in the area. With rapid innovations in refrigeration and packaging, meatpacking became more mechanized, and gradually, independent butchers began to decline in number. (Courtesy of the University of Louisville Photographic Archives.)

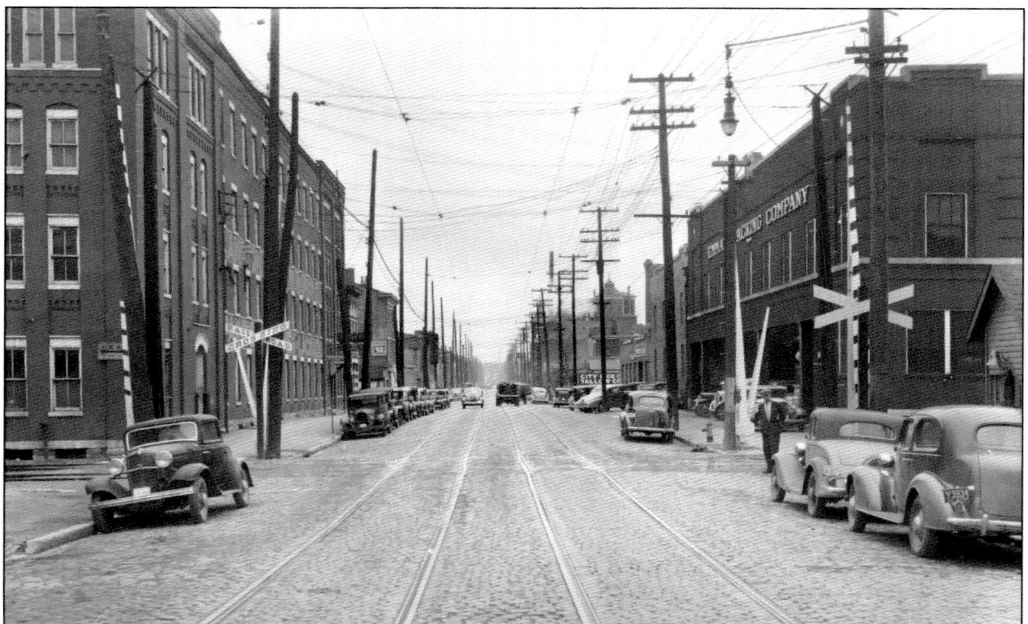

Emmarts Packing Company, located at 1200 Story Avenue, is seen in 1937. This property has long been utilized for meatpacking operations, with the Armour Meatpacking Company, the Taggart Company, the Cuddahy Packing Company, and the Louisville Packing Company all located here at points in time. (Courtesy of the University of Louisville Photographic Archives.)

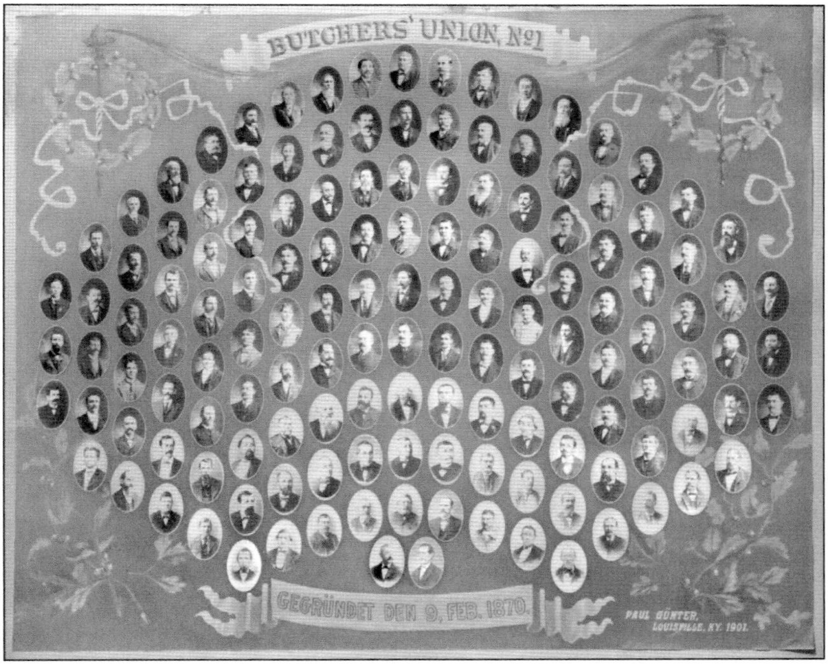

Louisville meatpacking has a long history of unions. In 1870, the Butchers Union No. 1 was organized. In 1902, the Local 227 union, still in existence, organized and carried out strikes to leverage better wages and working conditions in meatpacking plants. The image below shows the 1993 strike against Fischer's Meatpacking Plant, formerly located at 1862 Mellwood Avenue. Strikers were so effective that the union was eventually forced to make a video telling consumers that the strike was over and they should buy Fischer's Meat products again. (Both, courtesy of UFCW Local 227)

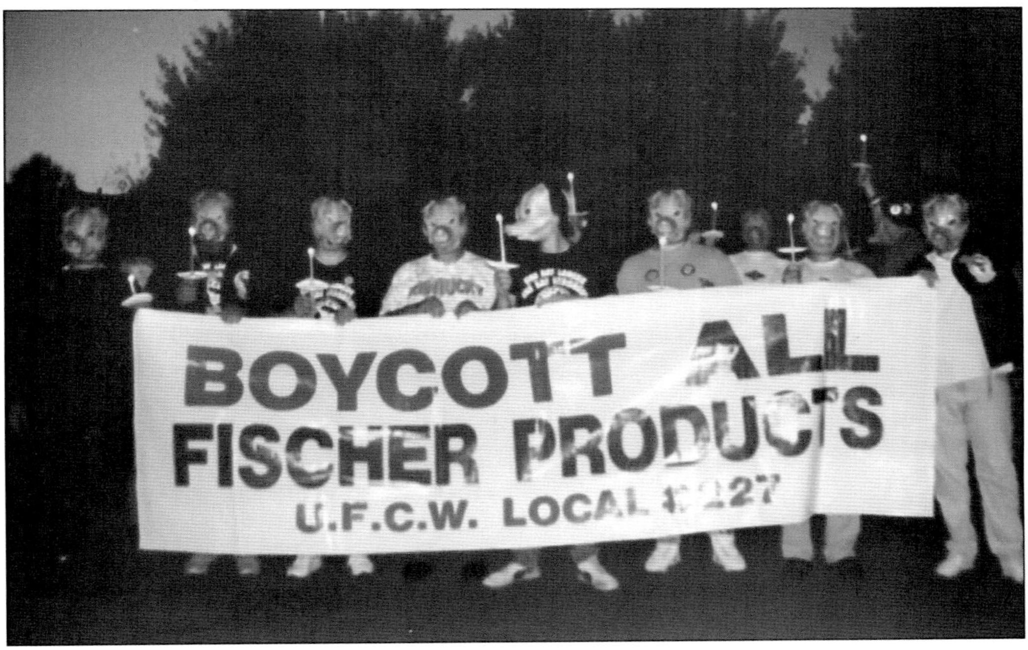

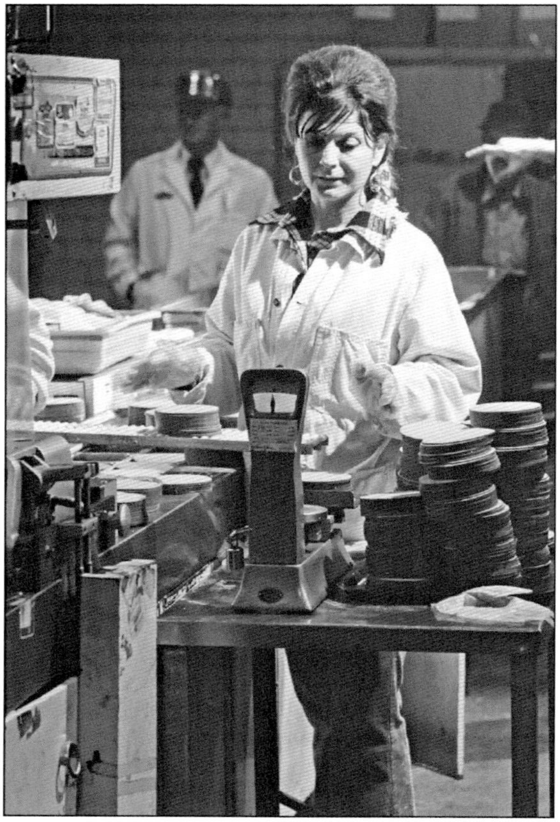

These images show the inside of the former Armour Meatpacking Company plant at 1200 Story Avenue in 1977. Workers weighed and packaged sliced meat and hung salami to cure dry in storage areas. Improved packaging allowed longer storage times for meats and less frequent store trips by the public. (Both, courtesy of John Beckman.)

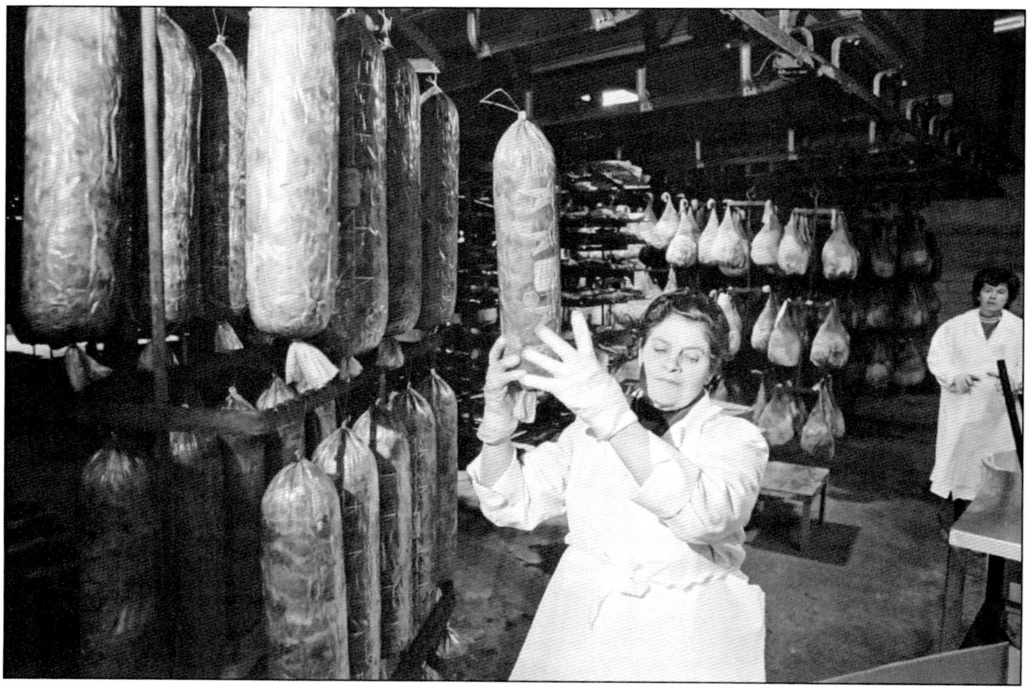

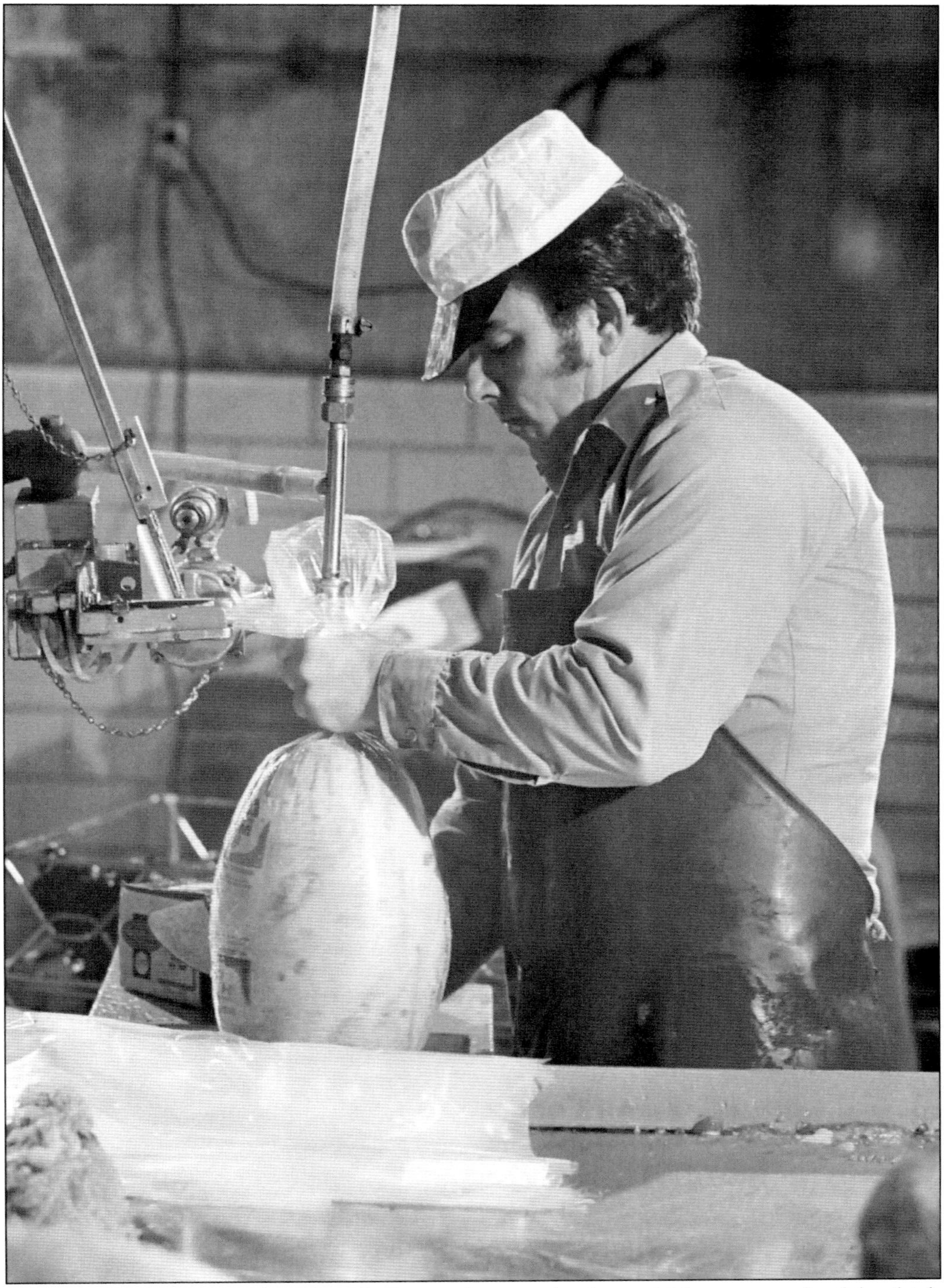

A worker is seen sealing a large ham before sending it to be shipped. Hams are made of the thigh and rump of pork and are generally cured by adding salt, sugar, and other preservatives to prevent spoilage. Ham used to be cured with large amounts of salt and cured in smokehouses or cool, dry storage areas. (Courtesy of John Beckman.)

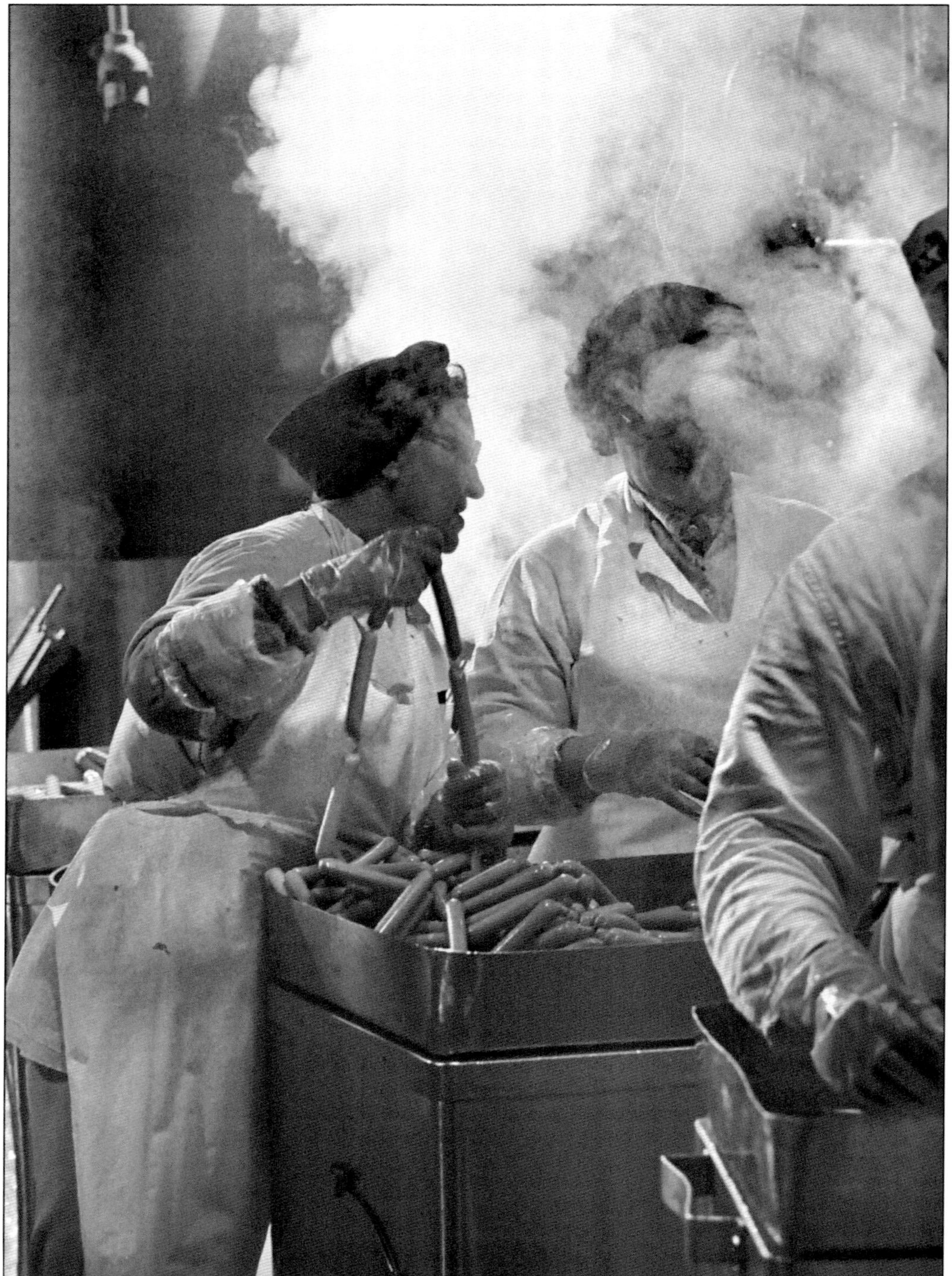

With mechanization and automation, modern meatpacking is a far cry from its humble beginnings, when butchers sold their wares from pushcarts, and a poor family could buy a bushel basket of soup meat and bones for 10¢. In the old days, butchers created a signature product for their meat shop, using their own blend of spices, curing style, and meats. (Courtesy of John Beckman.)

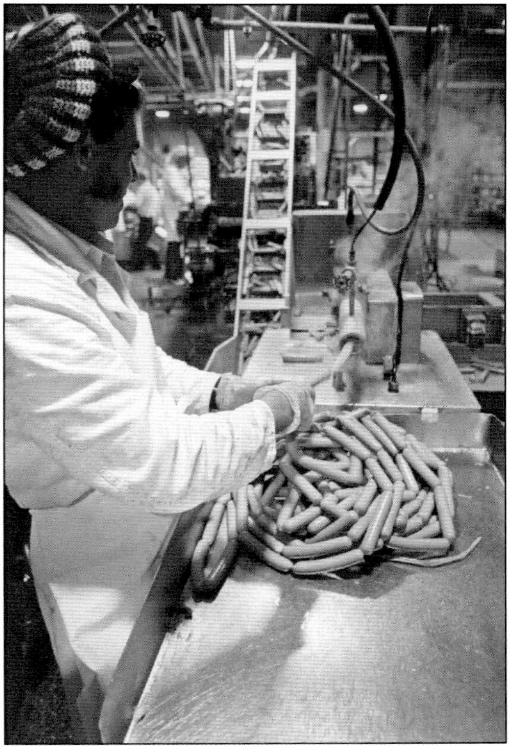

A worker is cleaning the production area. Hot dogs became immensely popular to both consumers and producers. Producers had a use for previously discarded small bits of meat that could be ground into a filling and packaged into easily transportable hot dogs. Consumers enjoyed the simple, precooked food that is still popular at baseball games and summer grill outs. (Both, courtesy of John Beckman.)

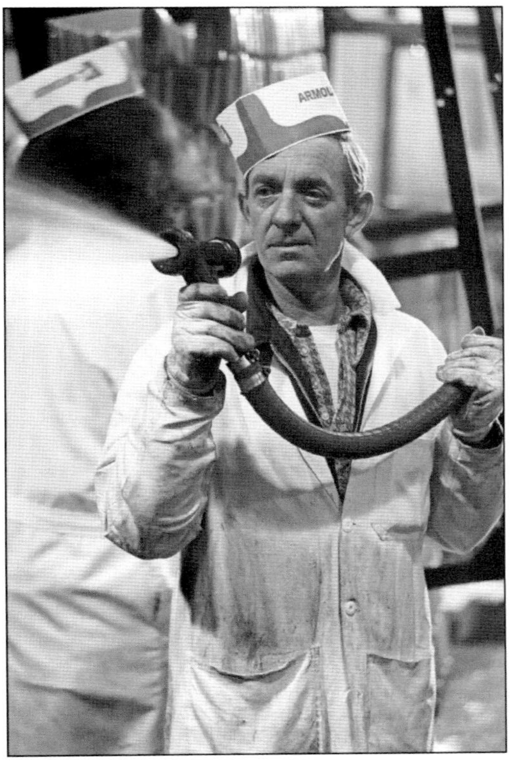

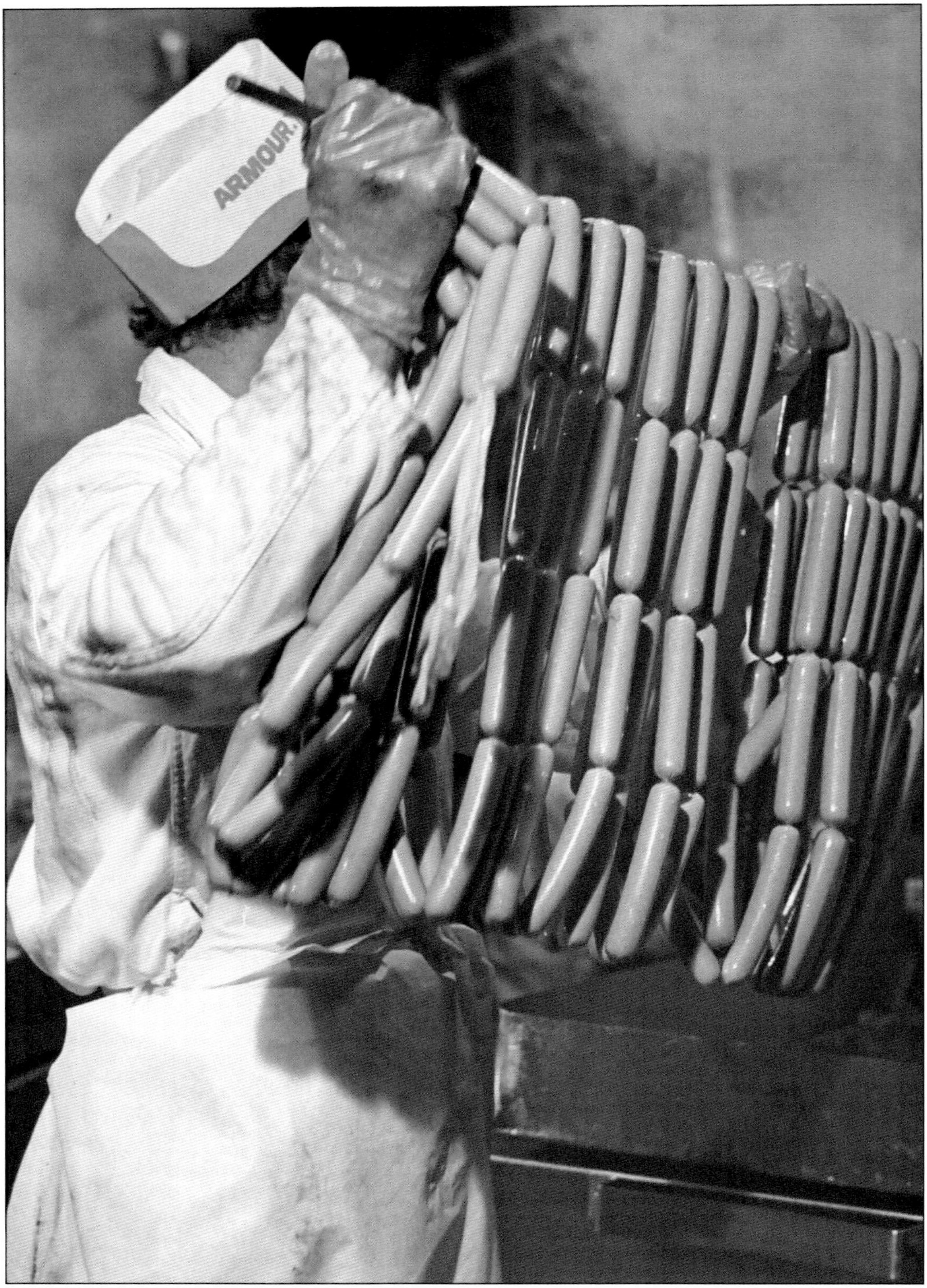

When advances in technology allowed for faster processing, longer storage, and wider distribution, many of the area's butcher barons ceded to the new conglomerates. (Courtesy of John Beckman.)

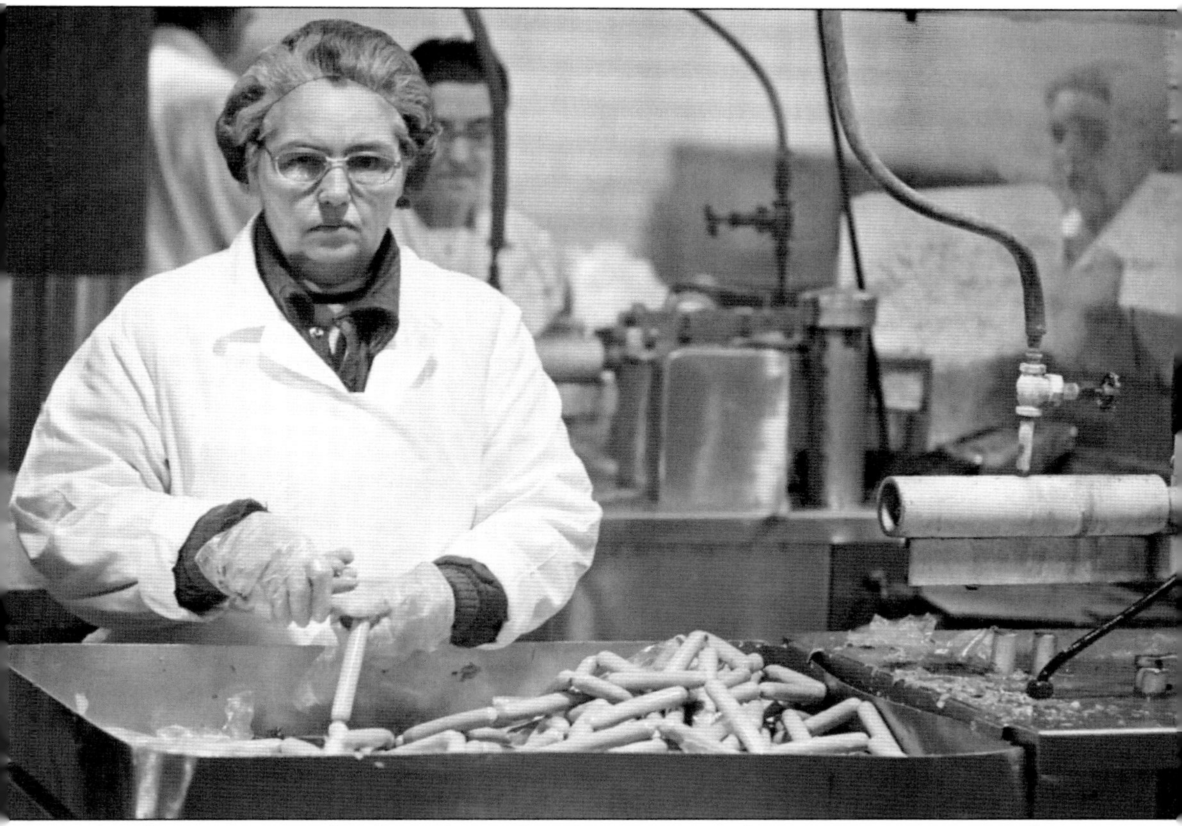

After the meat mixture has been chopped to the proper smooth consistency, it is pumped into casings. The casings are then twisted, as shown, to create a long, linked strand of equally sized hot dogs. These are hung up and cooked. (Courtesy of John Beckman.)

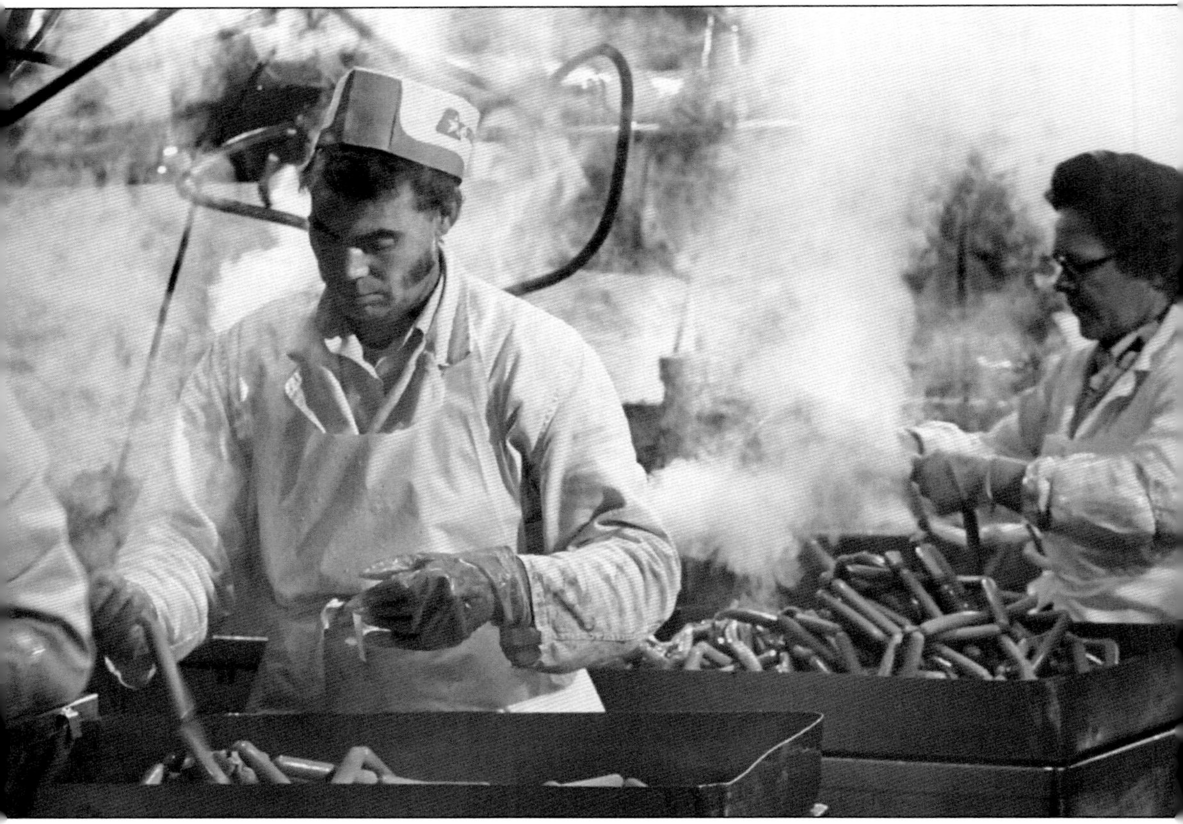

After the hot dog product is cooked, it is sent through cool water, and the hot dogs are separated. After the casing is removed, it is packaged and vacuum sealed before being sent to stores. (Courtesy of John Beckman.)

Two

BUSINESS

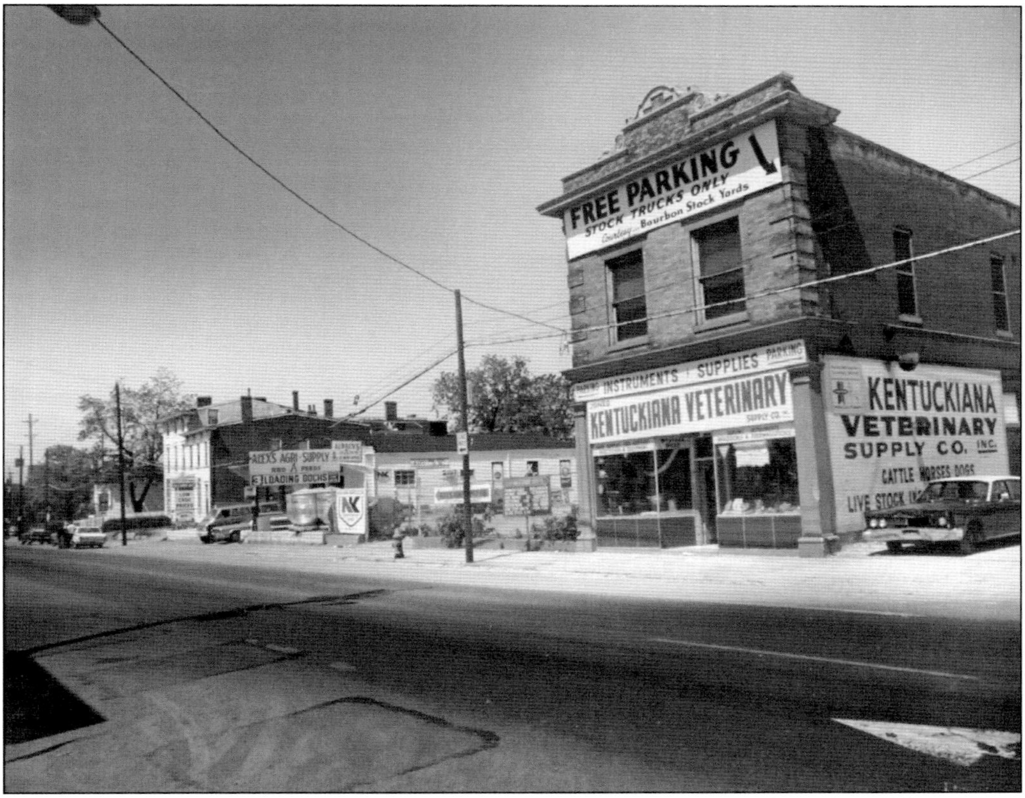

The mix of farmers, buyers, producers, and suppliers supported a number of small businesses. Farmers came with livestock and, after buying and trading, left with farm supplies, such as seed, fertilizer, and farm machinery, for the next year. Producers took by-products from the meatpacking process, such as lard and hides, to create soap, candles, and leather. This is the 1000 block of Story Avenue looking west, showing the ancillary industries that grew up around the stockyards. This store is now located on Mellwood Avenue across from the stockyards entrance. (Courtesy of Mark Thompson, NRHP.)

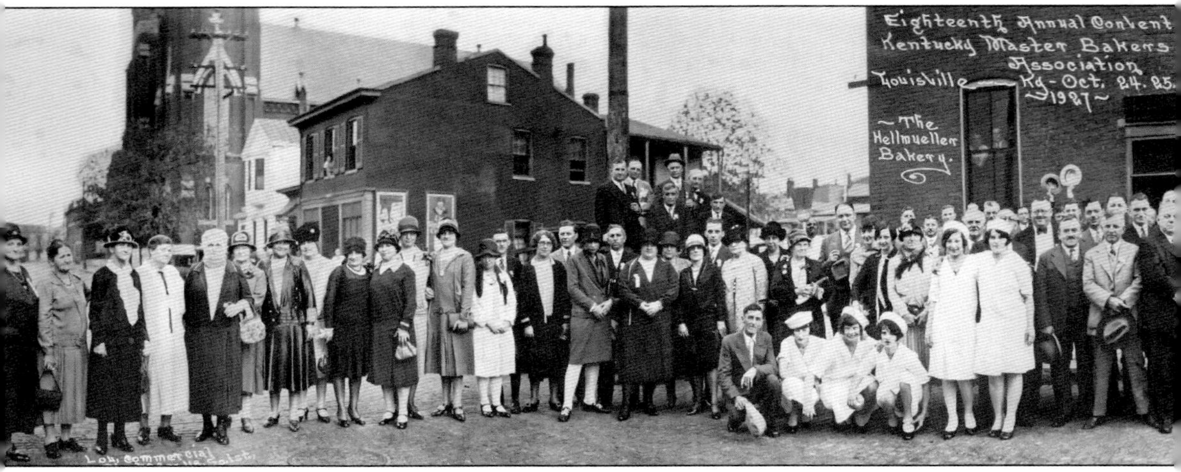

This 1927 picture shows the Kentucky Master Bakers Association at the then-named Hellmueller Baking Company located at 1324 East Washington Street. Irene Zehnder Bensing worked at the bakery and is on the right in front of the first left window, dressed in white. Built in 1870, the building has housed the O'Brian Tobacco Company, the Louisville Silvering and Beveling Company, and the Hellmueller Baking Company from 1926 to 1965. It is now Bakery Square, containing offices and shops. Many Butchertown residents have fond memories of getting a basket

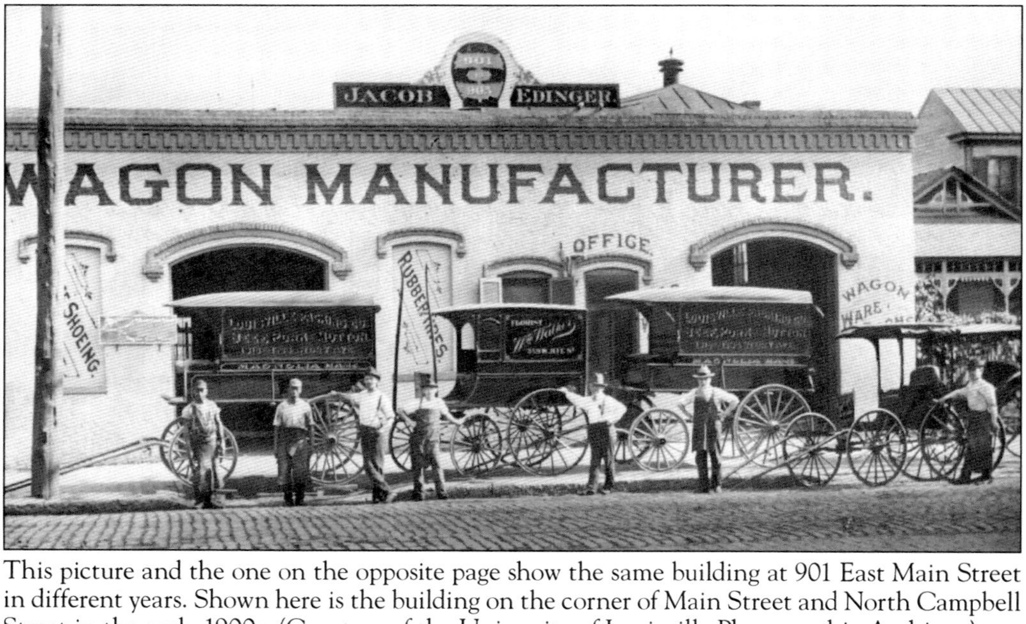

This picture and the one on the opposite page show the same building at 901 East Main Street in different years. Shown here is the building on the corner of Main Street and North Campbell Street in the early 1900s. (Courtesy of the University of Louisville Photographic Archives.)

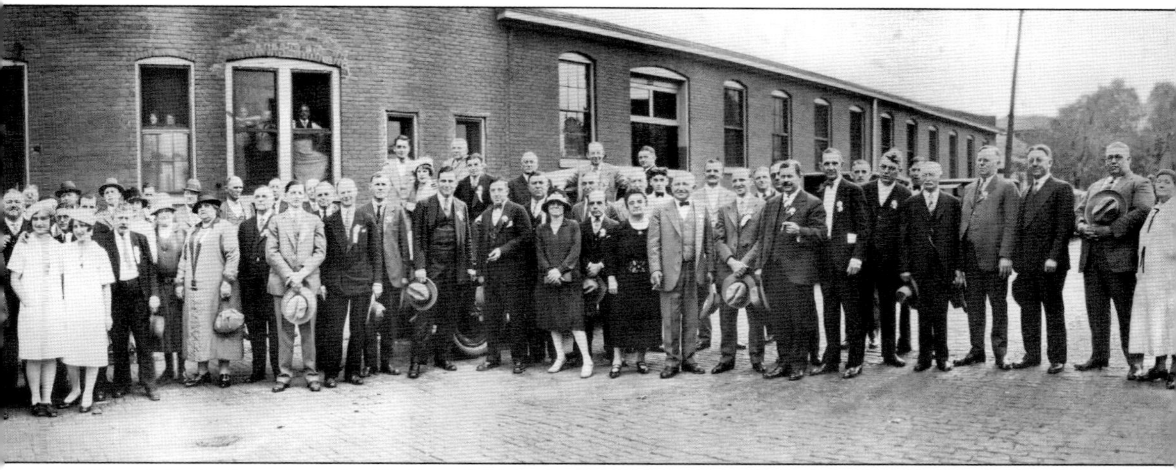

of day-old baked goods at the Hellmueller's bakery for 25¢ during the 1930s and 1940s. The basket might have contained donuts, bread, and cinnamon or apple kuchen. Many families stretched tight grocery budgets with these baked goods. During the 1937 flood, the building's first floor area was completely submerged and heavily damaged. Neighborhood families arrived by boat and took refuge in the second and third floors until flooding subsided. (Courtesy of Denise Wizor.)

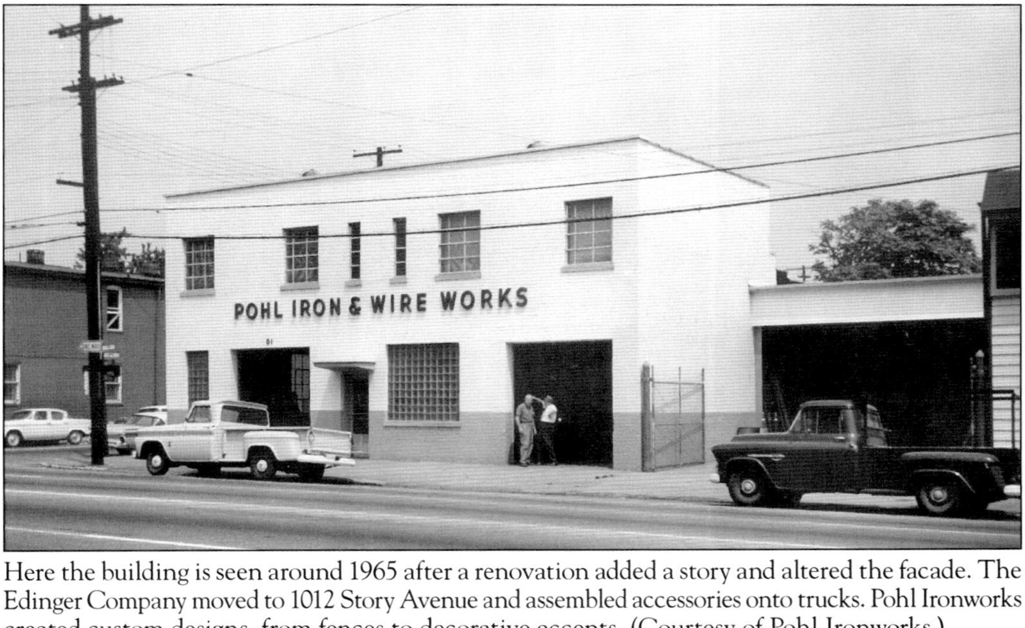

Here the building is seen around 1965 after a renovation added a story and altered the facade. The Edinger Company moved to 1012 Story Avenue and assembled accessories onto trucks. Pohl Ironworks created custom designs, from fences to decorative accents. (Courtesy of Pohl Ironworks.)

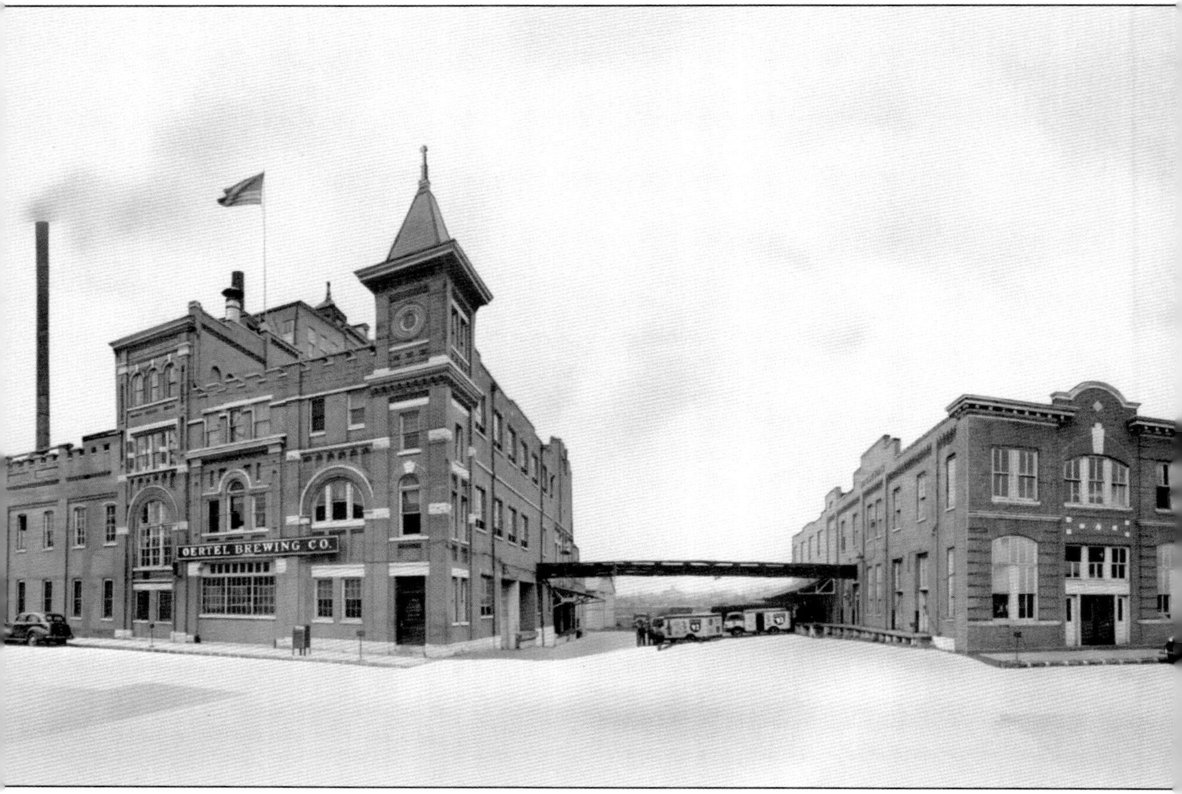

Butchertown was home to Oertel's 92 Brewery, first established as the Butchertown Brewery in 1865 by Franz Rettig. It was located at 1400 Story Avenue until it closed on December 1, 1967. After the death of Charles Hartmetz, John F. Oertel established a partnership with Hartmetz's widow, Magdalena Hartmetz, and eventually bought out her portion of the brewery in 1892. In 1903, a new brewery was built, but a fire burned it to the ground in 1908. Beer was temporarily brewed at the Phoenix Brewery until the building could be reconstructed. After the death of Oertel in 1929, his son succeeded him as president of Oertel's brewery until his death in 1961. In 1964, the Brown-Foreman Distillers Corporation bought the brewery but was unable to revive the lagging beer company, so in 1967 it was sold off. (Courtesy of the University of Louisville Photographic Archives.)

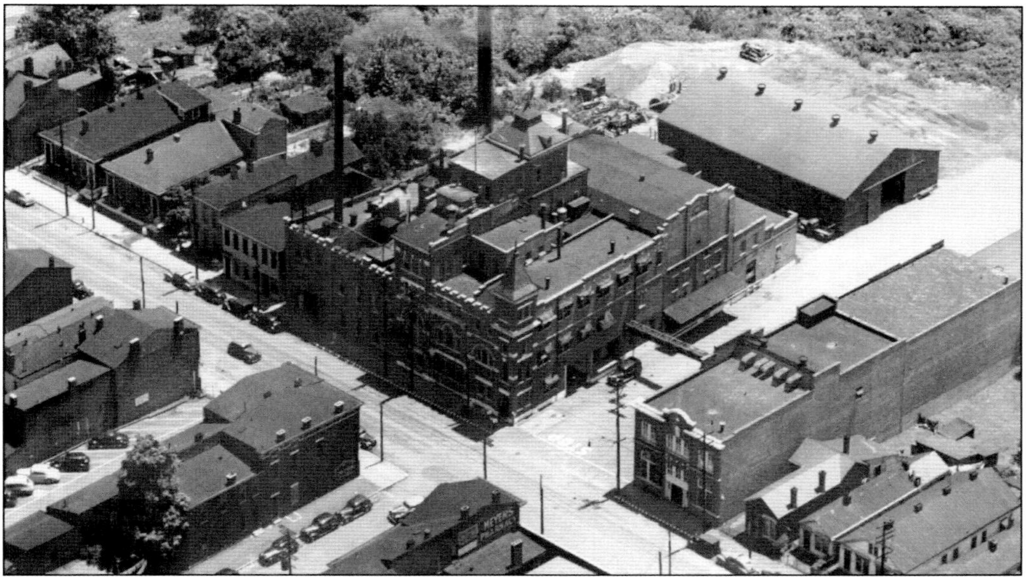

Prior to Prohibition, the majority of beer sold was draft beer, and residents remember going to the corner saloon and filling a bucket for 5¢. During World War II, civilian use of beer cans was discontinued, as aluminum was needed for the war effort; however, the military still shipped flat-topped cans to soldiers on the front lines. When bottling beer became cheaper and more homes had refrigerators, draft beer consumption fell from almost 90 percent in 1890 to less than 10 percent in 1953.

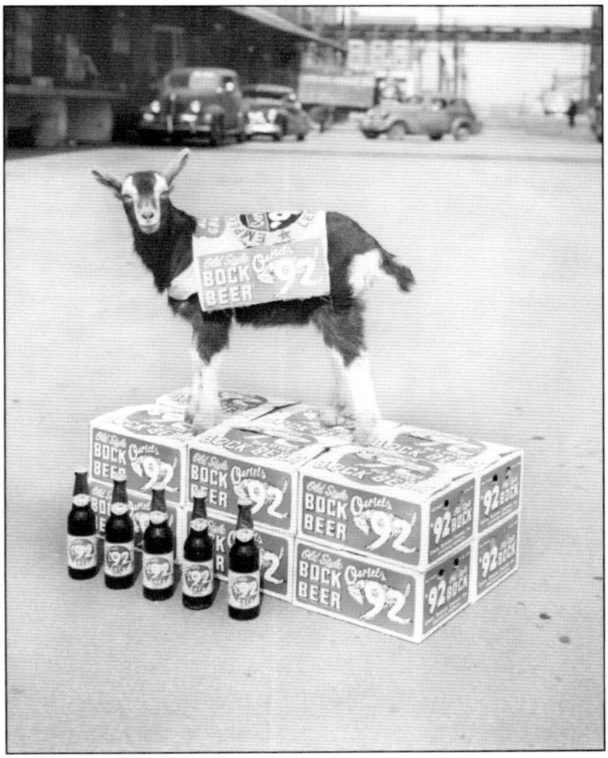

Every spring, brewers followed German tradition and made a batch of bock beer for sale in late March. This popular style sold out in a matter of days, and a billy goat—*bock* in German—was a popular advertising mascot. In 1992, a special batch of Oertel's Brewery's beer was contract brewed by the Huber Brewing Company in Wisconsin and served at the Oktoberfest in Butchertown. (Courtesy of the University of Louisville Photographic Archives.)

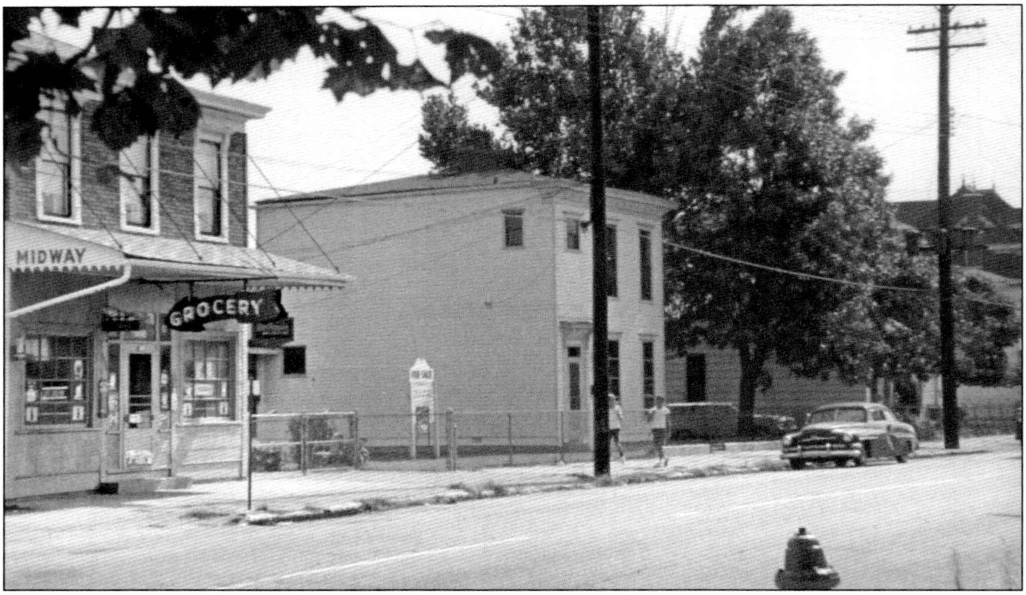

Grocery stores were found on nearly every block in Butchertown. Each one had a small variety of items different from other stores just down the block. Many families had a store in the front of a house to help supplement income. The image above shows Midway Grocery in the 1500 block of Story Avenue. The image below shows Sams Grocery in 1943 on the corner of Shelby and Washington Streets across from the Wesley house. Pictured from left to right are Jenny Kays Rigsby, Ruby Phelps, "Babe" Marshal Daniels, Marcelia Lewis, and Leon Lewis. Ethel Stoke recalls going for a weekly ride to the river and back because of the slightly larger wartime gasoline rations received by the grocery store owners. (Above, courtesy of the Eye Care Institute; below, courtesy of Ethel Stoke.)

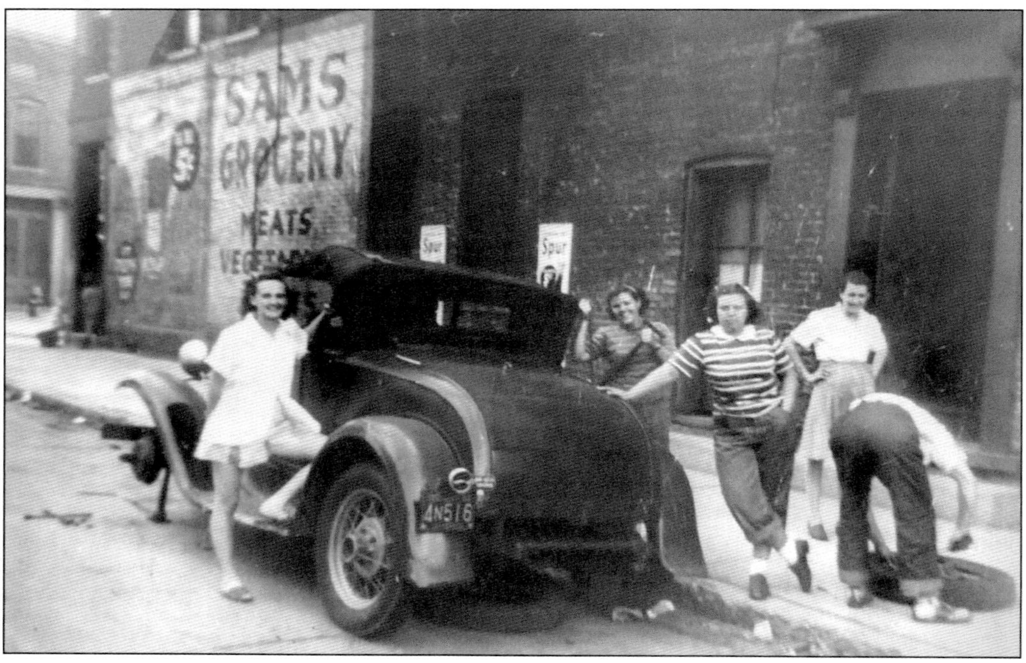

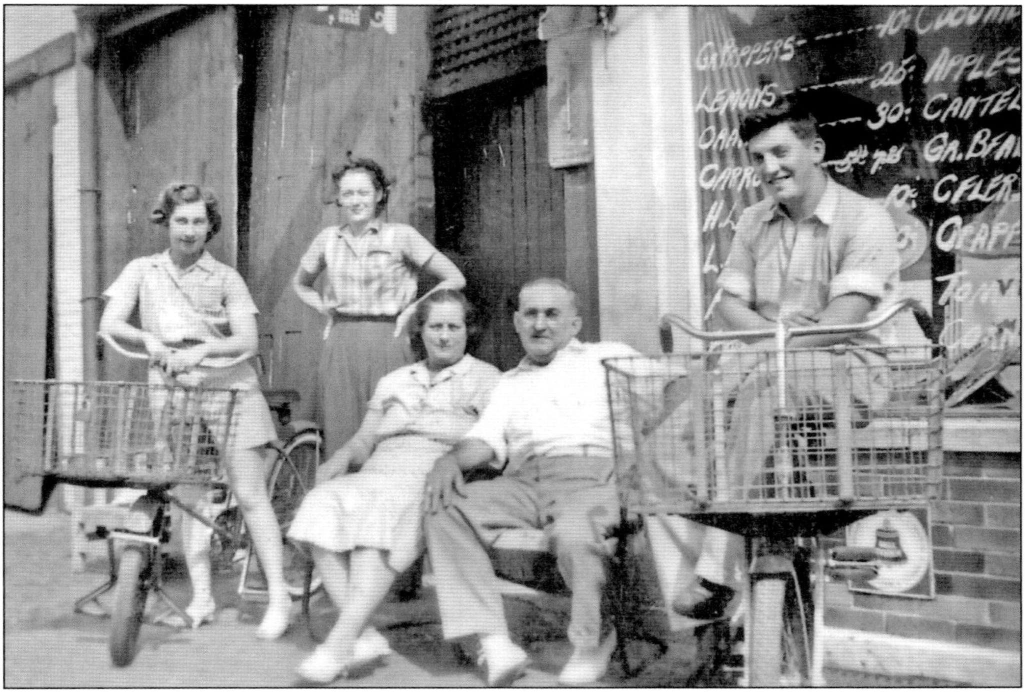

Members of Tommy and Dorothy Lutes's family are pictured in front of Kochs Grocery and Lutes Meats at 1604 Story Avenue around 1946. (Courtesy of Carl and Charles Lutes.)

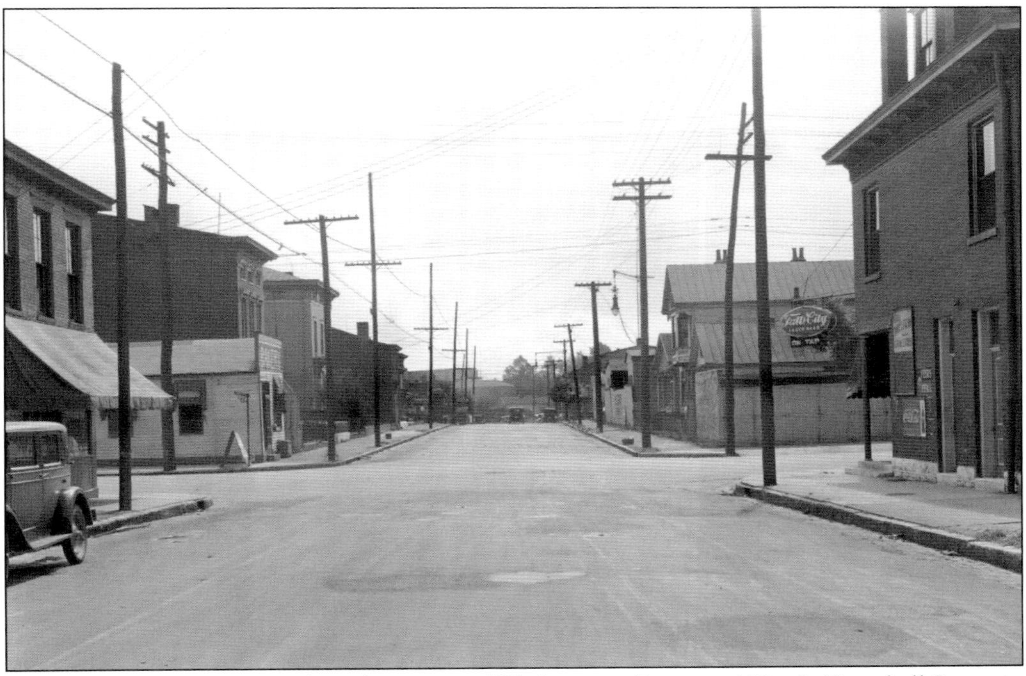

This grocery store is pictured on the corner of Washington Street and North Campbell Street in 1934. On one corner is the George Woelflin grocery store, on the left corner is a bakery, and on the far left is another store. (Courtesy of the University of Louisville Photographic Archives.)

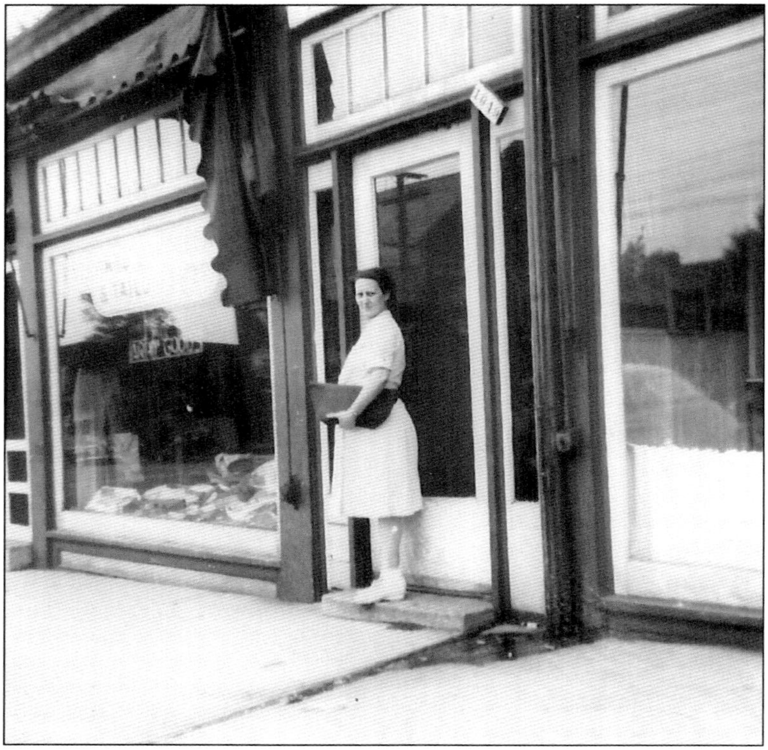

A dry goods shop at 1049 Story Avenue is seen in the 1950s. (Courtesy of the Kimpflein family.)

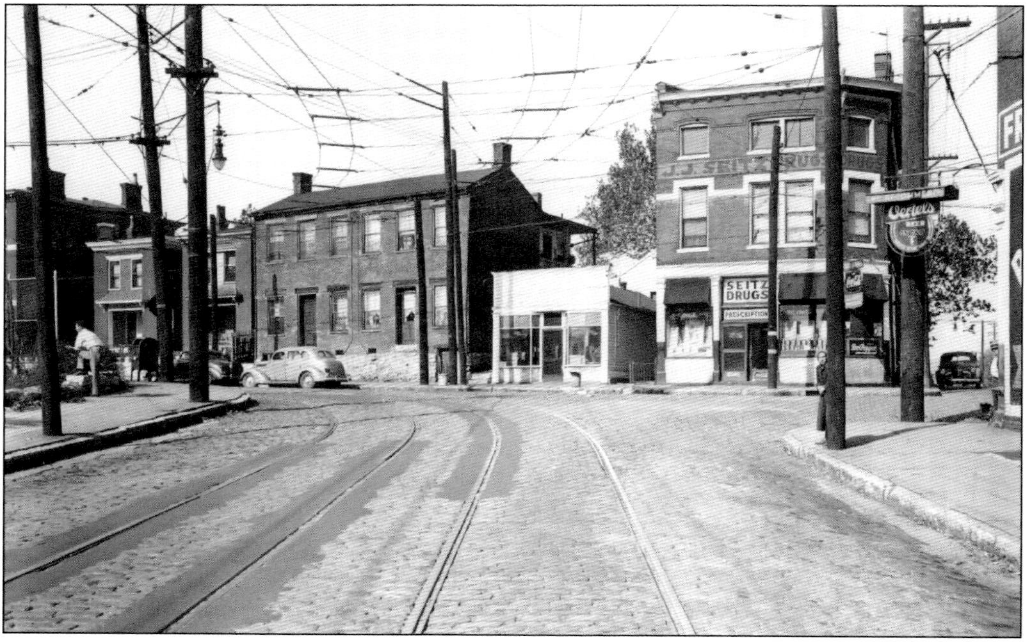

Here is a street view of Frankfort Avenue as it turns into Story Avenue in 1945. The corner structure, Seitz drugstore, sold candies, ice cream, and sickroom supplies. The small structure to its left was a barbershop, and both were torn down to reroute Ohio Street. Notice the trolley tracks in the bricked street. (Courtesy of the University of Louisville Photographic Archives.)

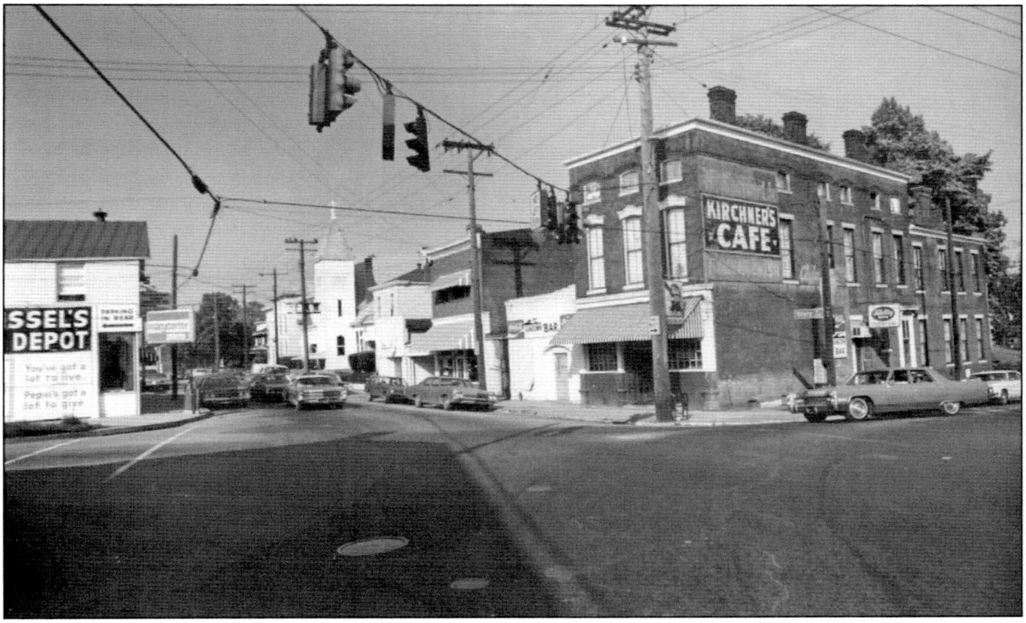

This photograph looks east on Story Avenue at the intersection of Frankfort Avenue. On the right is Kirchners Café at 1600 Story Avenue, which was a post office station in 1902 and a grocery store from 1904 to 1914. Various restaurants and cafes from 1920 to 1970, including Kirchners Café, Earl's Tavern, and the Sundown Bar, have occupied the building. The building with the striped awning farther east on Story Avenue was Lutes Meats. (Courtesy of Mark Thompson, NRHP.)

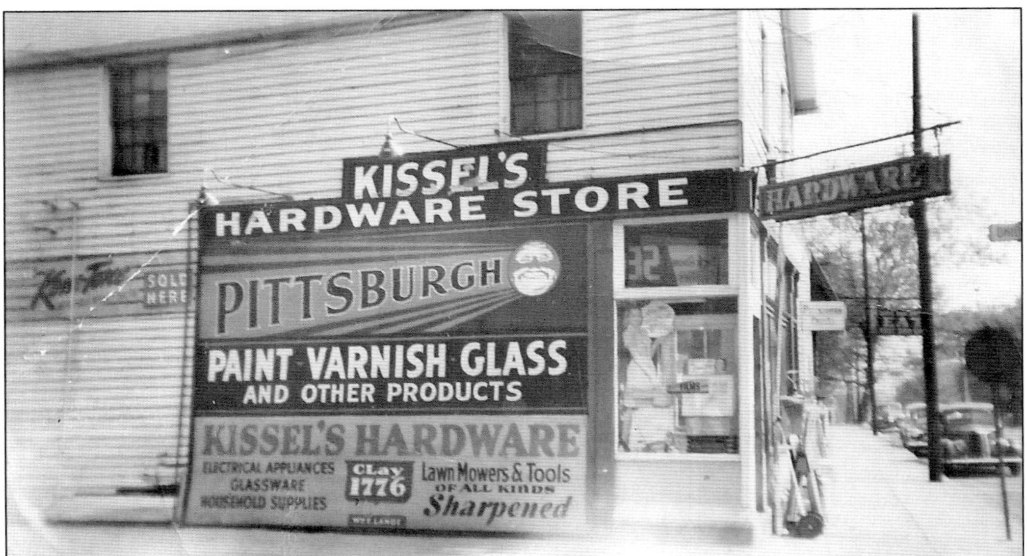

Kissels Hardware Store on the corner of Story Avenue and Ohio Street is seen here. The hardware store once housed a tavern in the back and was known as the beer depot. It was said to be the terminus for the mule-drawn Market Street Car Line, and a turntable was located there. (Courtesy of Charlie Johnson.)

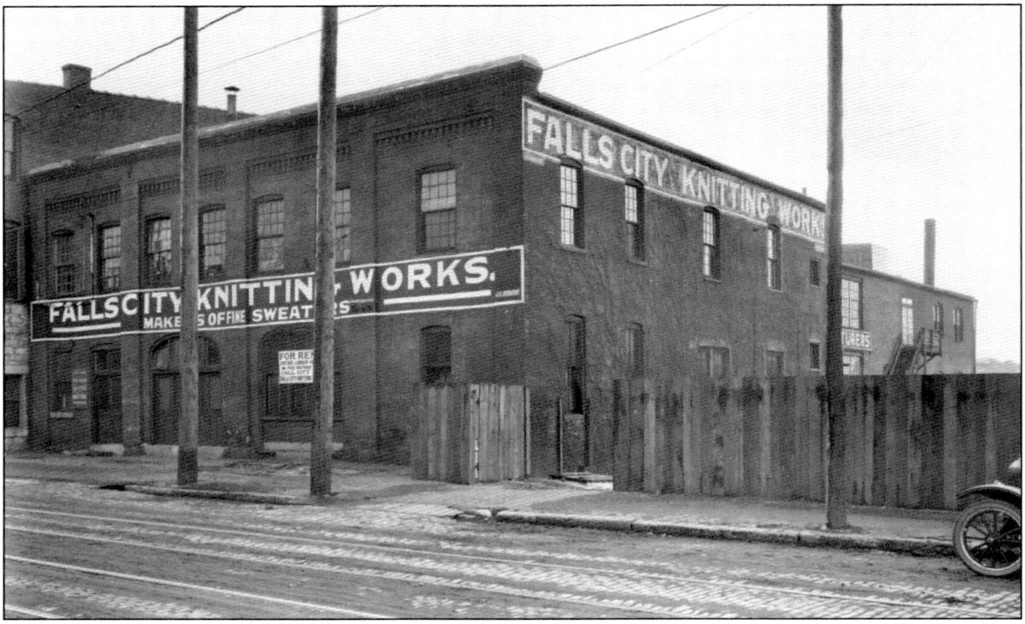

The Falls City Knitting Works at 1564–1566 Story Avenue is pictured in 1923. This structure was to the west of Hadley Pottery and was later torn down. The building at 1570 Story Avenue was said to be the first factory to get electricity in Louisville and was rumored to have been a station in the Underground Railroad during the Civil War. (Courtesy of the University of Louisville Photographic Archives.)

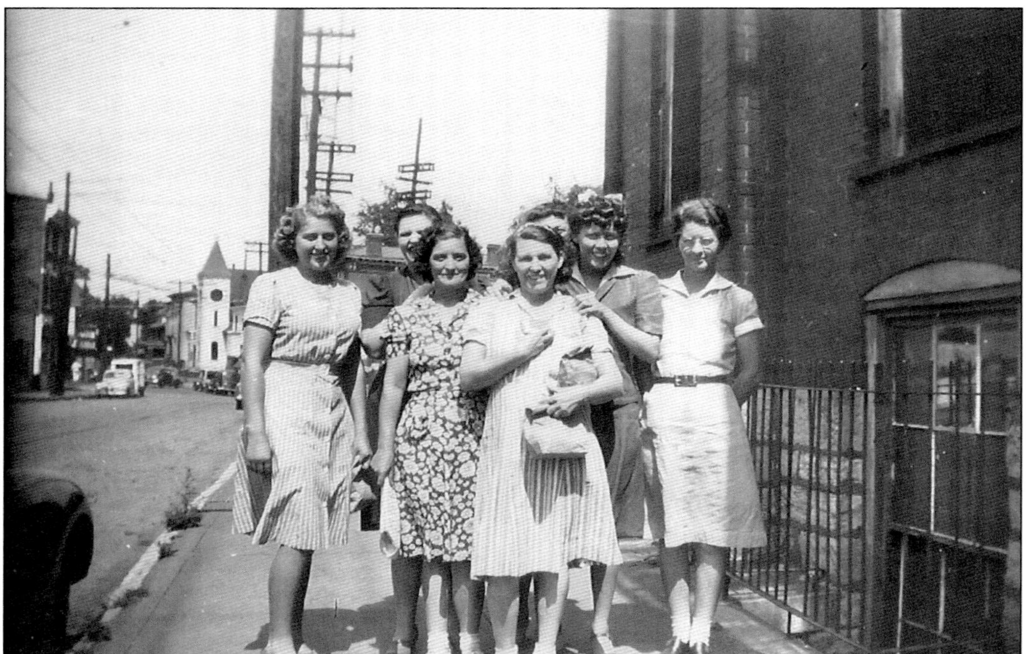

Workers are seen in the late 1930s at Semple Manufacturing, which was located at 1570 Story Avenue from 1917 to 1943 and created cordage, twine, and mops. (Courtesy of Wayne Miller.)

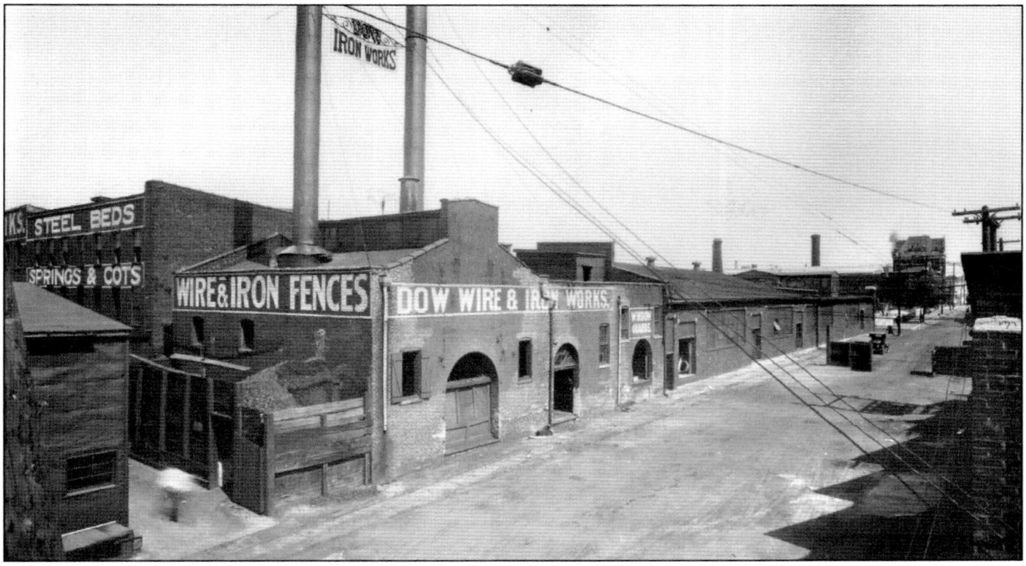

The location that was so convenient for butchers was also appropriate for industrial operations, such as the Dow Iron Works, founded in 1876 by A. G. Dow. It created ornamental iron pieces, fireplaces, and mattress springs. William H. Logan, owner of the Whitehall mansion on Lexington Road, later bought Dow Iron Works and renamed it the Logan Company in 1910. As it expanded, the offices moved to 200 Cabel Street, and the company employed some 600 people. It was one of the first to develop conveyor belts and was at one time the fifth largest package-handling conveyor company in the world. (Courtesy of the University of Louisville Photographic Archives.)

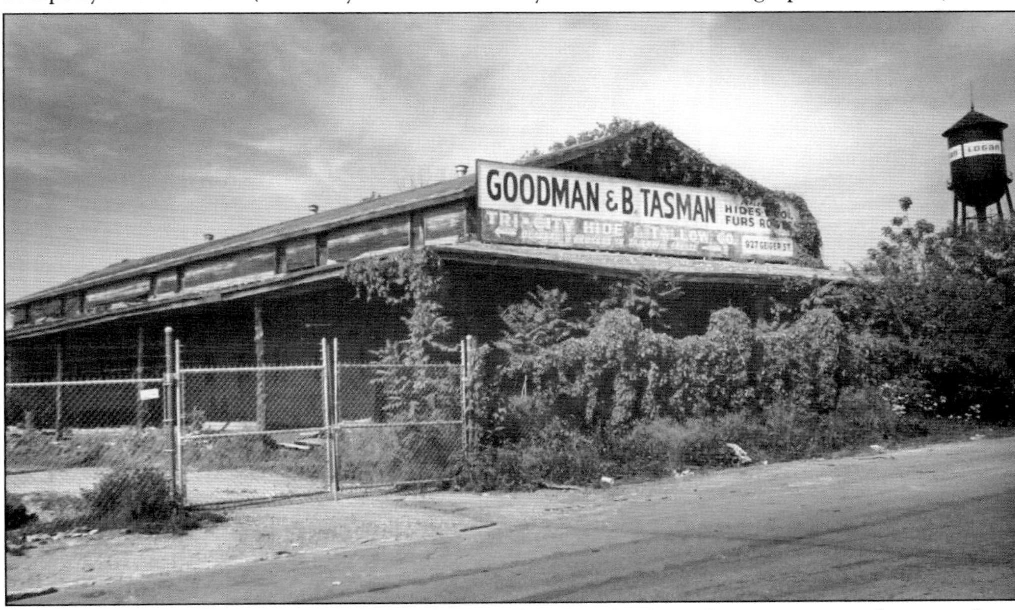

The same conditions that attracted butchers to the area also brought tanneries and soap makers. Located at 926 Geiger Street, Tri City Hide and Tallow Company was one of many local tanneries making leather, using animal hides leftover from the meatpacking business. Geiger Street was named after Col. Frederick Geiger, whose estate, Geigers Enlargement, was subdivided by his son Jacob and includes parts of Butchertown today. (Courtesy of Mark Thompson, NRHP.)

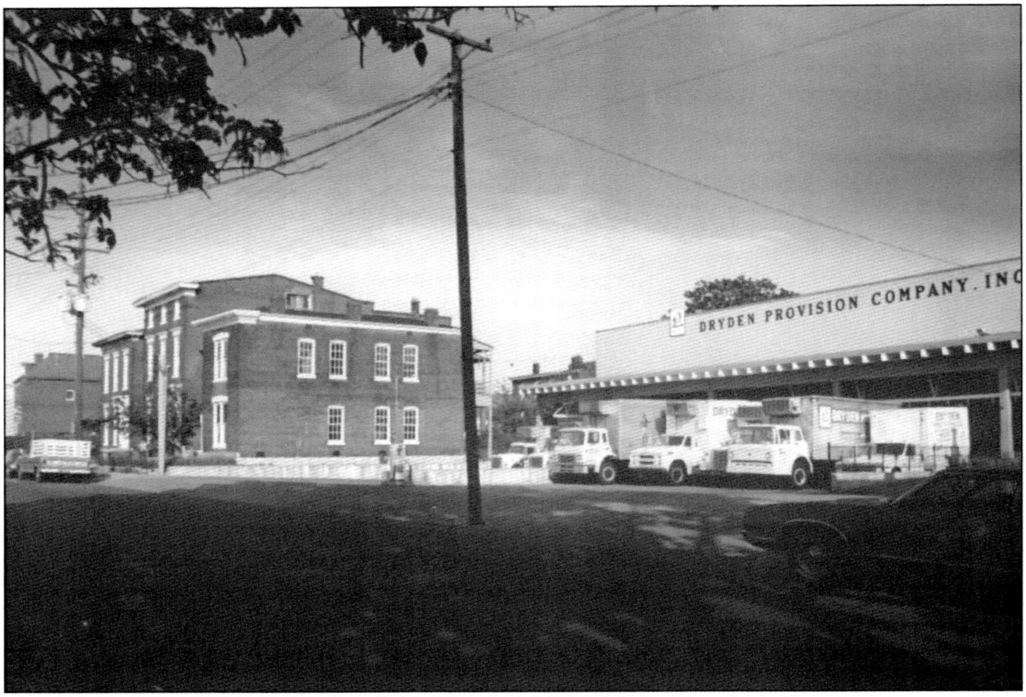

Dryden Provision at 1016 East Washington Street is a distributor of meats and cheeses and has been family operated since 1960. (Courtesy of Mark Thompson, NRHP.)

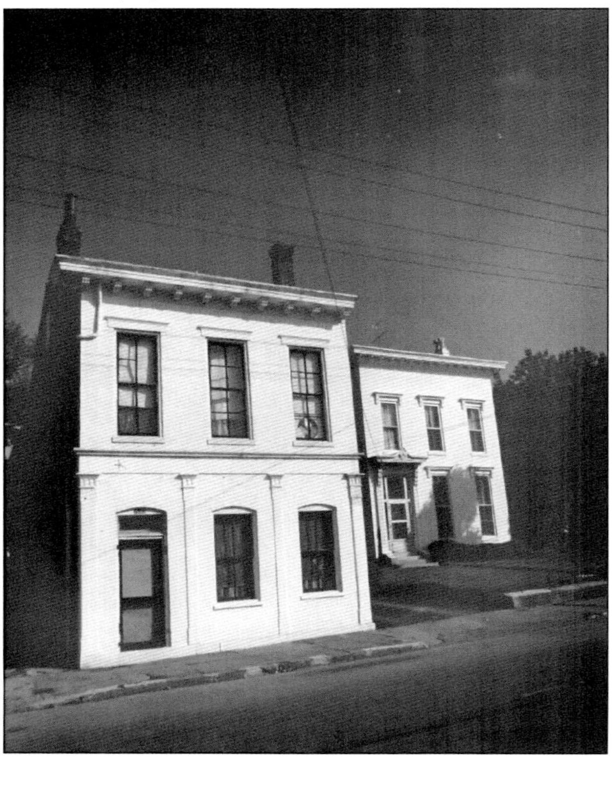

The former Last Chance Tavern, located at 1642 Story Avenue, used to be the "last watering hole" for travelers on their way out of Louisville along the Brownsboro Turnpike into Bluegrass farmland. (Courtesy of Mark Thompson, NRHP.)

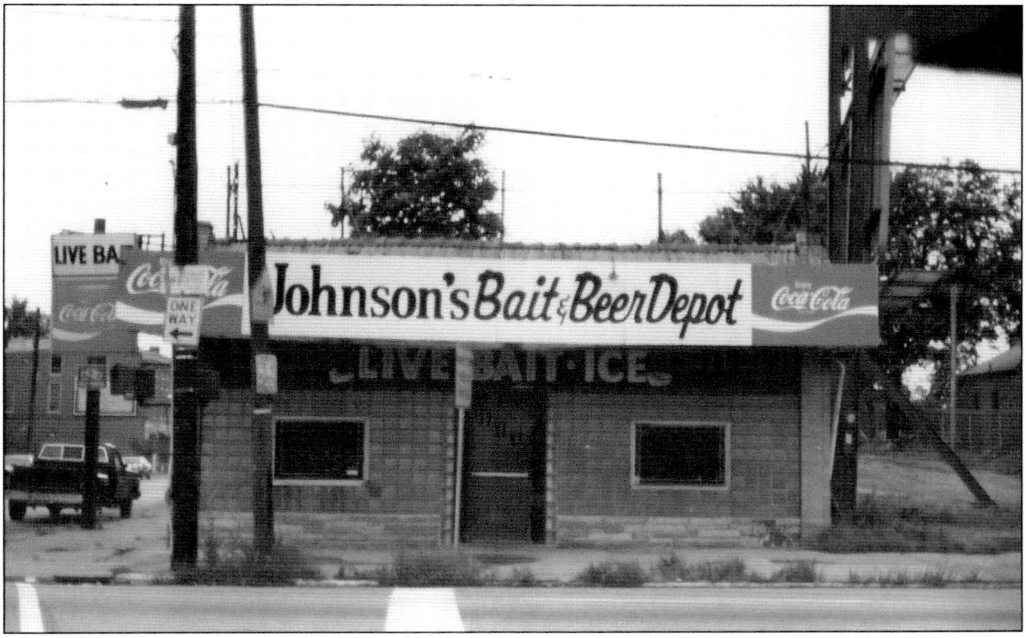

Johnson's Bait and Beer Depot was located at 1501 Story Avenue on the corner of Adams Street. Previously this had been a blacksmith shop from 1902 to 1918. From 1930 to 1941, it was the A&P. Between World War II and 1968, it was Dutch's Grill and Tavern and then Stan's Café. This site is currently the Wesley Wear house. (Courtesy of Leslie Tichenor.)

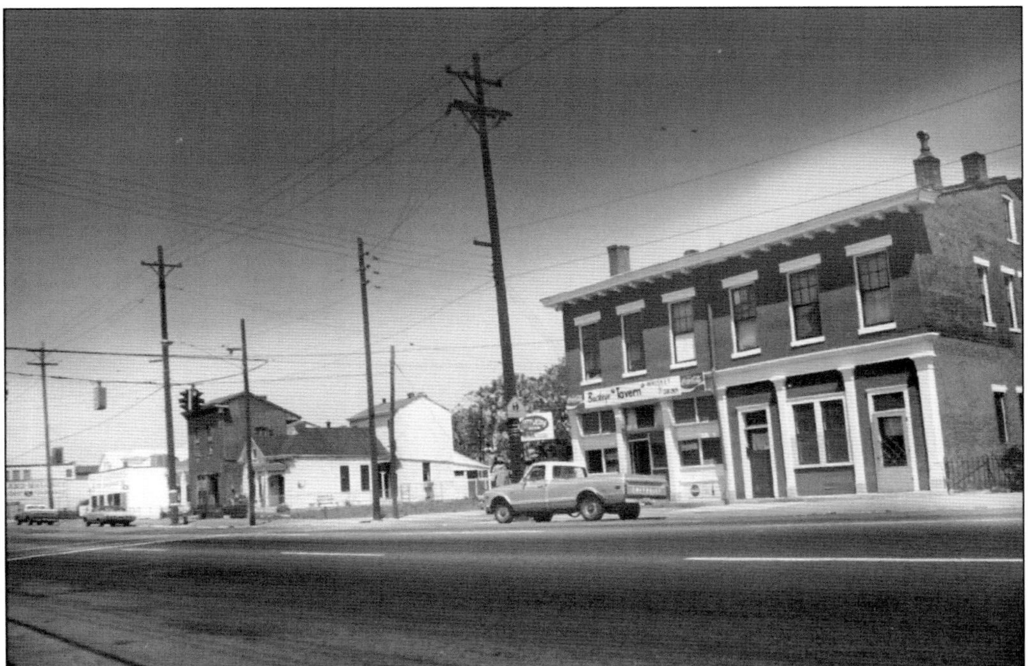

Buckeyes Tavern on Main Street was another bar visited by Butchertown residents. (Courtesy of Mark Thompson, NRHP.)

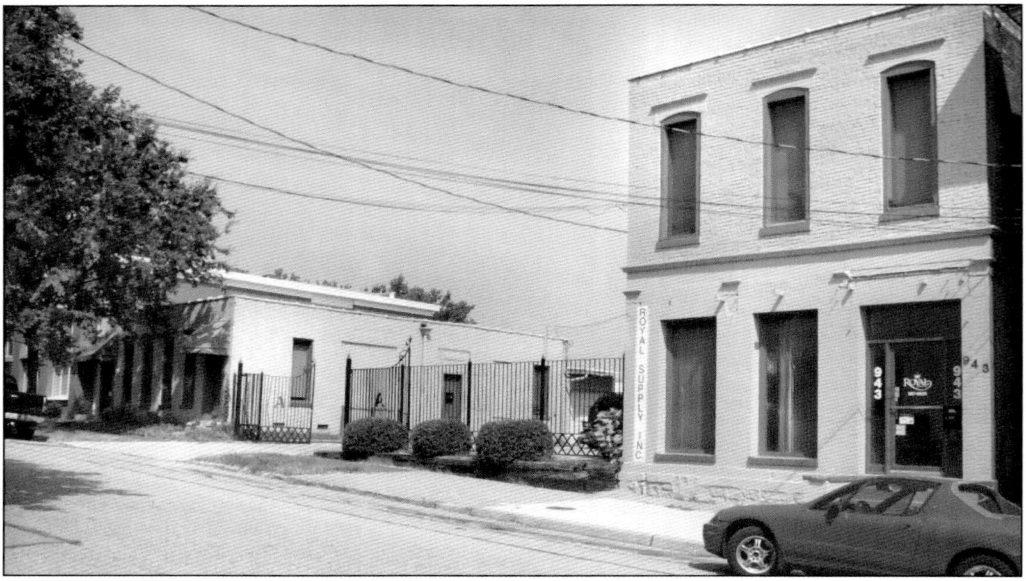

With a large number of European immigrants, especially Germans, it should come as no surprise that Butchertown was home to several local breweries. The picture of 941–943 Franklin Street shows the site of the former Franklin Street Brewery, which operated from 1865 to 1877. Other breweries located in Butchertown were X (Xavier) Joseph and Company on the north side of Geiger Street between Campbell and Wenzel Streets, from 1859 to 1865; Thomas and Gentner on Washington Street between Campbell and Wenzel Streets, from 1865 to 1866; Jacob Steuer Brewery at 1372 Story Avenue between Webster and Cabel Streets, from 1866 to 1905, and Charles Hartmetz and Brothers on Main Street between Campbell and Wenzel Streets, from 1866 to 1873. (Courtesy of author's collection.)

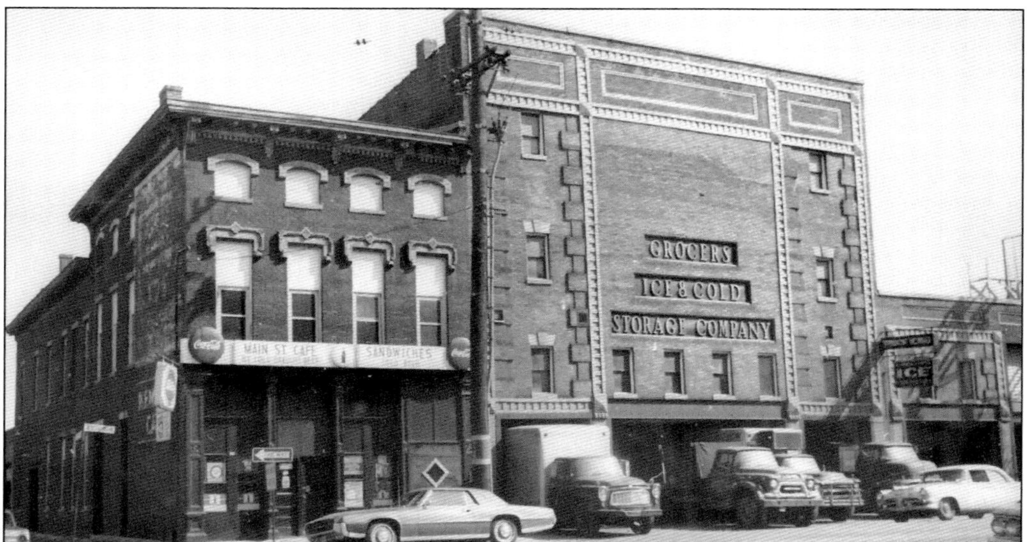

The former Grocers Ice and Cold Storage building at 609 East Main Street was used to store goods and ice cut from the rivers and ponds. A fire damaged the top story of the storage building, and the Main Street Café to its left was torn down. It is now Creation Gardens, a store that sells regional products to local restaurants. (Courtesy of Leslie Tichenor.)

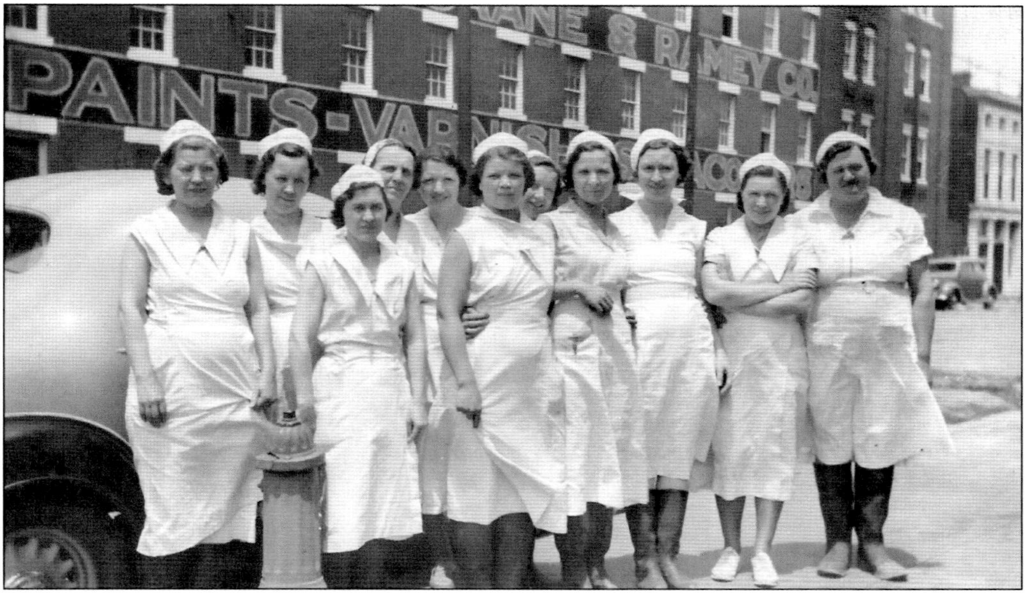

The former Varnish Company at 1201 Story Avenue employed many area residents and is now the Butchertown Market building, which houses galleries, local stores, and offices. (Courtesy of the Collett brothers.)

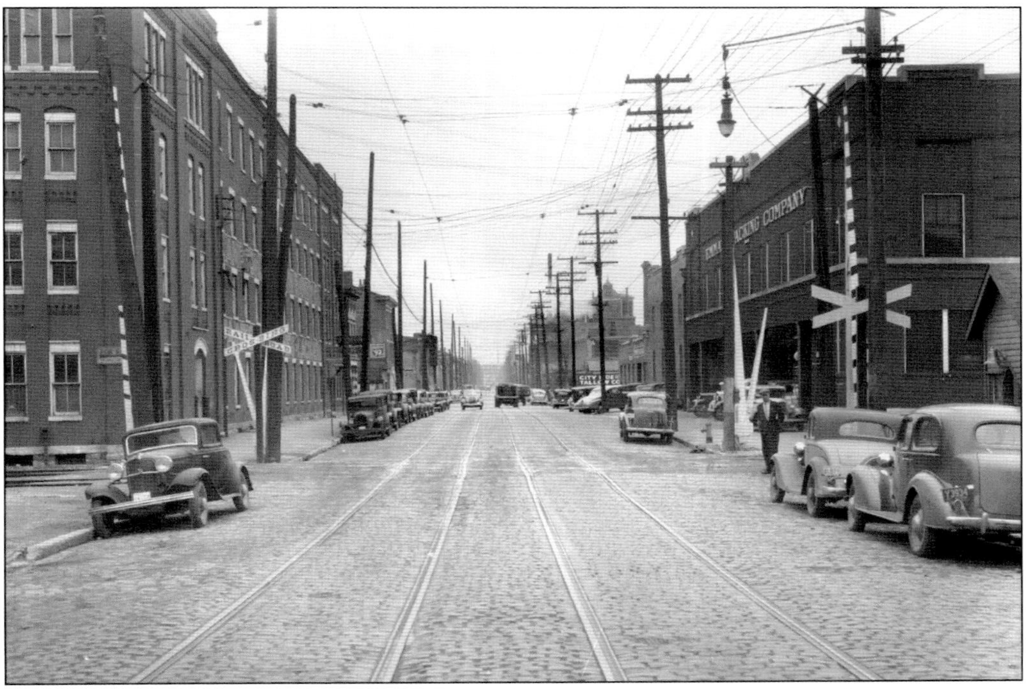

This photograph looks east on Story Avenue from Pocahontas Street, with the trolley tracks in the bricked road. On the north side of Story Avenue is the Varnish Company, shown in the previous picture. On the south side of Story Avenue are Emmarts Packing Company, the City Hide and Tallow Company, and Oertel's in the distance. (Courtesy of the University of Louisville Photographic Archives.)

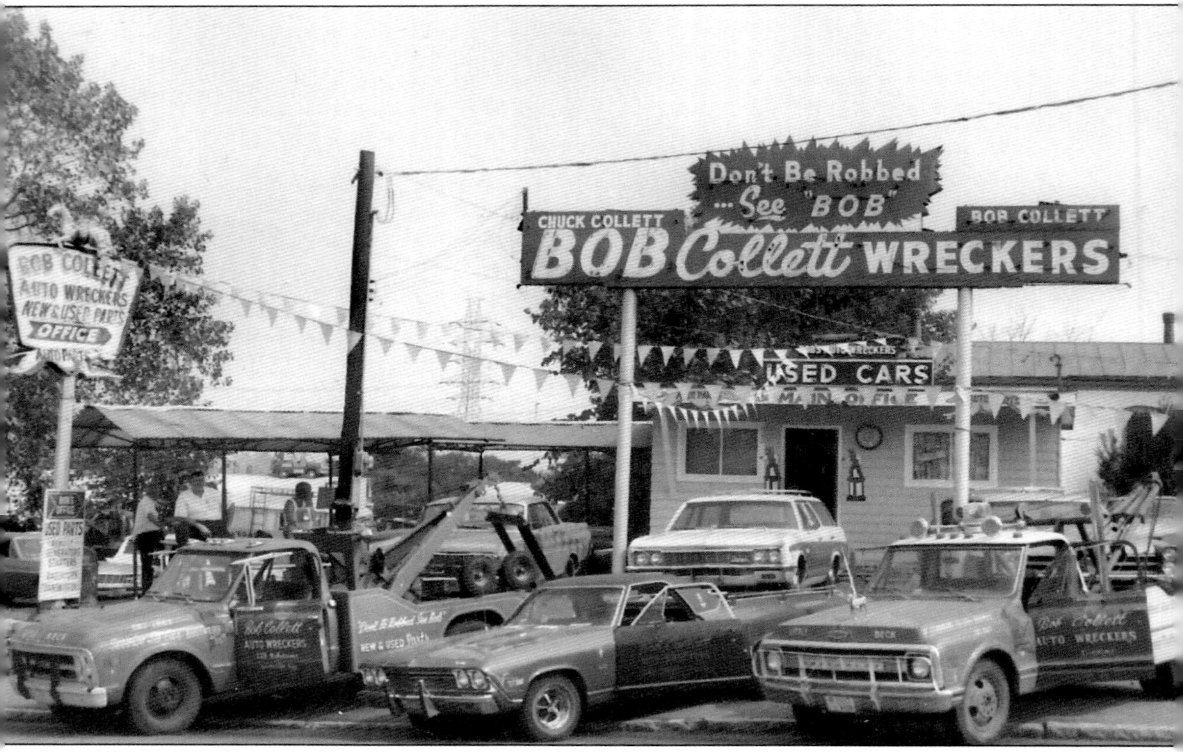

The Collett brothers have been in the automobile business in Butchertown for many years. Their store was located on River Road before moving to the corner of Adams and Quincy Streets. They now operate on Frankfort Avenue between Story and Mellwood Avenues by Beargrass Creek. (Courtesy of the Collett brothers.)

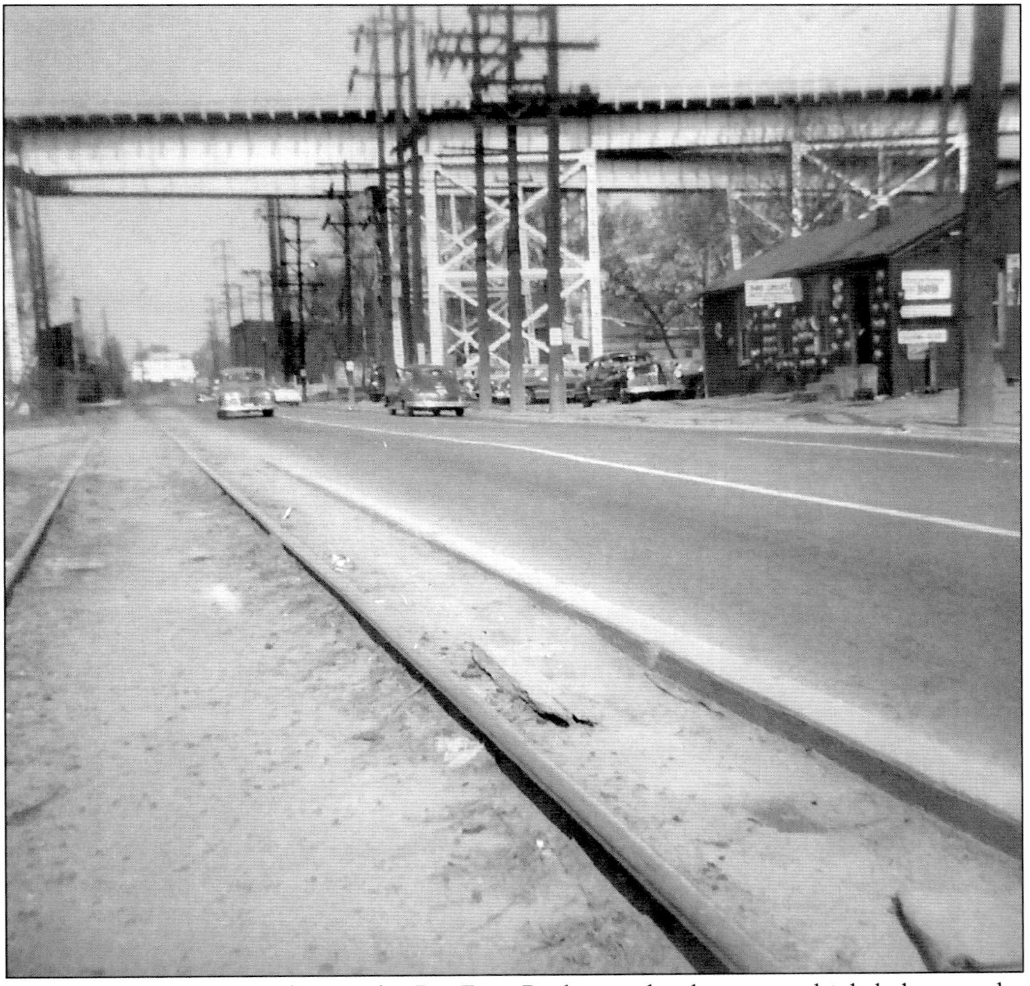

Notice the steel approaches to the Big Four Bridge in the distance, which led up to the single-track bridge. The original Big Four Bridge was completed in 1895 and replaced in 1929 to allow for heavier trains. When the bridge closed to traffic in 1968, after the Big Four Railroad entered a merger with the Pennsylvania Railroad, the steel approaches were removed. (Courtesy of the Collett brothers.)

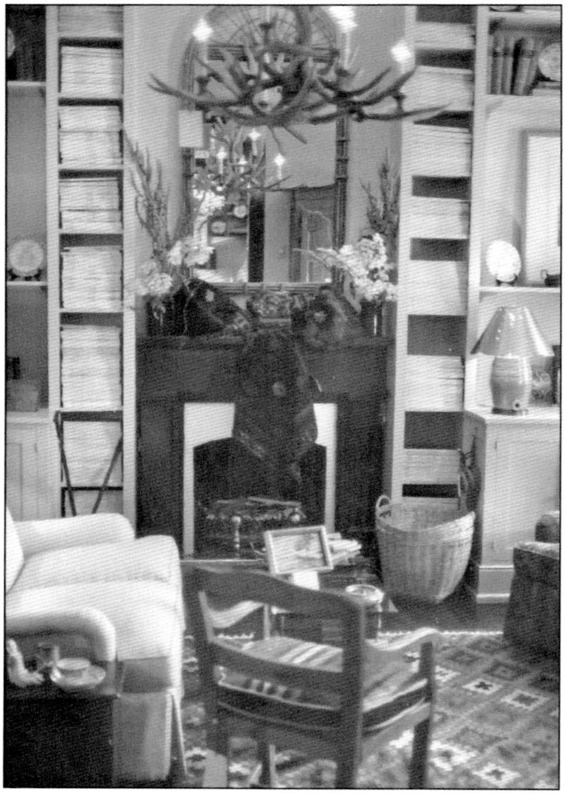

Above is the inside of Tichenor's Interior Design Store. Attracted to the low rent, Scott and Leslie Tichenor moved to Butchertown in 1969 and fell in love with the neighborhood. They opened their interior design business and store at 122 Adams Street and began work renovating an apartment above. The building, pictured below, was constructed in the 1800s and housed the Gnau Feed Store and Grocery until 1938, the Good Luck Polish Company from 1939 to 1947, Union Market Meats from 1948 to 1949, R. Mason Meats from 1950 to 1951, the Clarence Awles Grocery from 1952 to 1958, and Pop's Grocery until 1969. Leslie painted a black-and-white checkerboard pattern on the hallway floor of the residence, a feature that remained after the residence was recently converted to condominiums. (Both, courtesy of Leslie Tichenor.)

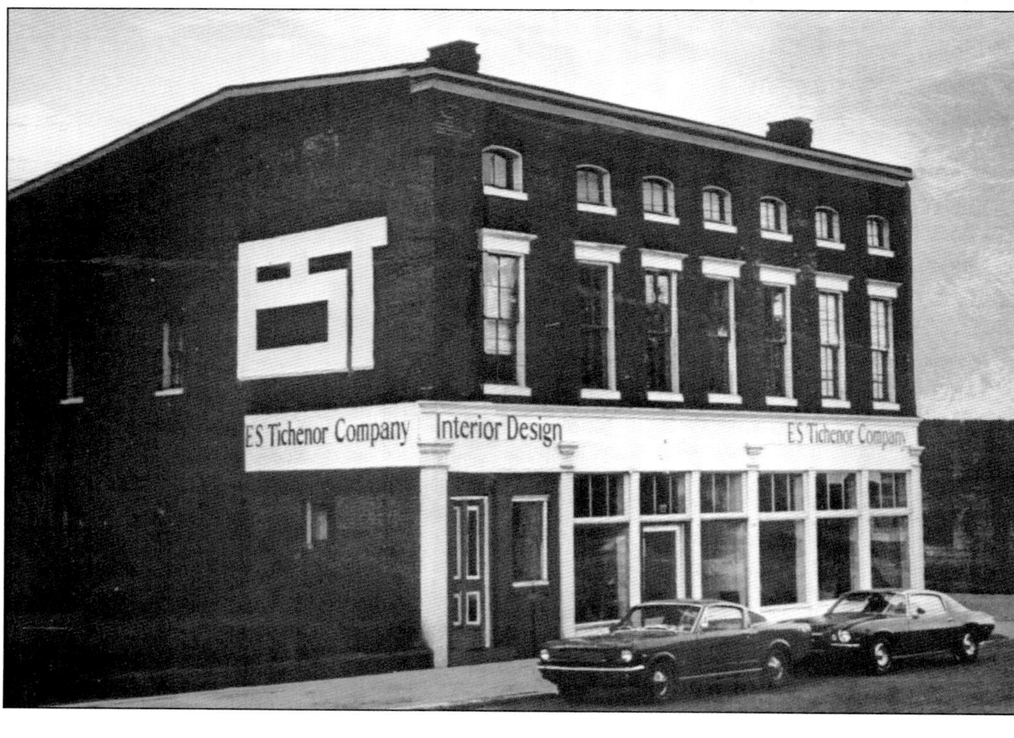

Three

Disastrous Flooding

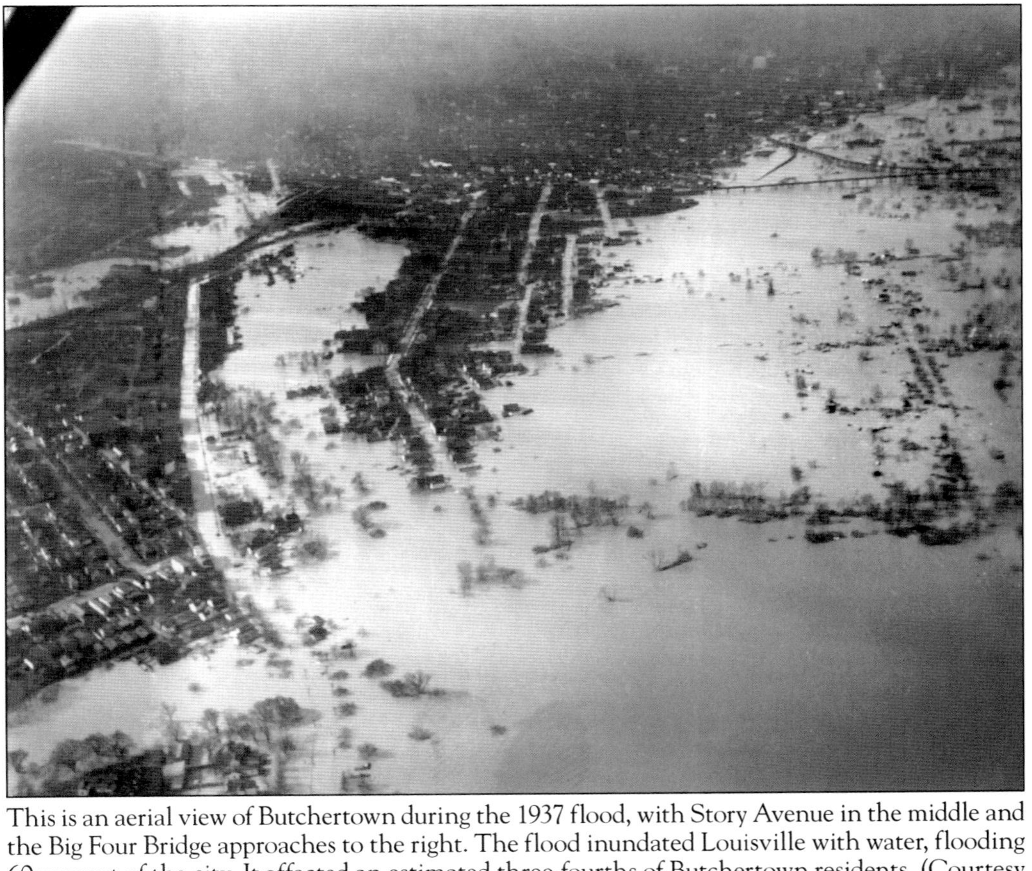

This is an aerial view of Butchertown during the 1937 flood, with Story Avenue in the middle and the Big Four Bridge approaches to the right. The flood inundated Louisville with water, flooding 60 percent of the city. It affected an estimated three-fourths of Butchertown residents. (Courtesy of the University of Louisville Photographic Archives.)

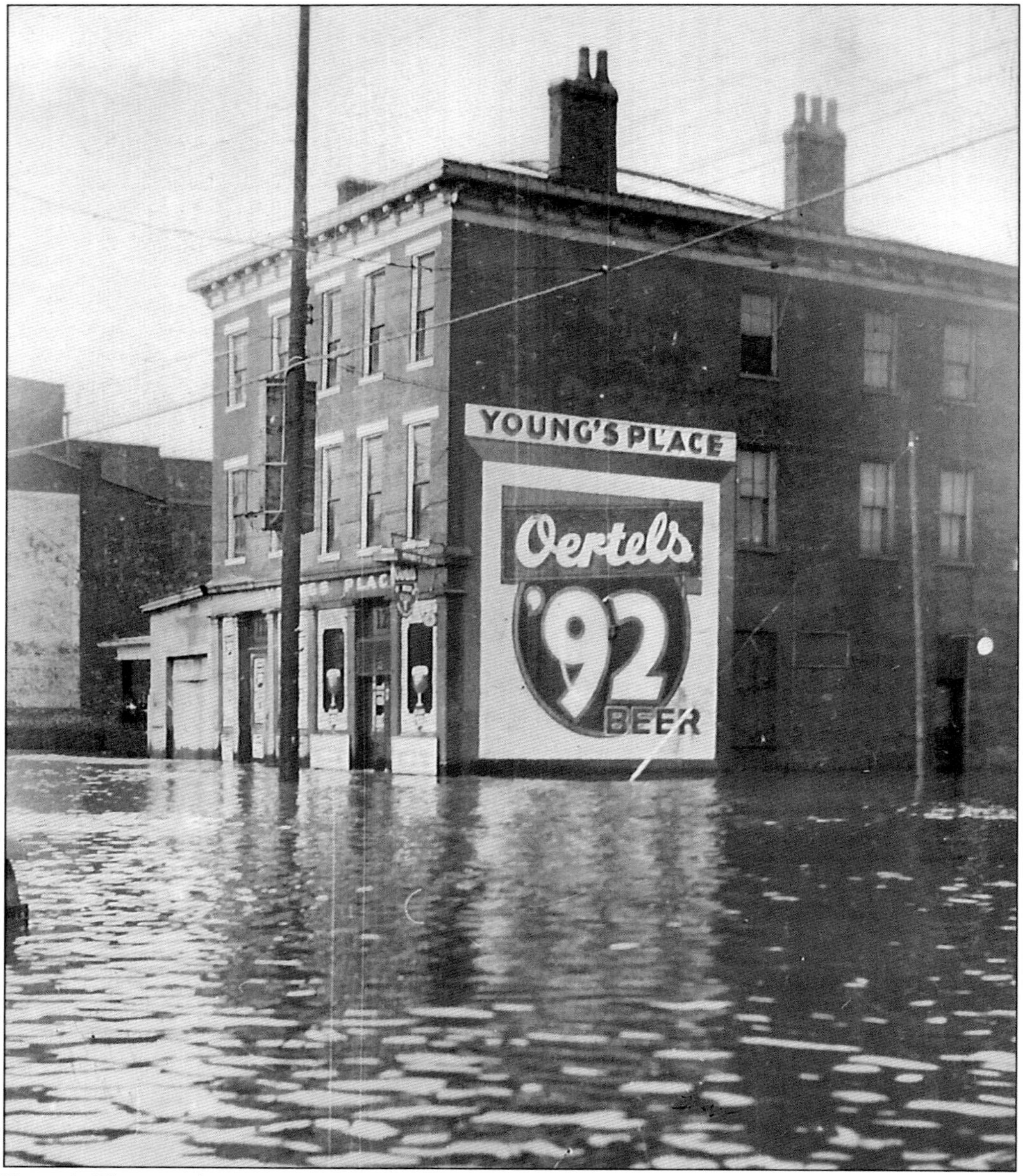

Young's Place at the corner of Story Avenue and Cabel Street is pictured in the 1937 flood. Rain began falling on January 9, and the river rose steadily until cresting on January 27 at 57.15 feet. Residents were stranded in their homes without electricity, surrounded by freezing water. (Courtesy of the Kimpflein family.)

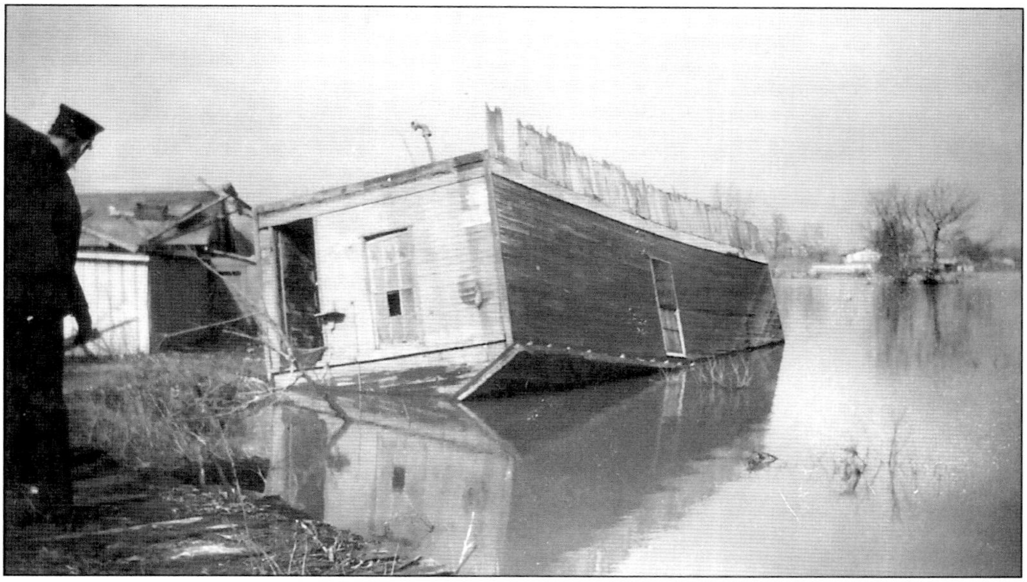

Damage from the 1937 flood is being surveyed in the photograph above. Always prone to flooding as a result of its low-lying land, the 1937 flood devastated most of Butchertown. Water was so high, houses floated off their foundations into the middle of the street, and people were evacuated from their homes by boats. Below, a boat on Story Avenue is near Webster Street. Gov. Albert Benjamin Chandler declared martial law on January 25, 1937, and people were pulled from their homes and taken to higher ground by rescue agencies and troops. (Both, courtesy of the Kimpflein family.)

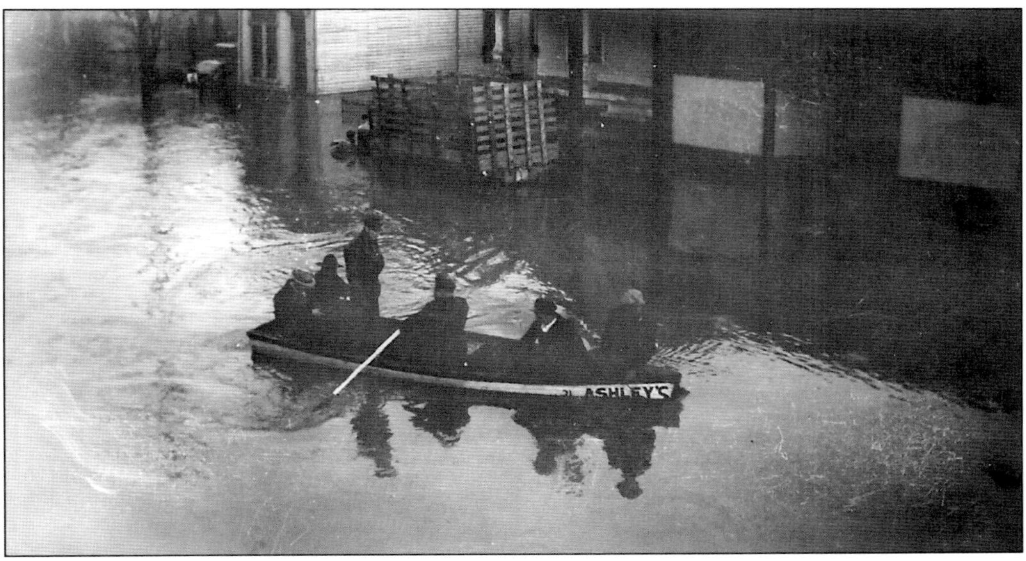

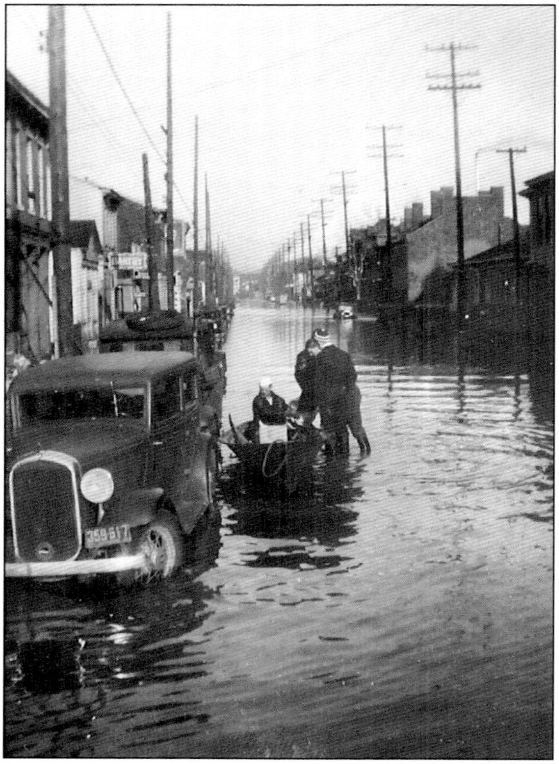

Story Avenue is shown looking east from Webster Street, with the floodwaters receding. After 23 days, the river returned to below flood level on February 6. (Courtesy of the Kimpflein family.)

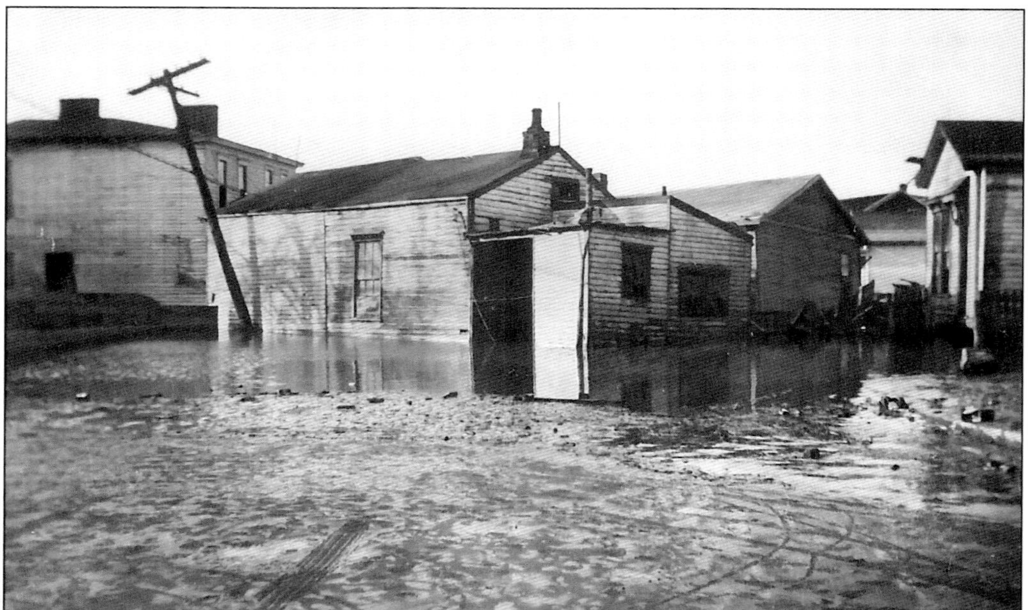

The clean-up following the 1937 flood left residents with a host of problems. These houses on Adams Street near Quincy Street floated off their foundations and were a complete loss. Debris and residual sludge required many homes to be completely gutted and rebuilt; some homes were completely destroyed. (Courtesy of the Kimpflein family.)

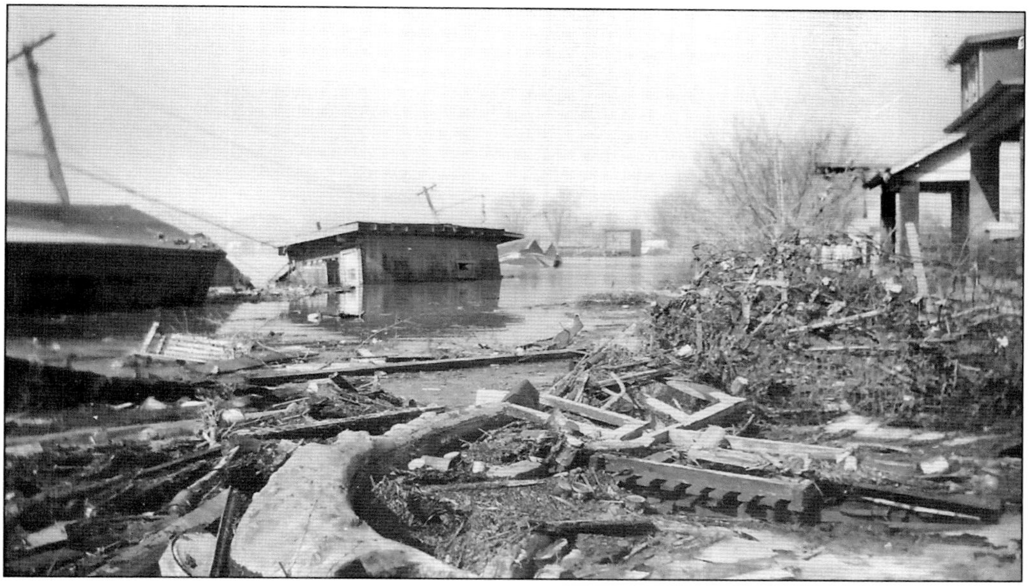

Seen above is Adams Street during the 1937 flood. The water brought debris into the yards and lifted sheds off their foundations. The photograph below is labeled, "Aunt Katie's Backyard." This picture shows the high water with floating debris in 1945. (Both, courtesy of the Kimpflein family.)

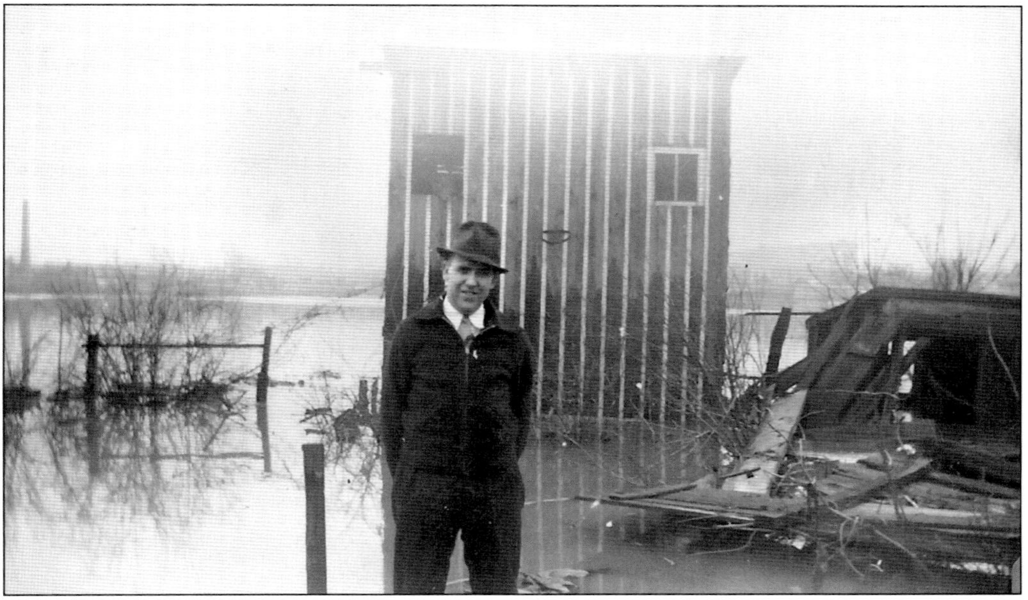

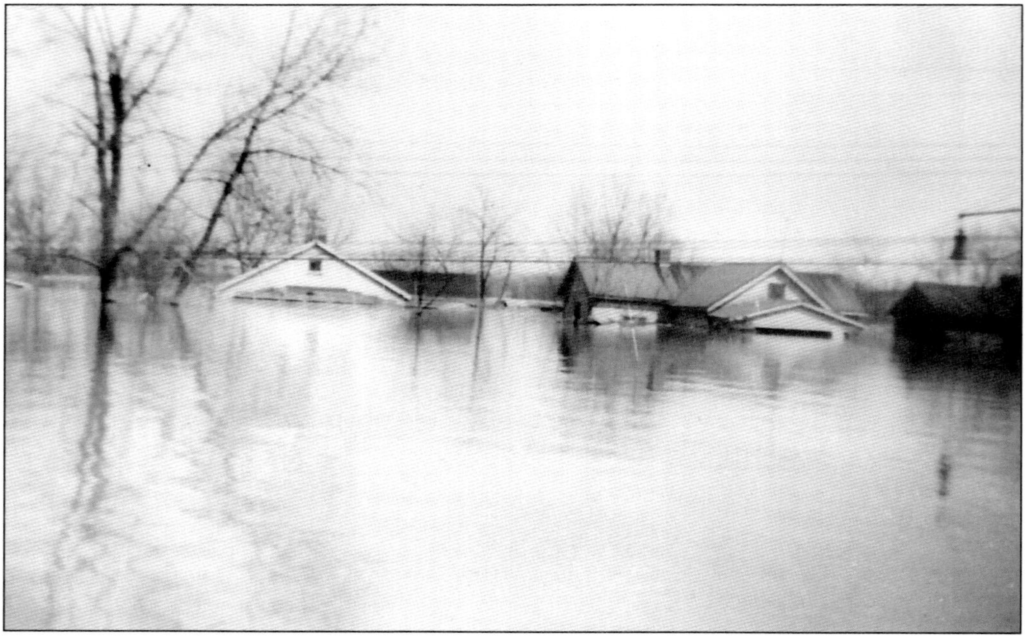

Houses are submerged in the Point neighborhood in the 1945 flood. (Courtesy of the Kimpflein family.)

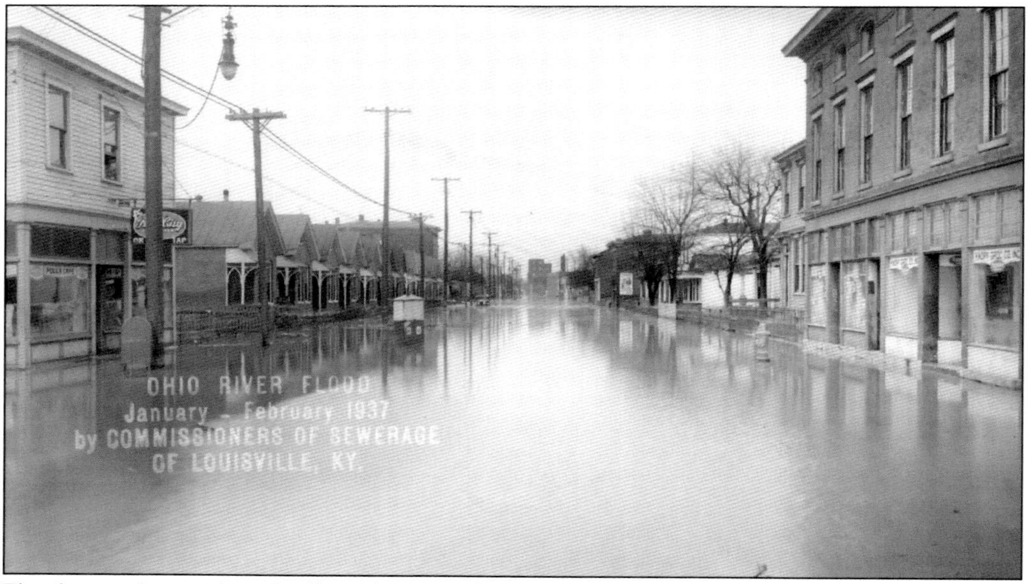

Flooding is shown along Mellwood Avenue looking east by the Metropolitan Sewer District in 1937. Charles Stoecker constructed the row of 24 identical shotgun homes between 1912 and 1915 as rental properties to serve the nearby railroad workers. The Louisville and Nashville Railroad yards were located across the street, and rail workers paid $8 a month for 15 of the cottages. A shotgun home is typically one story high, one room wide, and three- to four-rooms long. Its name is attributed to the alignment of doors being such that a shot fired from a shotgun could pass from the front door to the back door without hitting any walls. (Courtesy of the University of Louisville Photographic Archives.)

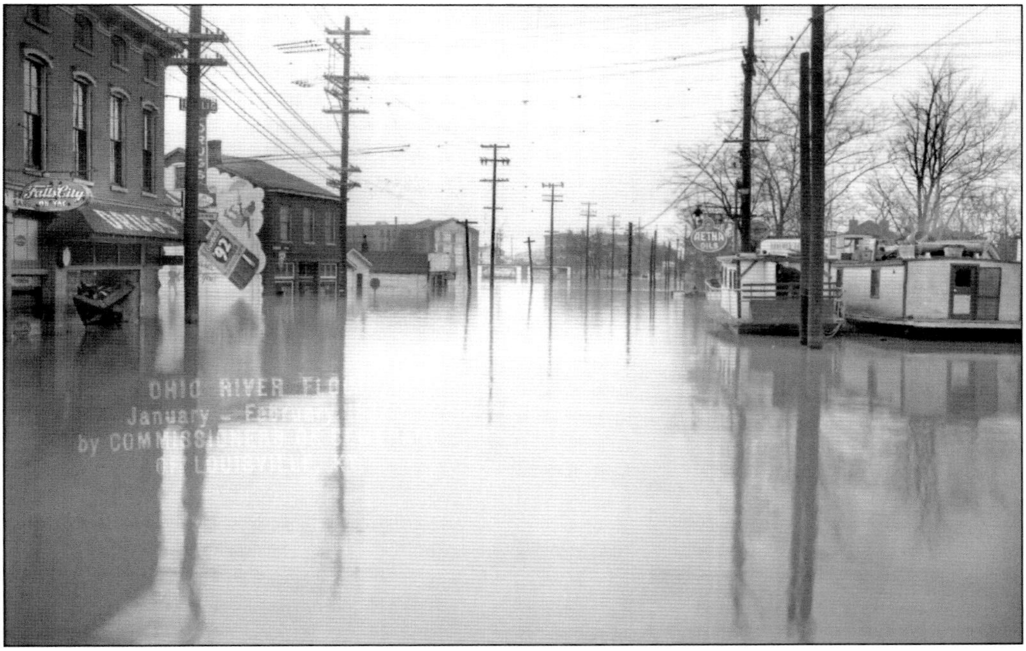

The photograph above looks north into Butchertown from Clifton from the intersection of Frankfort Avenue and Pope Street in 1937. Hadley Pottery can be seen in the far distance. An estimated three-fourths of Butchertown families had flooded homes. The photograph below was taken at the intersection of Brownsboro Road and Mellwood Avenue looking north toward Story Avenue in 1937. (Both, courtesy of the University of Louisville Photographic Archives.)

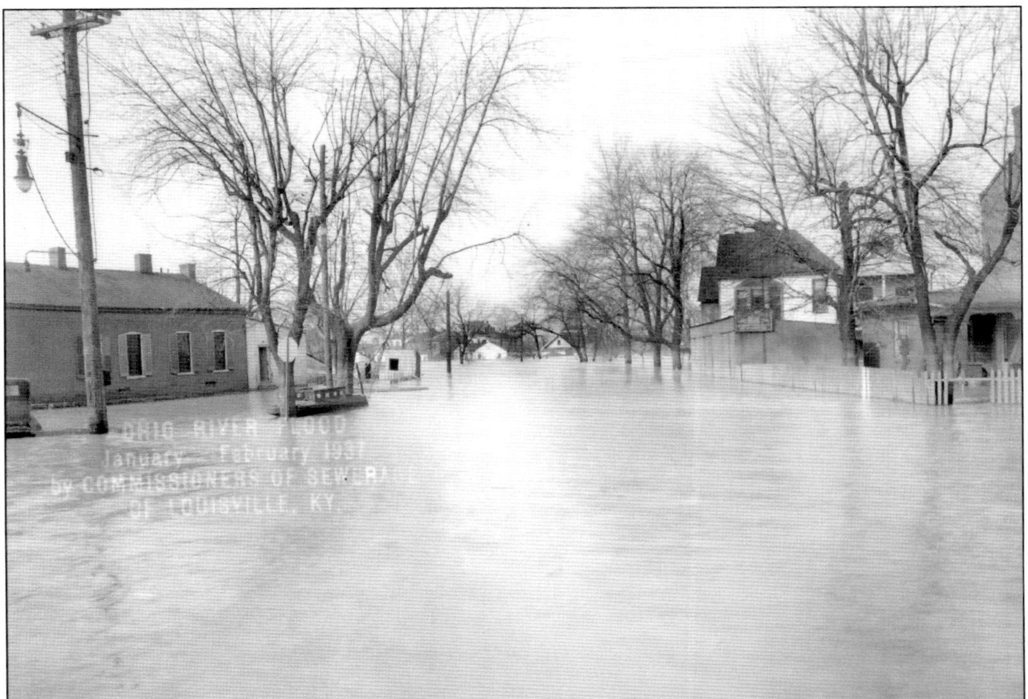

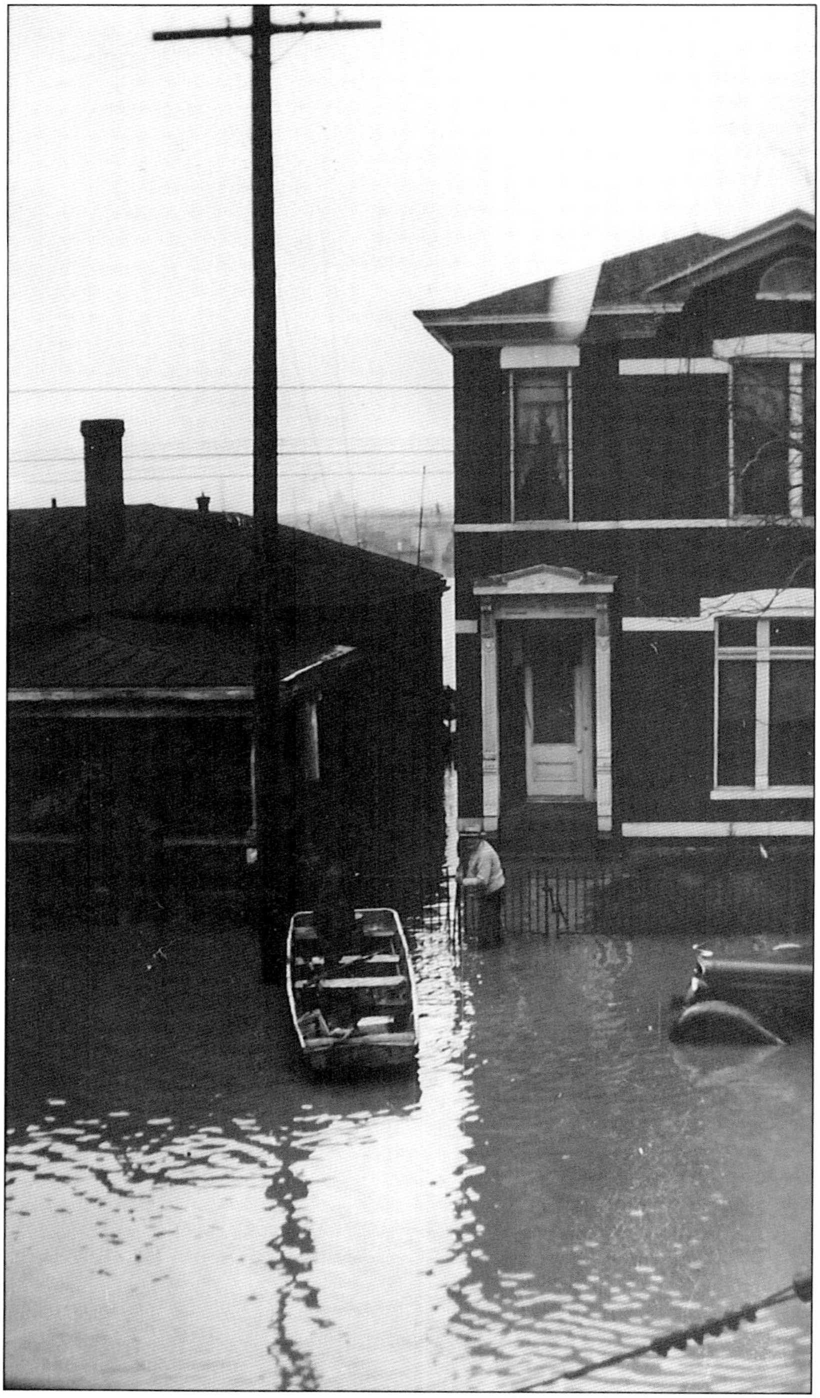

Above, neighbors visit by boat to the residence at 1308–1306 Story Avenue in 1937. Flooded families moved to higher ground. A few area families moved into St. Joseph's school with their furniture; others took refuge in the Vernon Club and the upper floors of Bakery Square. (Courtesy the Kimpflein family.)

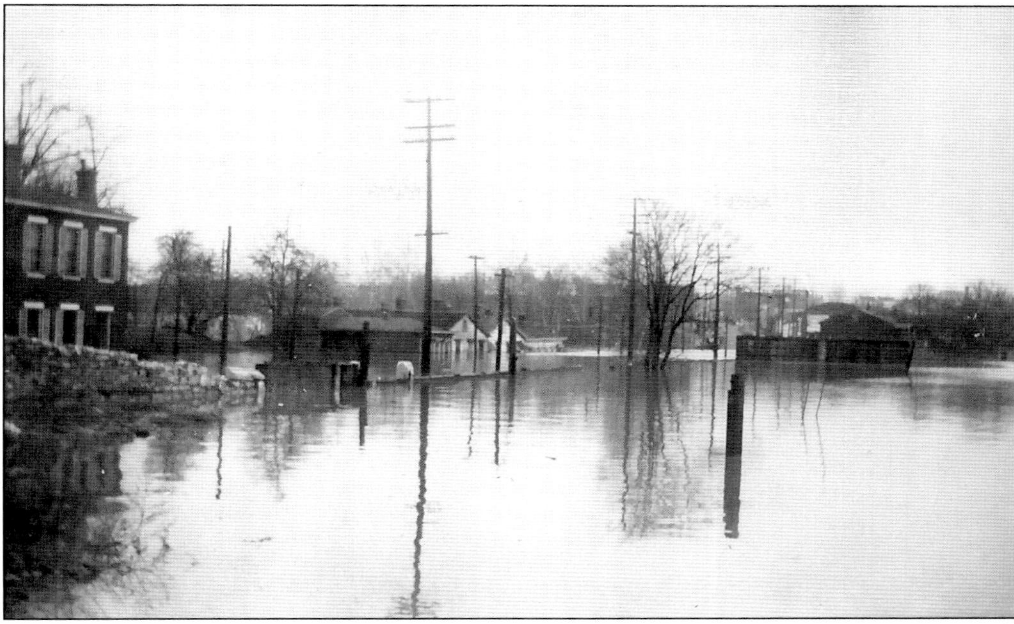

Here is the corner of Frankfort and Story Avenues, with the field next to Hadley Pottery completely underwater in 1937. Frame shotgun homes between Blue Horse Alley and Beargrass Creek bridge are barely visible. (Courtesy of the Kimpflein family.)

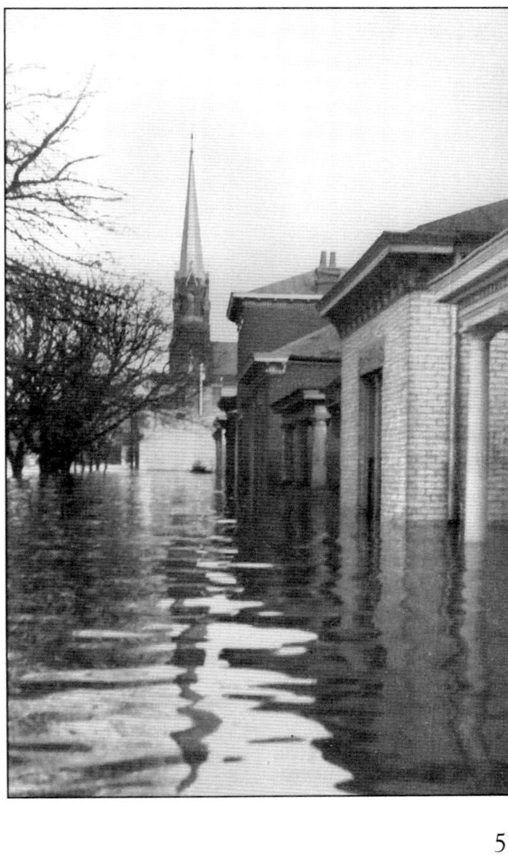

Floodwaters are seen on Washington Street with St. Joseph's Catholic Church visible in the background. During the 1937 flood, 2.5 feet of water covered the rectory. (Courtesy of St. Joseph's Catholic Church.)

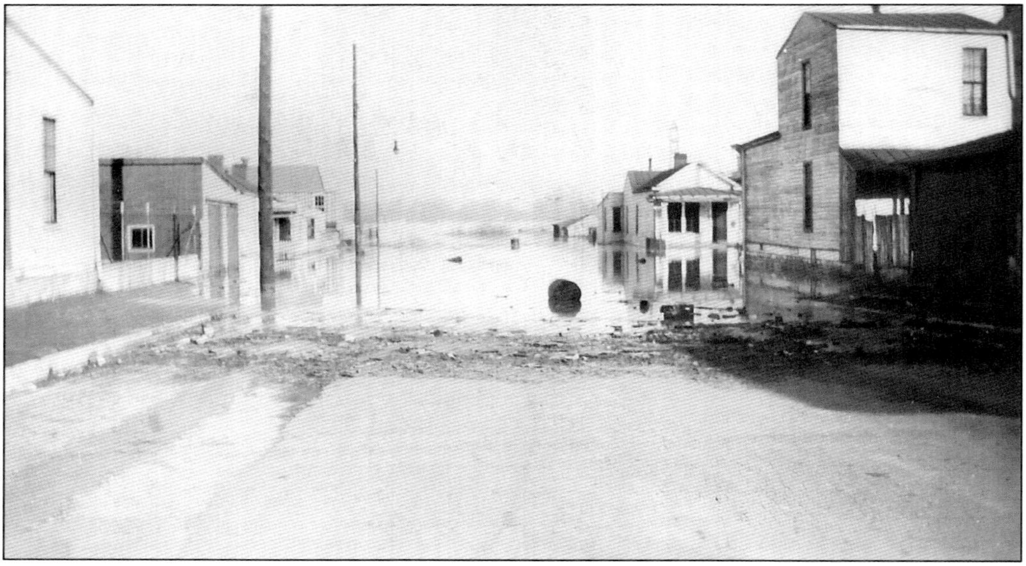

This view looks north on Webster Street from Washington Street at the debris and floodwaters in 1945. (Courtesy of Wayne Miller.)

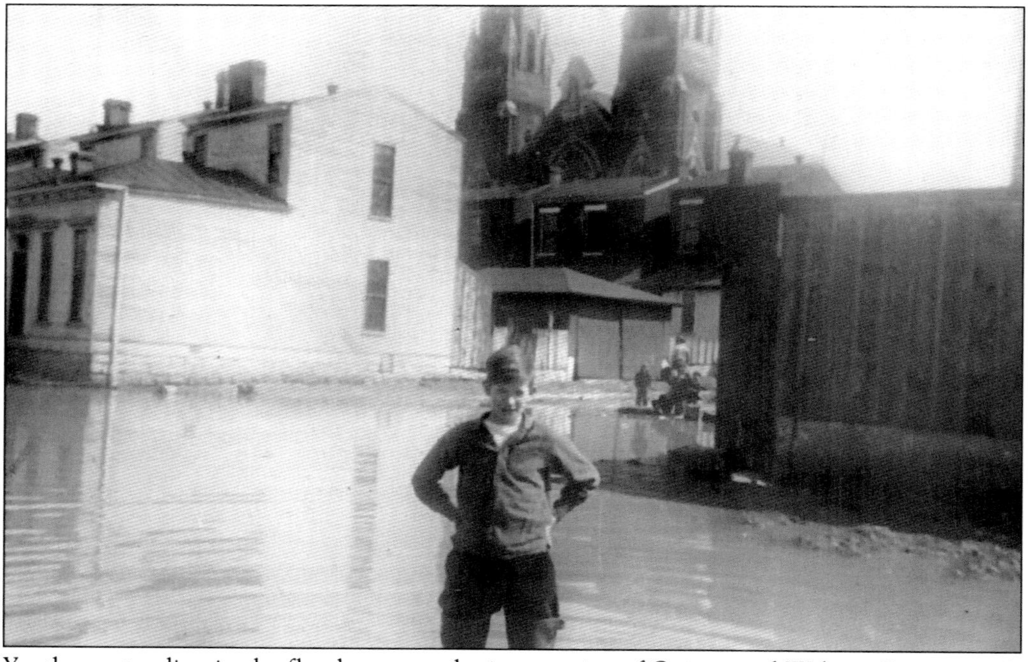

Youth are standing in the floodwaters at the intersection of Quincy and Webster Streets north of the flood wall in 1945. Built to protect Louisville from another flood, the flood wall divides Quincy Street in half. (Courtesy of the Kimpflein family.)

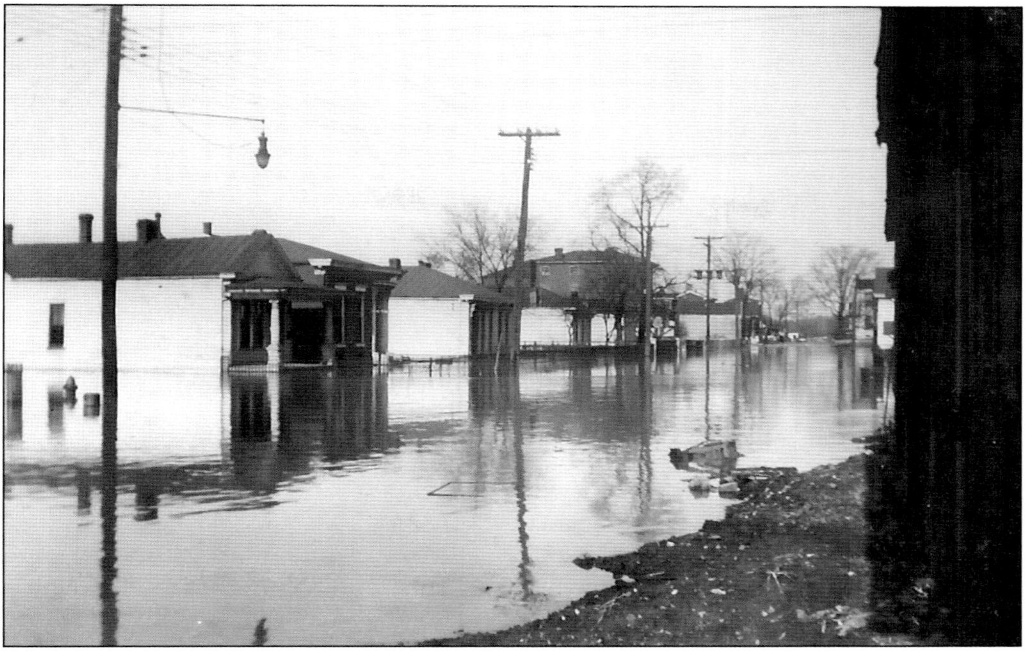

The above image looks east along the flood wall on Quincy Street in 1945. The image below looks back at St. Joseph's Catholic Church from north of Quincy Street during the 1945 flood. (Both, courtesy of the Kimpflein family.)

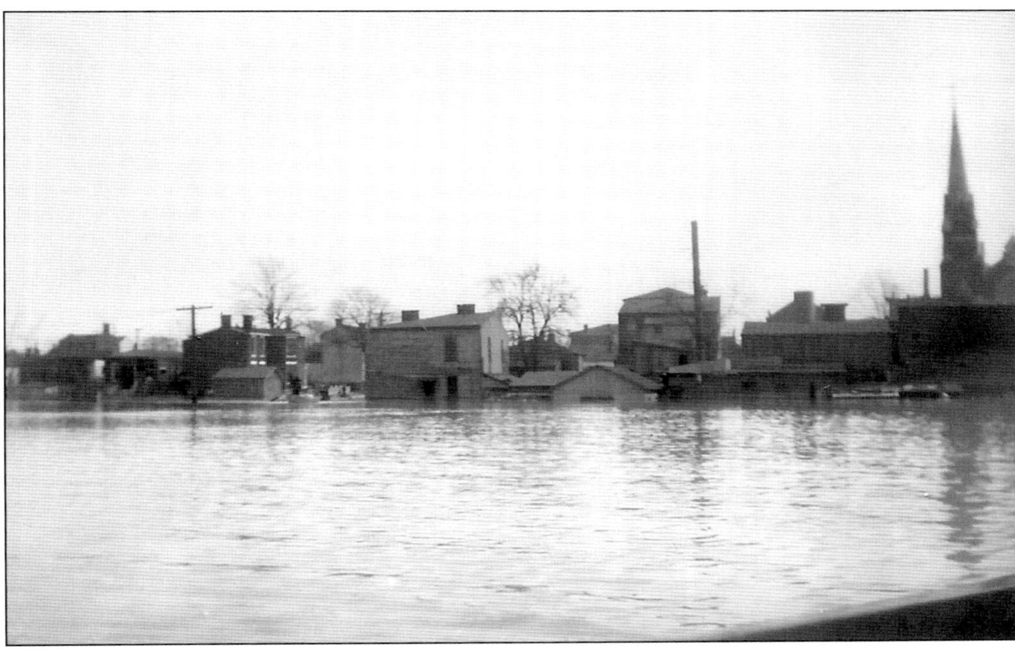

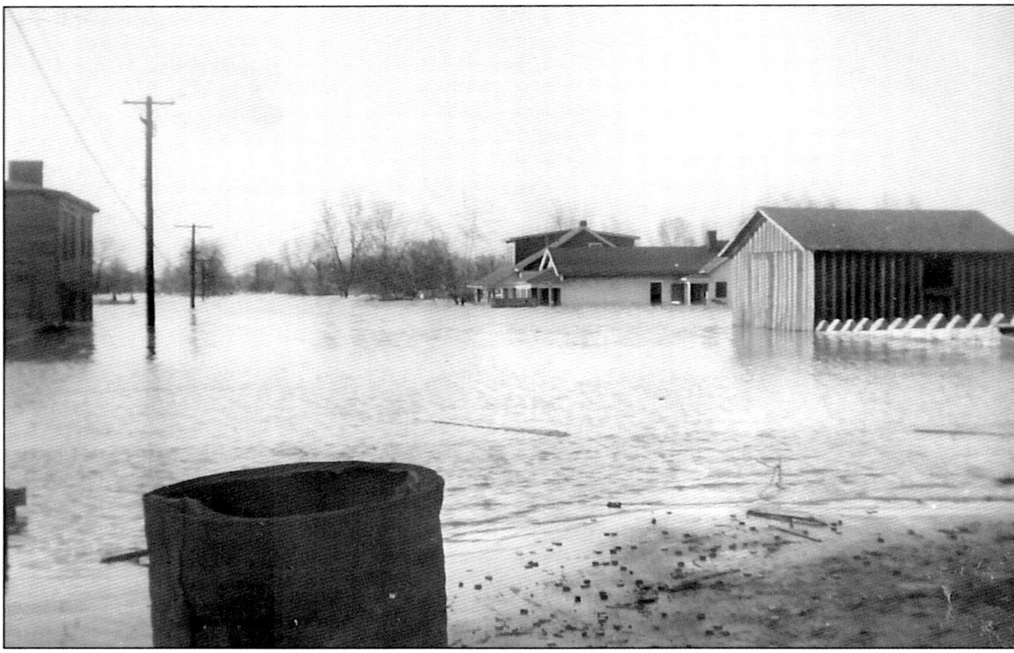

High water is seen on Adams Street close to Quincy Street in 1945. (Courtesy of the Kimpflein family.)

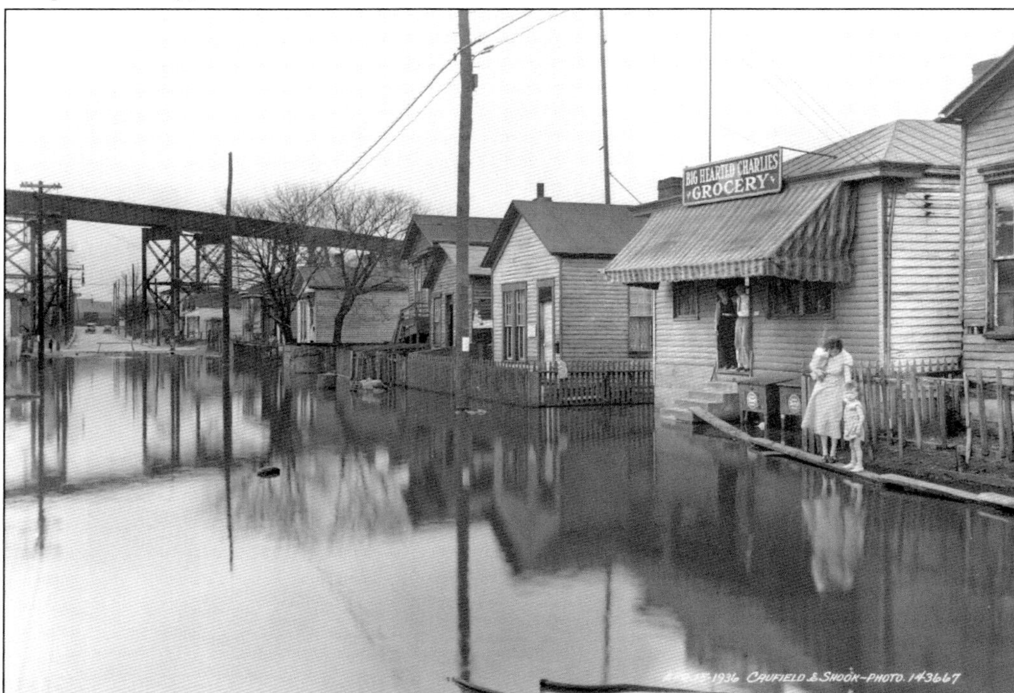

Flooding is shown in 1945 north of Adams Street in Butchertown. After the flood, Meyers Pharmacy on Story Avenue released a commemorative booklet of photographs taken by their members. (Courtesy of the University of Louisville Photographic Archives.)

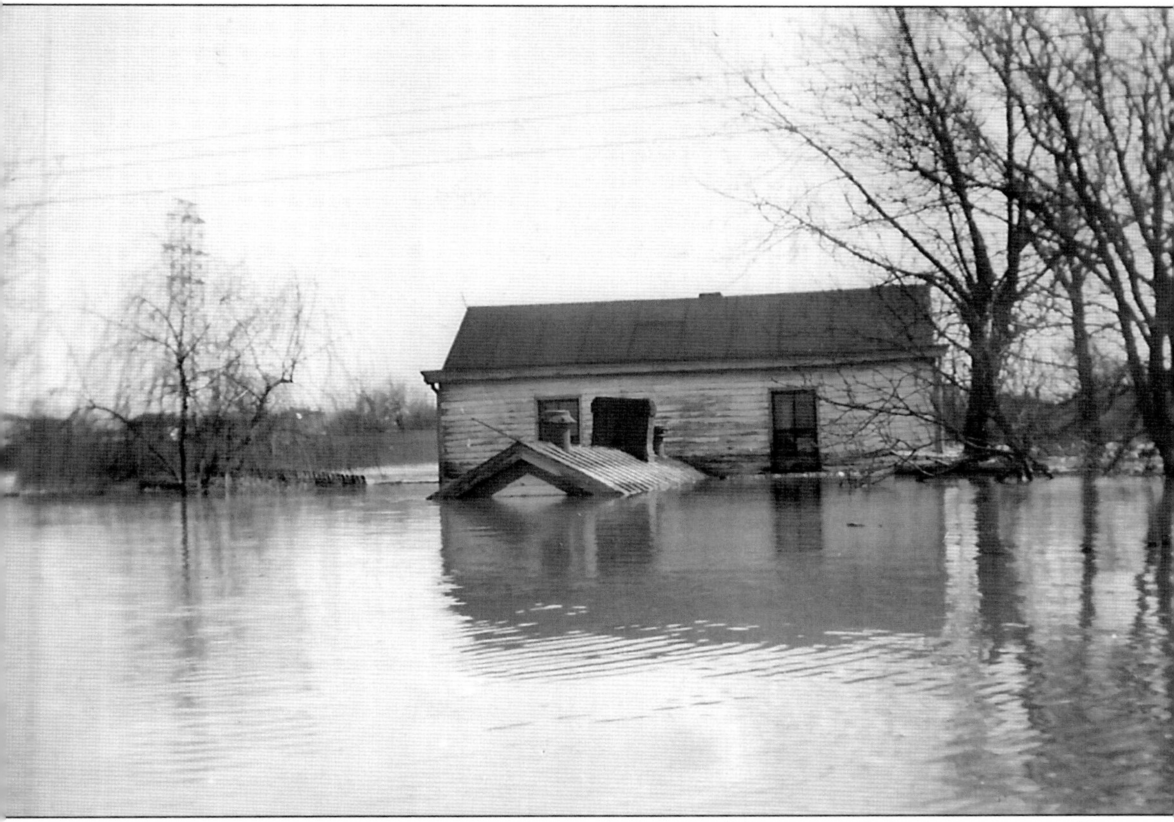

In 1945, local residents ventured into floodwaters by boat and documented the high water and submerged homes by camera. Meyers Pharmacy, formerly located at 1335 Story Avenue, put out a commemorative book with pictures of the flooding throughout Butchertown and the Point neighborhood for 50¢. (Courtesy of the Kimpflein family.)

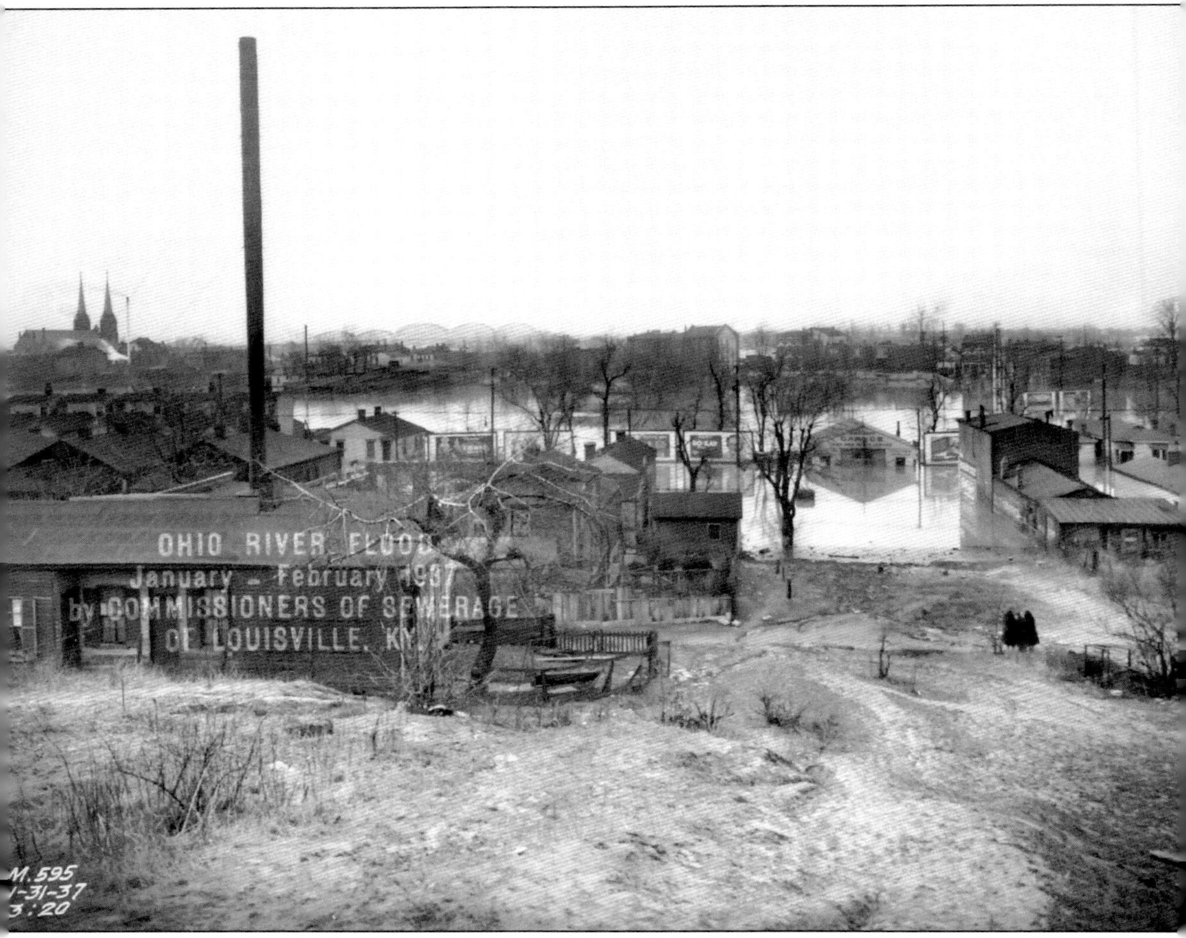

This view looks north from Stevenson Street at flooding along Beargrass Creek in January or February 1937. Mellwood Avenue is underwater, and Hadley Pottery and Vernon Lane can be seen in the center of the image in the distance. (Courtesy of the University of Louisville Photographic Archives.)

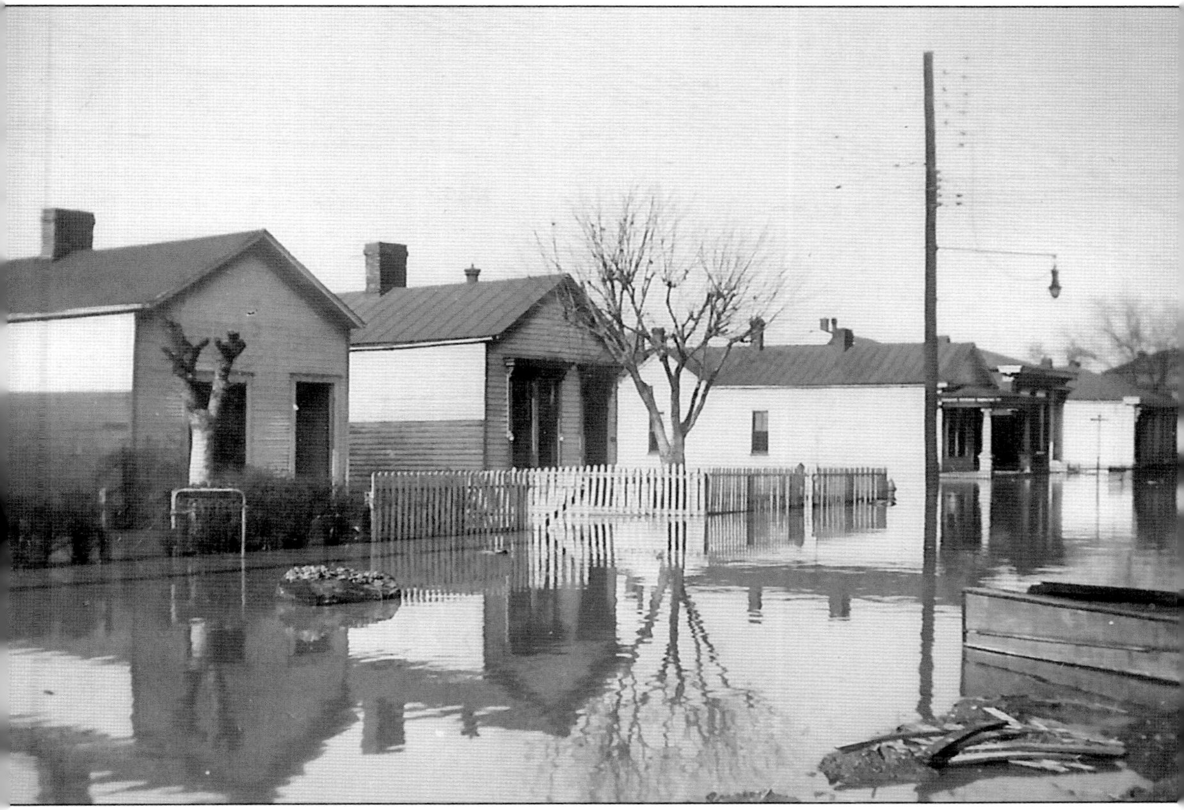

Quincy Street west of the flood wall opening at Webster Street is shown above. While this part of the flood wall was already standing in 1945, the Army Corps of Engineers did not complete the remainder until 1957. The floodwaters left 4 inches of mud throughout many people's homes. (Courtesy of the Kimpflein family.)

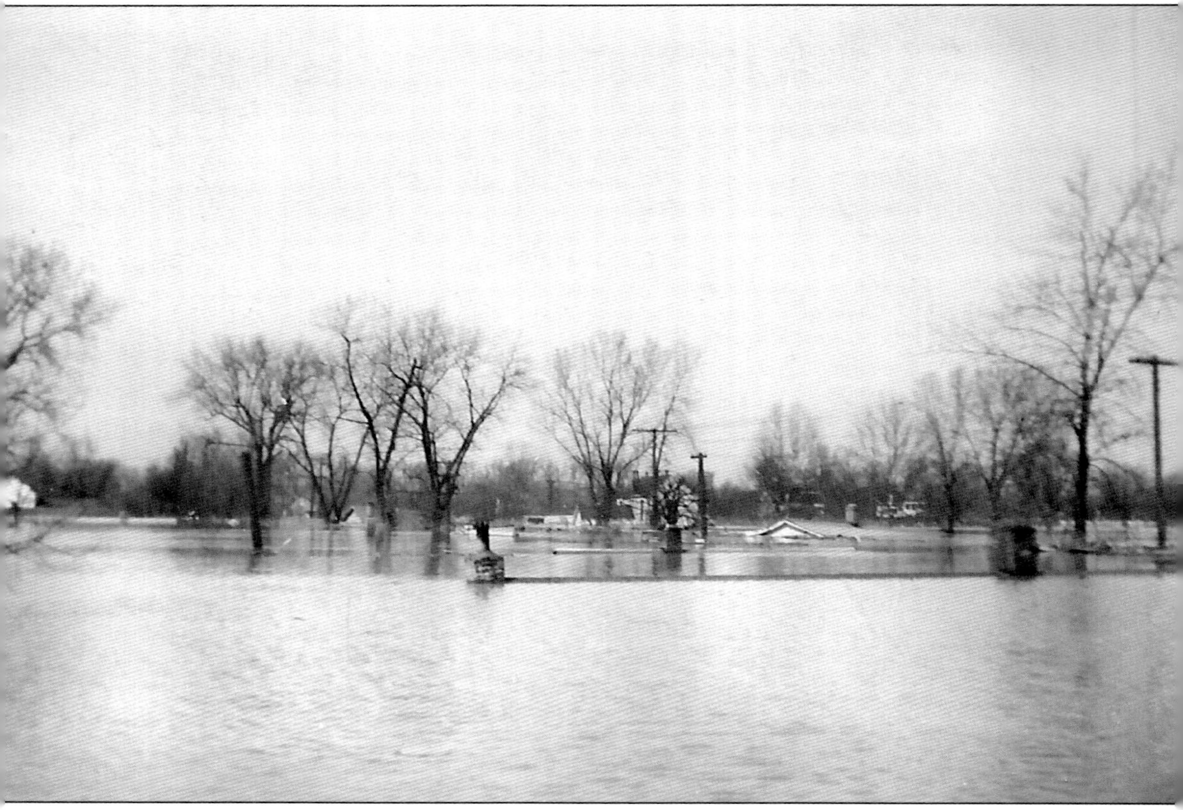

With water blanketing houses, streets, and other features, the Kimpflein family was not able to identify this picture other than stating it was taken in the Butchertown/Point neighborhood in 1945. Many residents believed that the sandbags would hold back the floodwaters and did not evacuate. In the early morning hours it began to rain; people were caught in their homes when the water breached the barriers. They had to be rescued by boat. (Courtesy of the Kimpflein family.)

Four

Religious Life, Education, and Recreation

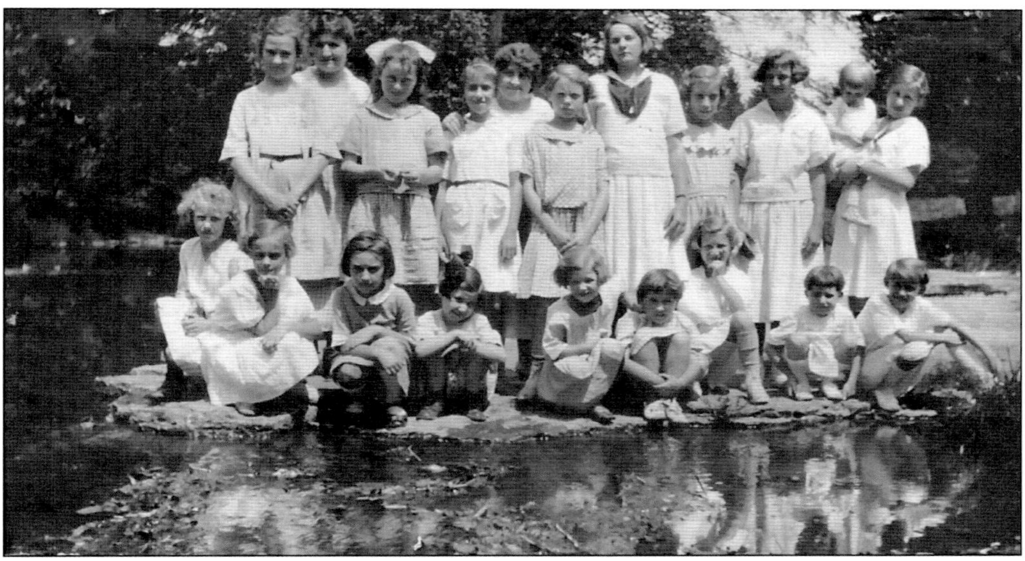

The Light Brigade, a children's missionary society of the Third Lutheran Church, visit Big Rock in Cherokee Park in 1922. Organized outings and activities by churches, schools, and clubs were very important in keeping children occupied. Pictured from left to right are (first row) Virginia Stiglitz, Bernice Kalkhof, Louis Schwenck, Mary Jane Spaid, Virginia Stoecker, Dorothy Herman, Nola Crabtree, and Agnes Crabtree; (second row) Margaret Lee Perkins, Mrs. J. E. Spaid, Grace Herman, Elizabeth Kalkhof, Elsie Haemish, Susie Martin, Anna Schoedinger, Virginia Watson, Verna Schwab, Grace Dillman, and Ruth Spaid. (Courtesy of Third Lutheran Church.)

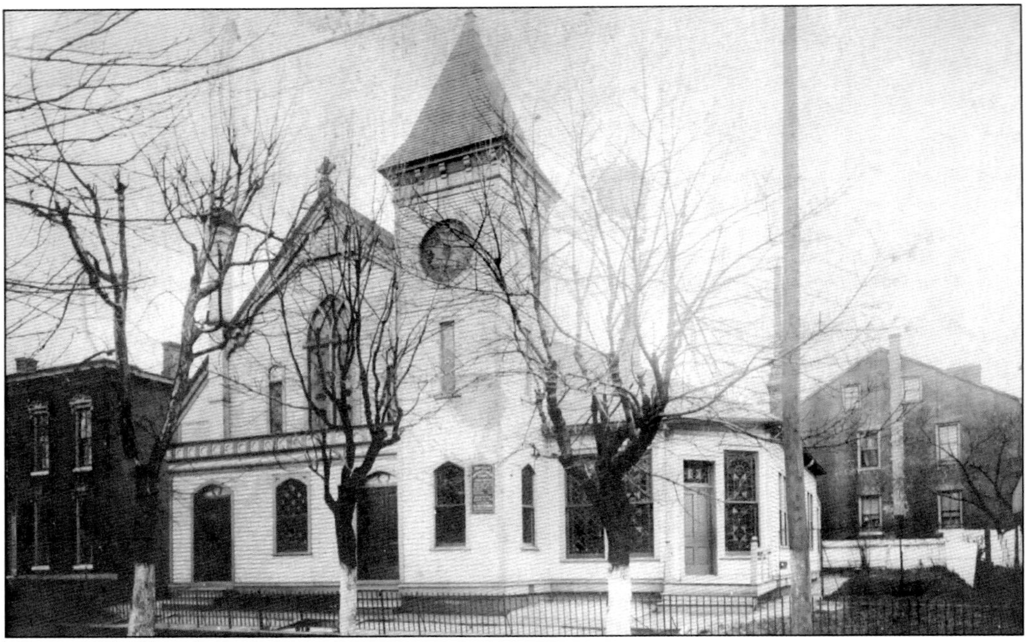

Third Lutheran Church traces its beginnings to 1870, when it was founded as a mission for the First Lutheran Church. In 1886, the Third Lutheran Church was organized and began building on the Story Avenue lot it bought. The frame structure, with its distinct steeple, was featured in 1909 on a *Louisville Evening Post* postcard. (Courtesy of Third Lutheran Church.)

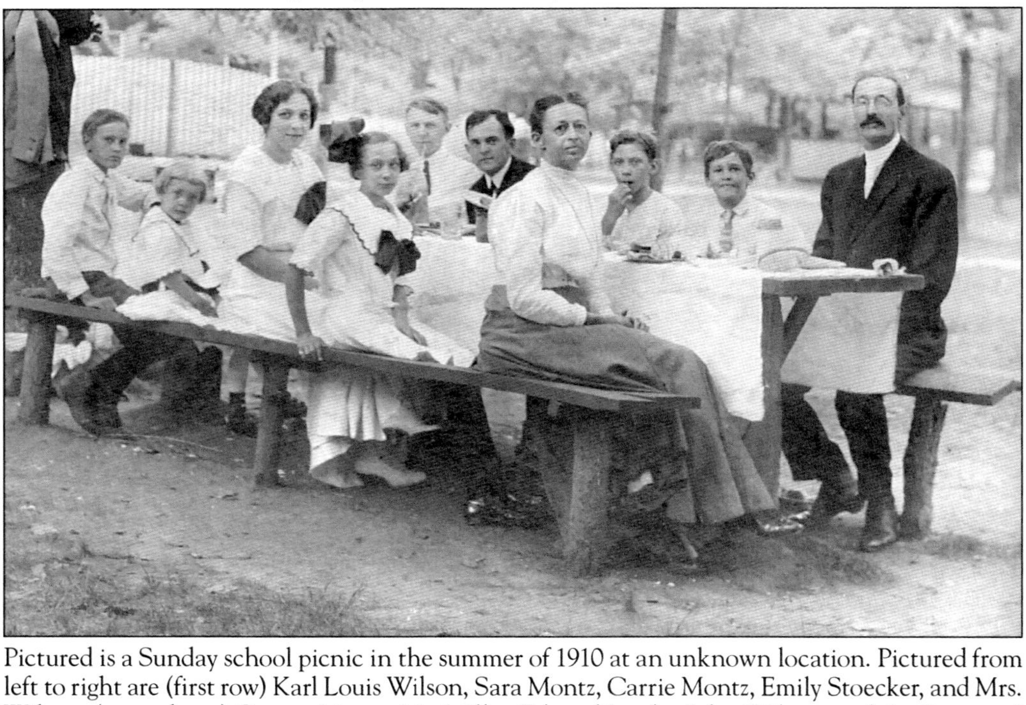

Pictured is a Sunday school picnic in the summer of 1910 at an unknown location. Pictured from left to right are (first row) Karl Louis Wilson, Sara Montz, Carrie Montz, Emily Stoecker, and Mrs. Wilson; (second row) George Montz, Mr. Miller, Edward Jacoby, John Wilson, and the Reverend Charles A. Wilson. (Courtesy of Third Lutheran Church.)

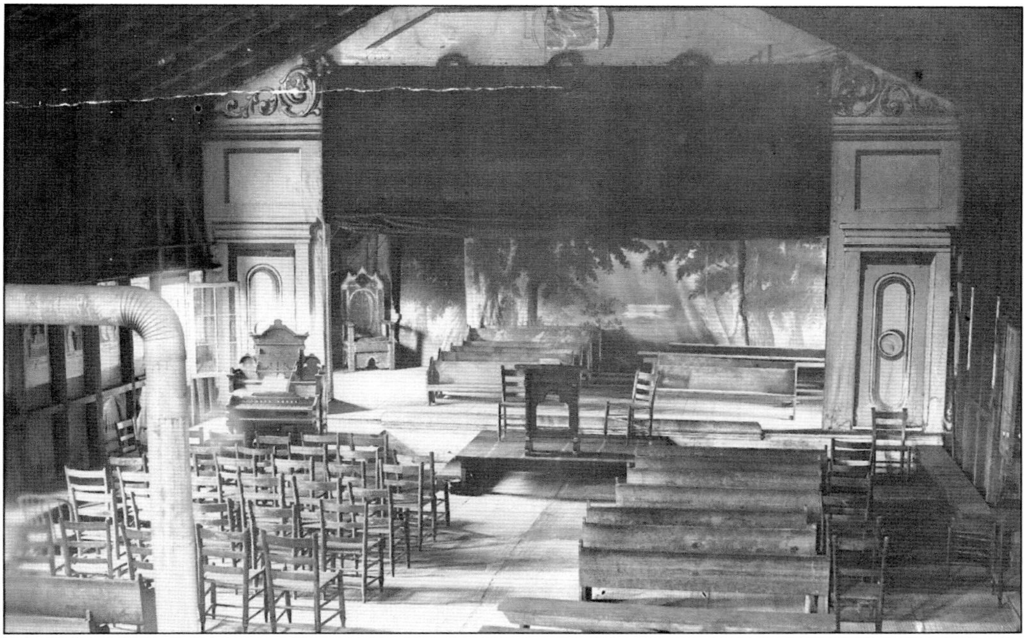

This is the interior of the old gymnasium, the interim meeting location of Third Lutheran Church from 1880 to 1887, before it moved to its present location. At that time, the church was looking to expand to Butchertown and set up a mission in the old gymnasium, a former meat-curing house behind the Letterle house on Adams Street. (Courtesy of Third Lutheran Church.)

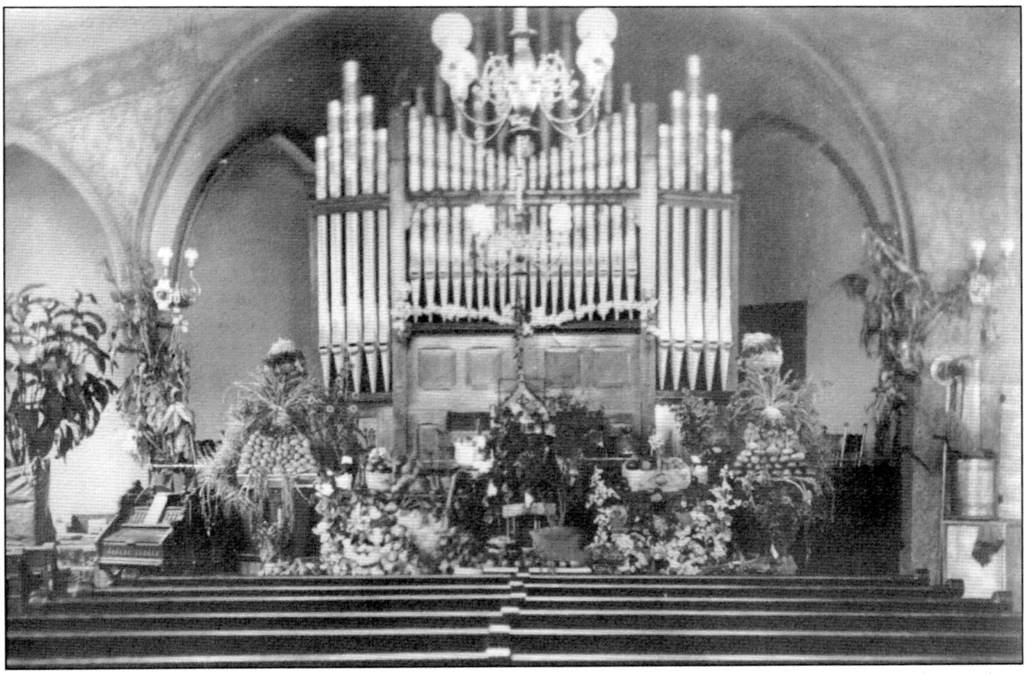

An early 1900s interior of Third Lutheran Church, with harvest offerings on the pulpit and a small stove to the right used to warm the building, is shown here. (Courtesy of Grace Immanuel United Church of Christ.)

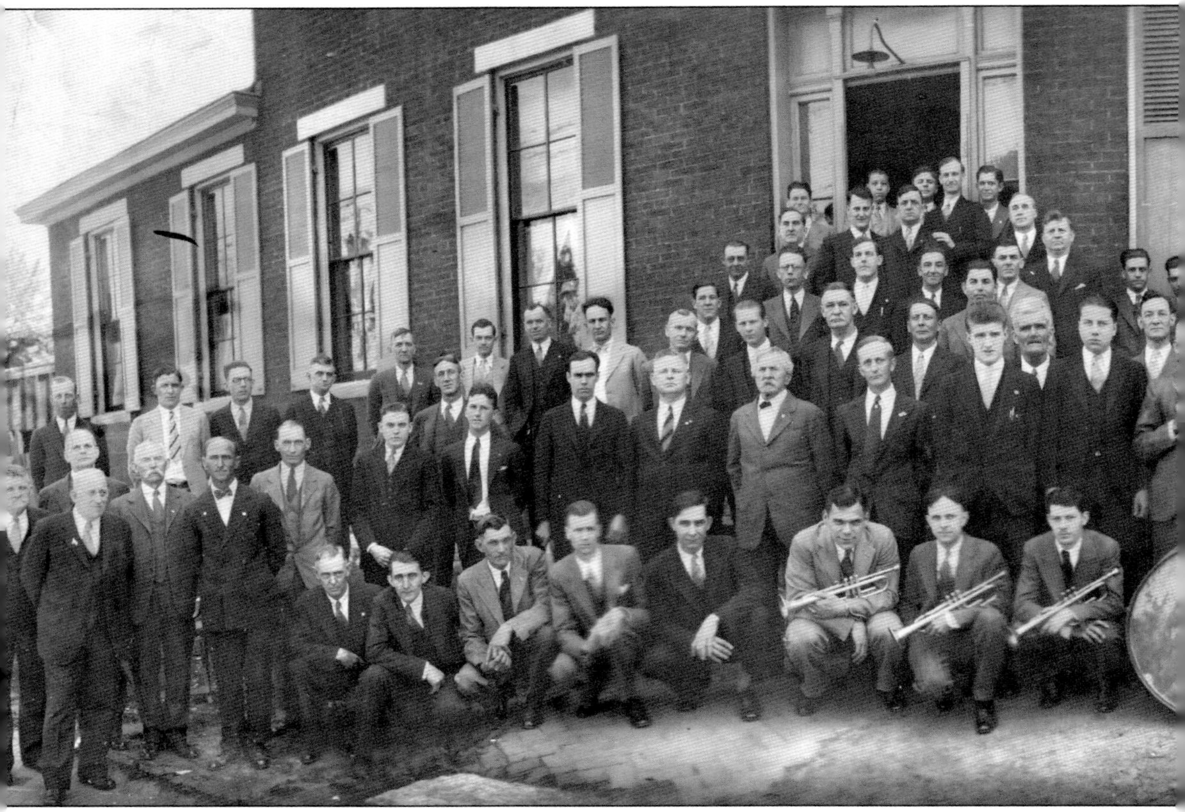

In 1929, the church split, and members of Third Lutheran Church built a new parish on Frankfort Avenue, while members that stayed to form the Grace Immanuel United Church of Christ were without a building and met in the basement of Rendezvous Inn until their former church

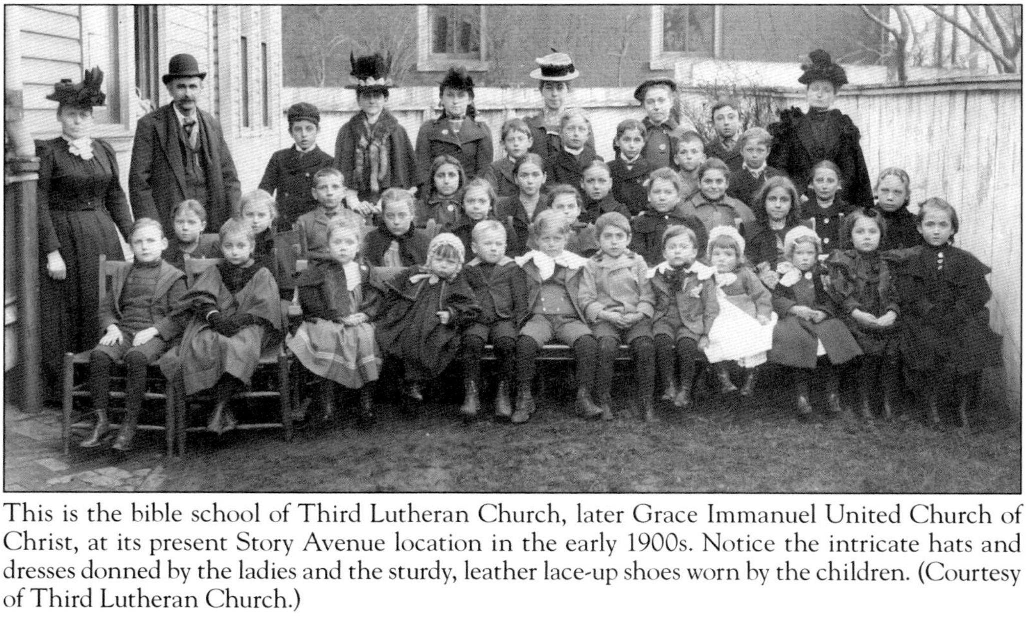

This is the bible school of Third Lutheran Church, later Grace Immanuel United Church of Christ, at its present Story Avenue location in the early 1900s. Notice the intricate hats and dresses donned by the ladies and the sturdy, leather lace-up shoes worn by the children. (Courtesy of Third Lutheran Church.)

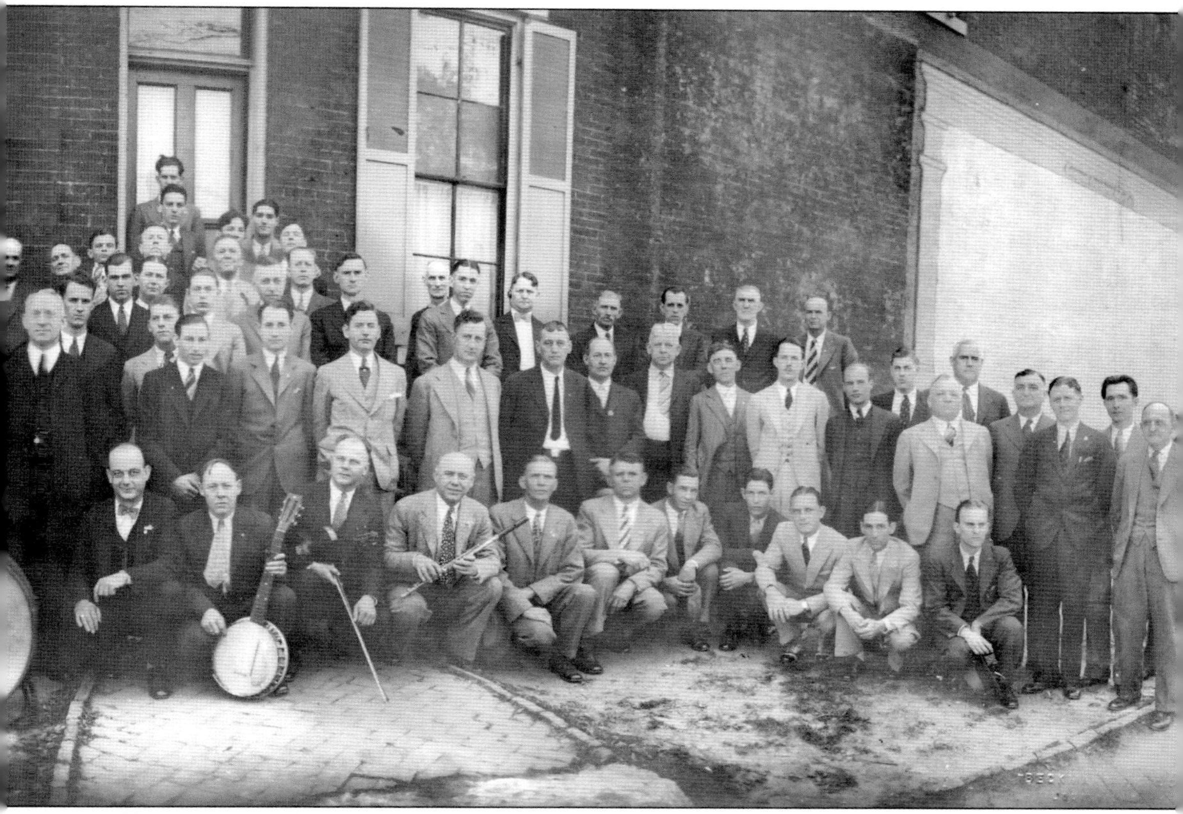

could be repurchased in 1931 from Third Lutheran Church. Pictured are members of the Men's Eveready Bible Class in front of the Rendezvous Inn at the intersection of Mellwood Avenue and Brownsboro Road. (Courtesy of Grace Immanuel United Church of Christ.)

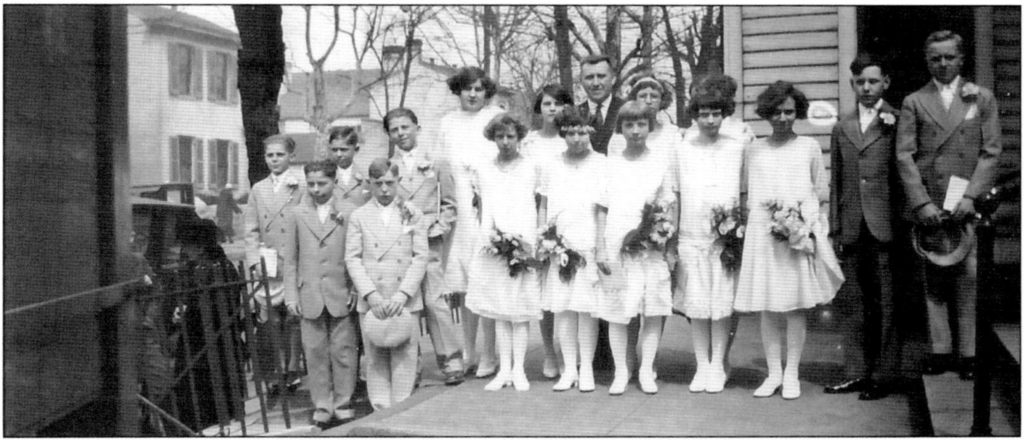

Here is a confirmation class at Third Lutheran Church on Story Avenue in 1926. The girls pictured are, from left to right, Edna May Biechert, Ethel Edwards, Anna Hepp, Bernice Kalkoff, Helen Kope, Katherine Lukemeier, Ethel Satori, Louis Schwenck, Eva Scoff, Evelyn Smith, and Lola Wheatley. The boys pictured are, from left to right, Cummins Childers, Harry Frantz, Gilbert Gutzel, Willis Herman, Edward Humphrey, Morton Kinker, Clarence Krauth, William Santori, Bernard Smith, and Charles Stoecker. (Courtesy of Third Lutheran Church.)

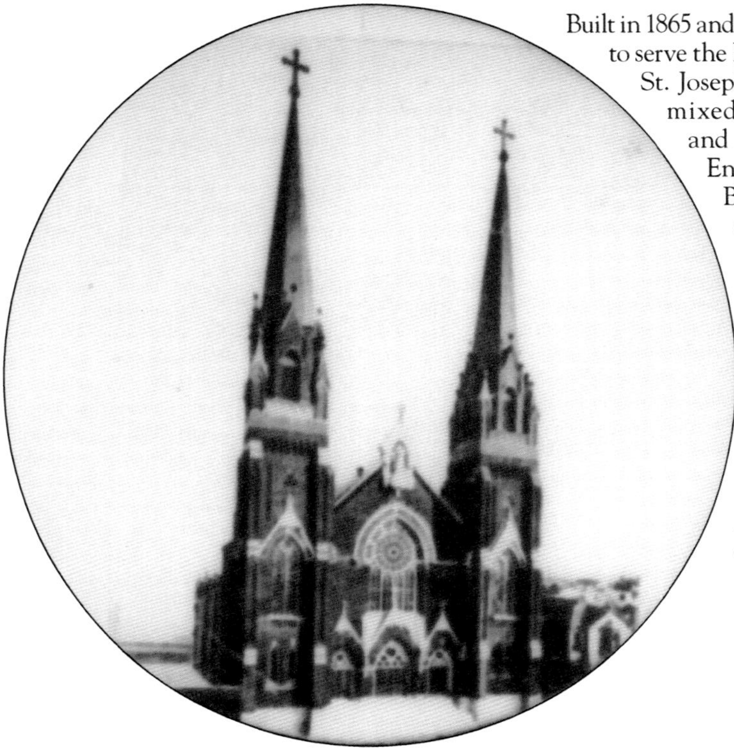

Built in 1865 and 1866 and established in 1866 to serve the large immigrant population, St. Joseph's Catholic Church was a mixed parish, serving German and Irish families. In 1876, the English-speaking Catholics of Butchertown built a church at the corner of Washington and Buchanan Streets. It was known as St. Columba's until 1893, when a new building was constructed and renamed Blessed Sacrament Church. After the last pastor died in 1933, the remaining members joined St. Joseph's. (Courtesy of St. Joseph's Catholic Church.)

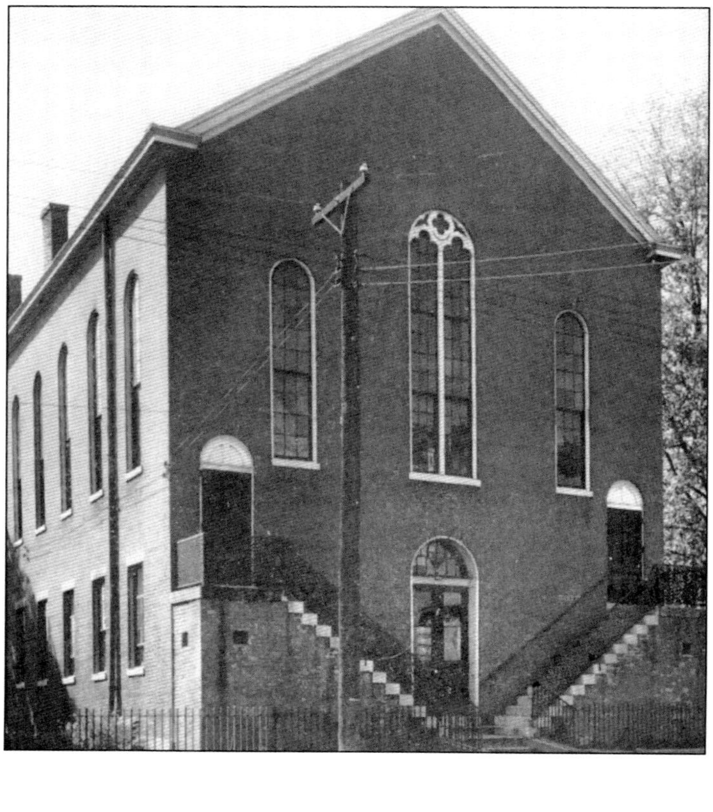

Having outgrown the original combination structure, pictured above, St. Joseph's Catholic Church deeded a piece of property to a brick factory in 1882 in exchange for one million building bricks to construct a permanent parish. Members selected architect Adolph Druiding to design plans for the new church and laid the cornerstone on October 21, 1883. The brick church built in the Gothic Revival style with stone and terra-cotta inserts was completed in 1885. In 1905 and 1906, the 175-foot-tall twin spires were added, making the church an easy landmark to spot from far away. (Courtesy of St. Joseph's Catholic Church.)

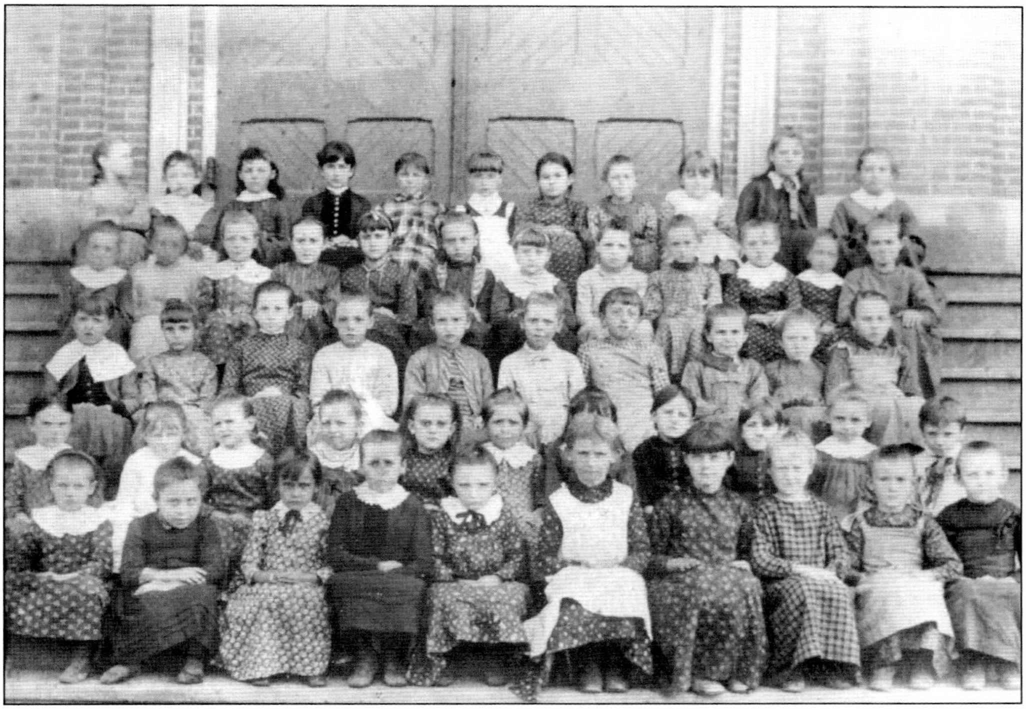

In 1867, the Ursuline nuns started teaching children at St. Joseph's Catholic Church. Until their home was built in 1926 at 114 Adams Street, they commuted by horse-drawn carriage from their headquarters at Shelby and Chestnut Streets. This building is now a day care center. The picture above shows grade school children sitting on the wooden steps in front the church in 1877. Below is the oldest picture of a wedding at St. Joseph's Catholic Church between John and Helen Fehr Peters in 1877. (Both, courtesy of St. Joseph's Catholic Church.)

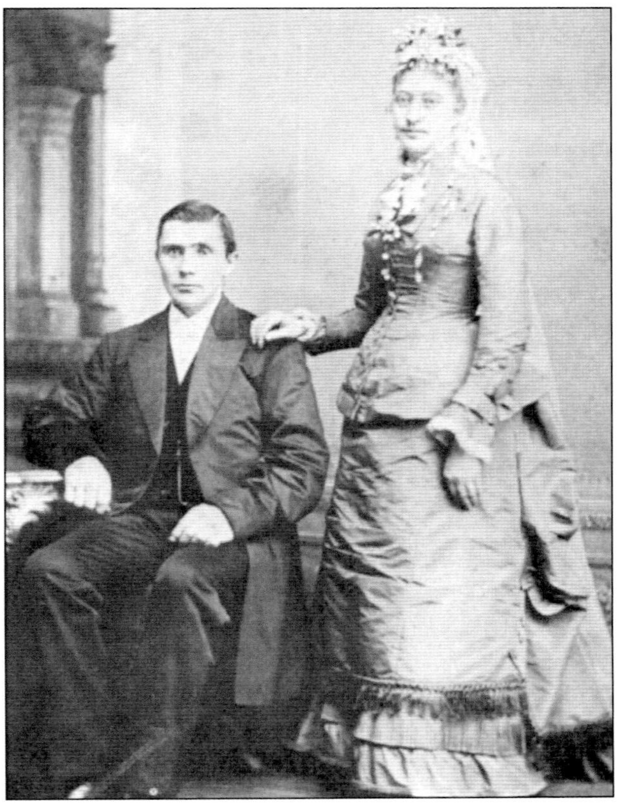

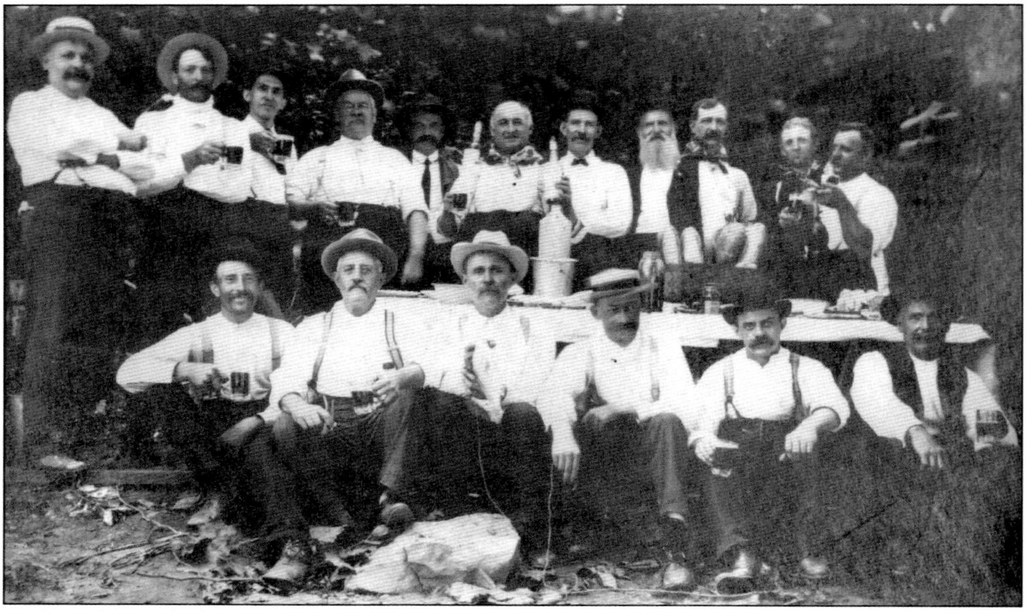

St. Joseph's Catholic Church trustees are relaxing at a picnic between 1906 and 1910. Pictured from left to right are (first row) George Lohmiller, Henry Smith, George Ecker, Joe Schmitt, Will Staeuble, and Charles Stoecker; (second row) Louis Kissel, Andy Mucklebaur, Louis Schmuckie, John Oertel Sr., Pete Hazley, Gus Schlacter, Joe Hillerich, Martin Kolb, August Georgel, Father Paulinus, and Charles Staeuble. (Courtesy of St. Joseph's Catholic Church.)

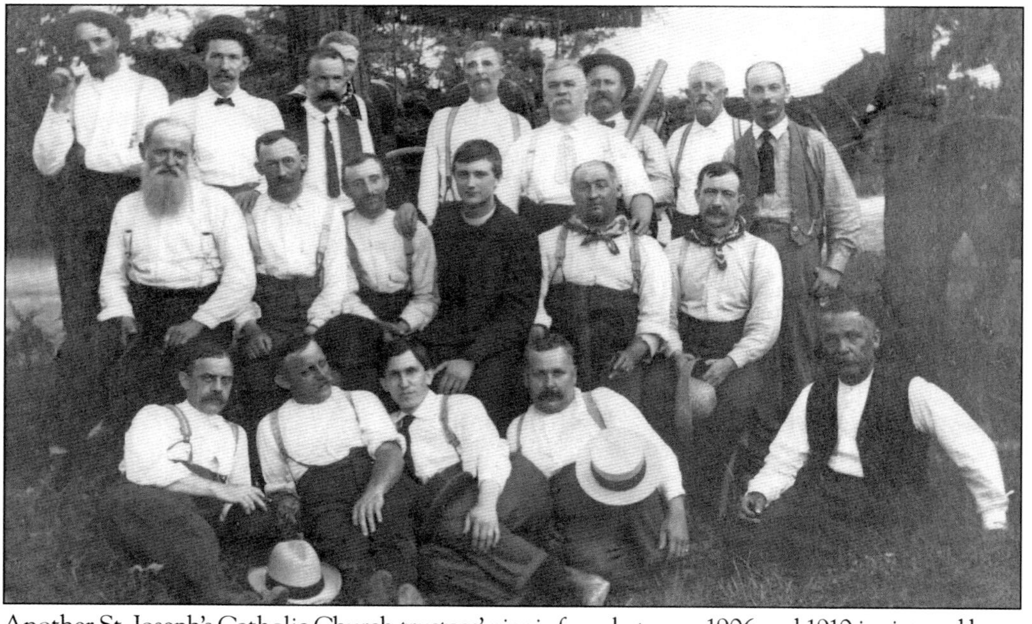

Another St. Joseph's Catholic Church trustees' picnic from between 1906 and 1910 is pictured here. From left to right are (first row) Will Staeuble, Charles Staeuble, Willie Mazer, Louis Kissel, and Charles Stoecker; (second row) Martin Kolb, Frank Gnau, George Lohmille, Father Alexander, Gus Schlacter, and August Georgel; (third row) Andy Mucklebauer, Joe Hillerich, three unidentified, John F. Oertel Sr., Joseph Blasi, Jacob Steurer, and Frank Ohlman. (Courtesy of St. Joseph's Catholic Church.)

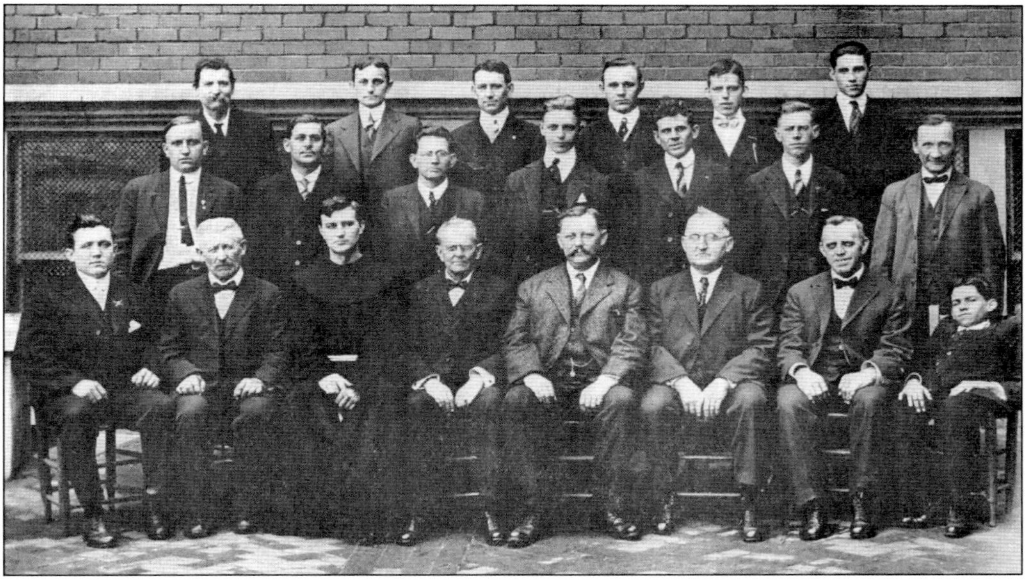

Here are trustees of St. Joseph's Catholic Church. (Courtesy of St. Joseph's Catholic Church.)

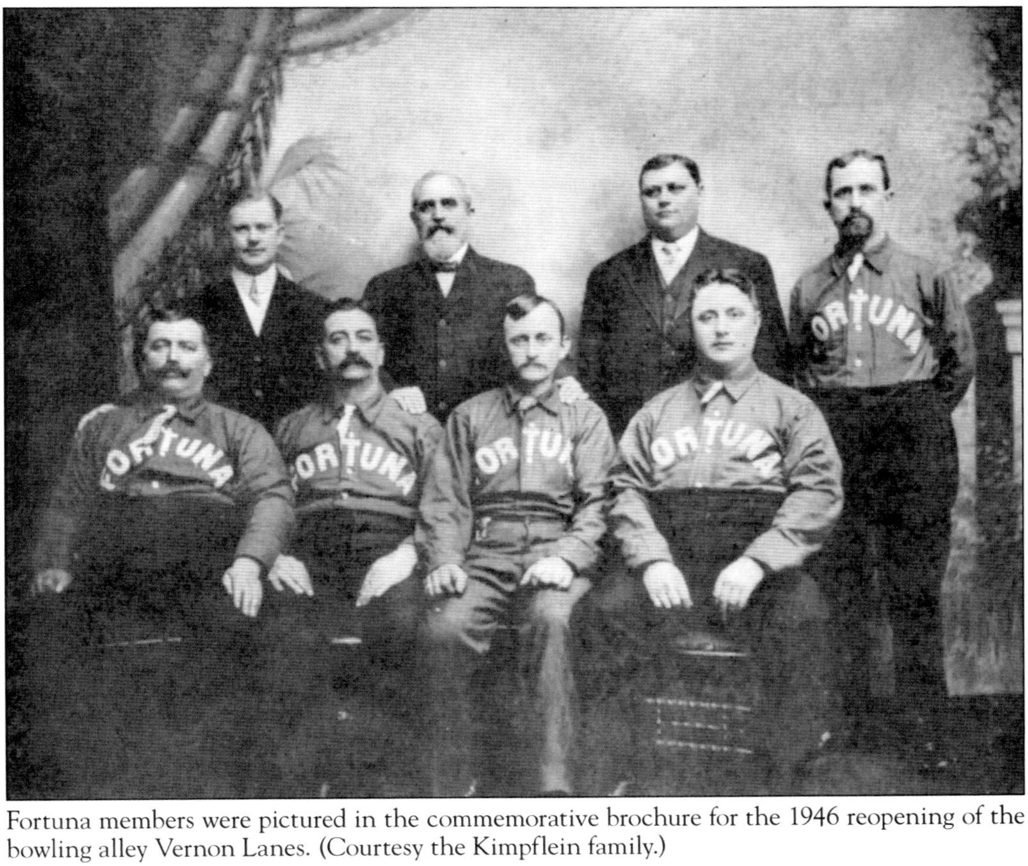

Fortuna members were pictured in the commemorative brochure for the 1946 reopening of the bowling alley Vernon Lanes. (Courtesy the Kimpflein family.)

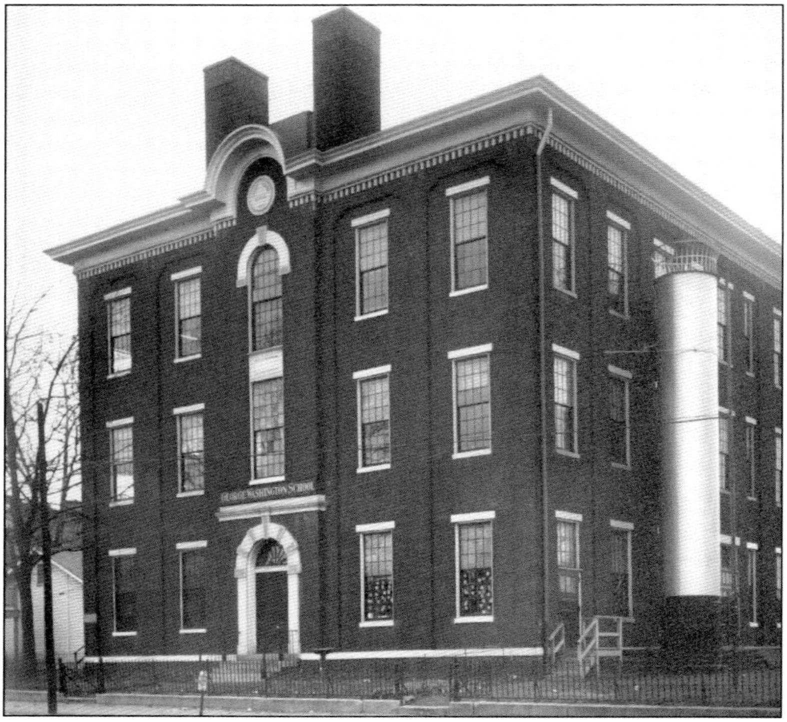

In 1866, the First Ward School, later renamed the George Washington School by its trustees in honor of the first American president, opened at Washington and Cabel Streets. Exactly 100 years after it opened, the George Washington School closed its doors. A meatpacking company acquired the lot, and the school was demolished. (Courtesy of the Jefferson County School System.)

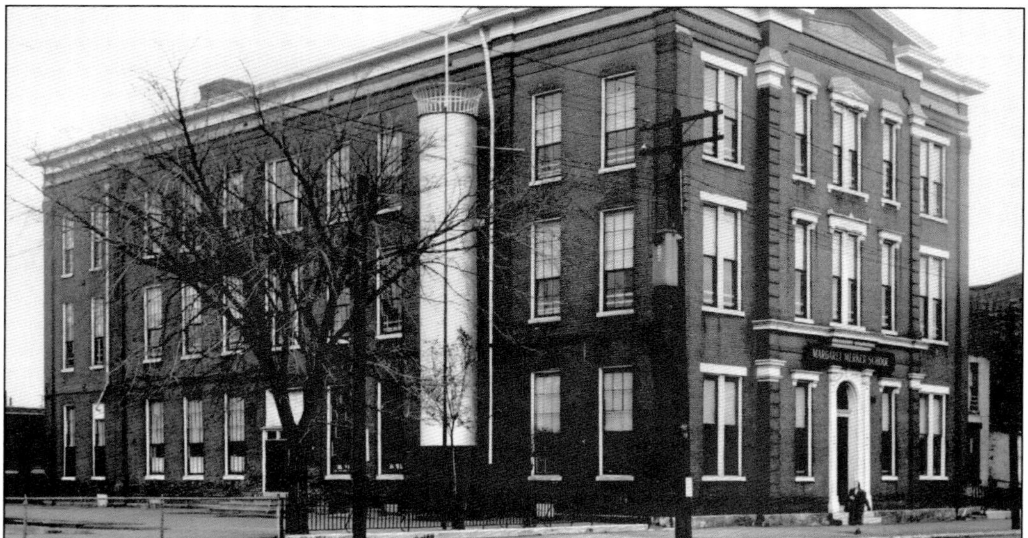

In 1853, the Second Ward School, later known as Margaret Merker School, was opened at 931 East Market Street. During recess, children were permitted to play in nearby Woodland Gardens. In the summer of 1863, the school was designated as Hospital No. 9 for the sick and wounded soldiers of the Civil War. After the war, the building was renovated and students once more attended classes there. In 1923, the school was renamed in honor of Merker, a scholar and social worker in Kentucky. A new neighborhood school, Abraham Lincoln Elementary, was built in 1966 on Main Street, and the Margaret Merker School was torn down. (Courtesy of the Jefferson County School System.)

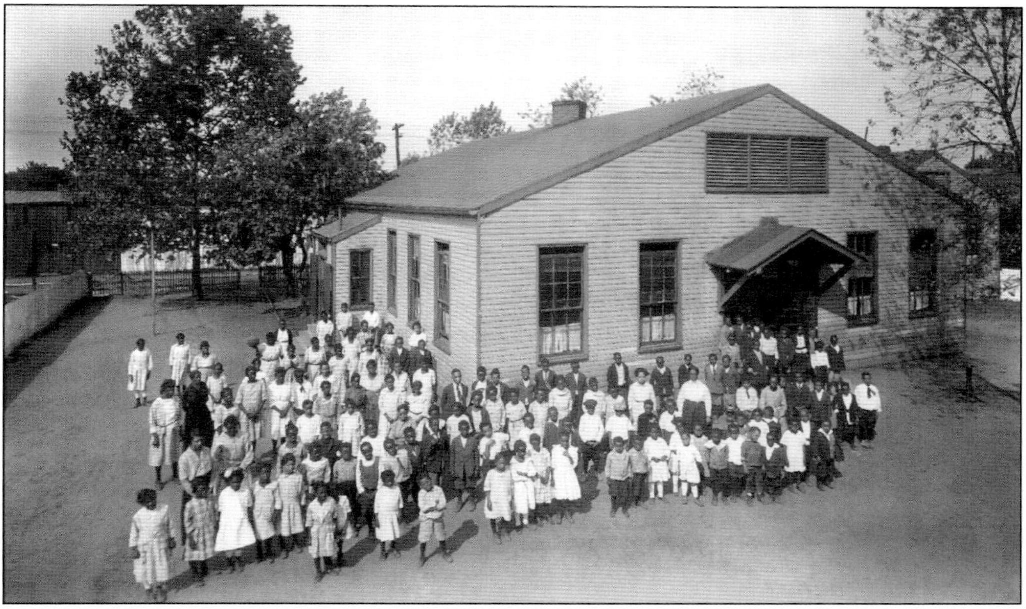

Maiden Lane Colored School was renamed Benjamin Bannecker Elementary School in 1911 in honor of the famous astronomer, naturalist, and author. Maiden Lane school replaced the Upper Fulton Street School, which was destroyed by flood in 1884. Bannecker school closed in 1956 with the end of segregation, and the building was later demolished. (Courtesy of the University of Louisville Photographic Archives.)

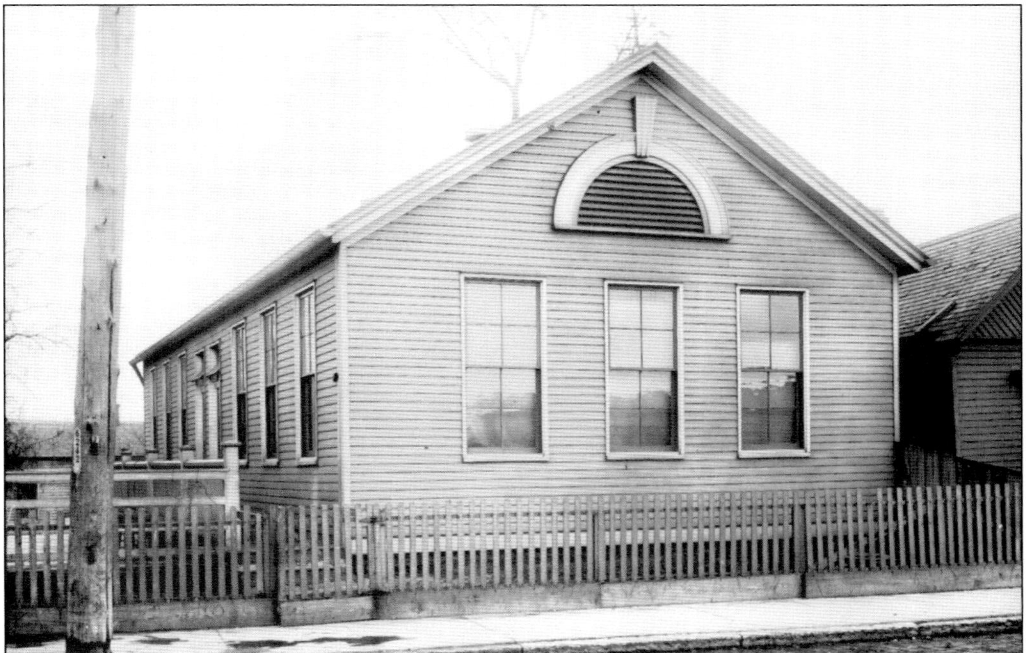

Located at 1560 Fulton Street, the Upper Fulton Street School was opened about 1838 and served the surrounding neighborhood. In 1912, Upper Fulton Street School had four classrooms. (Courtesy of the Jefferson County School System.)

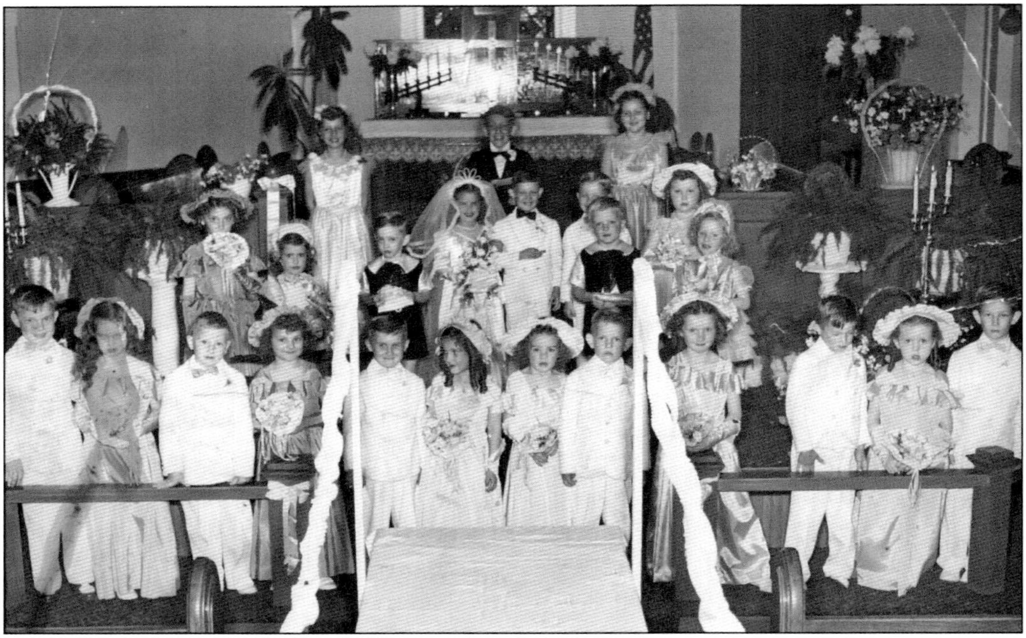

Pictured is a Tom Thumb wedding of several area children that was sponsored by and held in Grace Immanuel United Church of Christ around 1950. The wedding was held to raise funds for the George Washington School. Churches and the Wesley House worked hard to provide entertainment to area children with organized activities and excursions. (Courtesy of Eddie Mattern.)

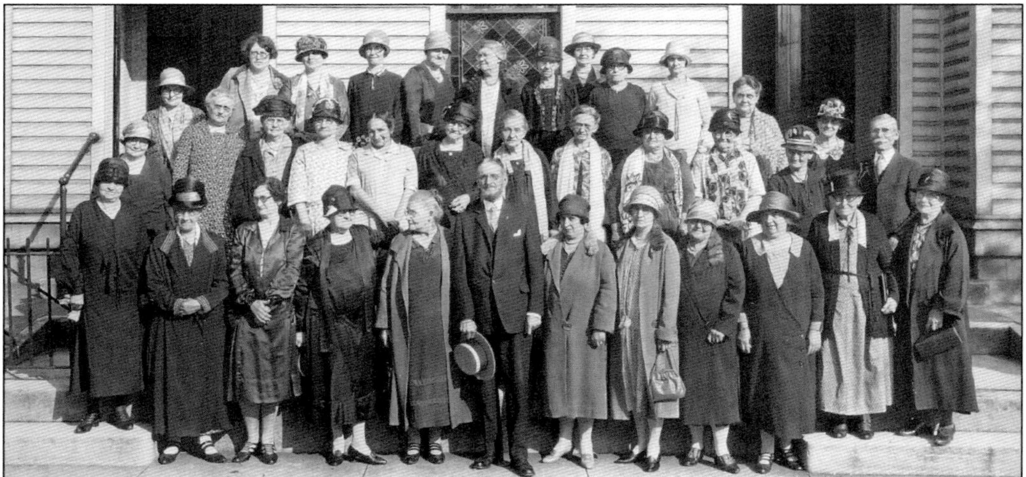

The Third Lutheran Church Ladies Bible Class is pictured in 1927. Pictured from left to right are (first row) Mrs. S. Zulauf, Mrs. M. Dillman, Mrs. W. Gregory, Mrs. A. Hitt, Mrs. W. F. Scholl, Dr. German (teacher), Mrs. Frillingsdorf, Mrs. S. Childers, Mrs. F. Herman, Mrs. L. Herman, Mrs. C. Zeiler, and Mrs. W. Scherer; (second row) Mrs. J. Humphrey, Mrs. Winkler, Mrs. J. Schaad, Mrs. Straub, Mrs. Schwegler, Mrs. D. Esterle, Mrs. Phillips, Mrs. M. Smith, Mrs. Perryman, Mrs. Frantz, Mrs. Hensel, and Mr. R. Zimmerman; (third row) Mrs. L. Schneider, Mrs. K. Holden, Mrs. E. Stoecker, Mrs. H. Mann, Mrs. A. Schwenck, Mrs. H. Land Sr., Mrs. R. Zimmerman, Miss C. Bollenbach, Miss L. Rehm, Mrs. Rosenbaum, Mrs. F. Dresel, and Mrs. Clausen. (Courtesy of Third Lutheran Church.)

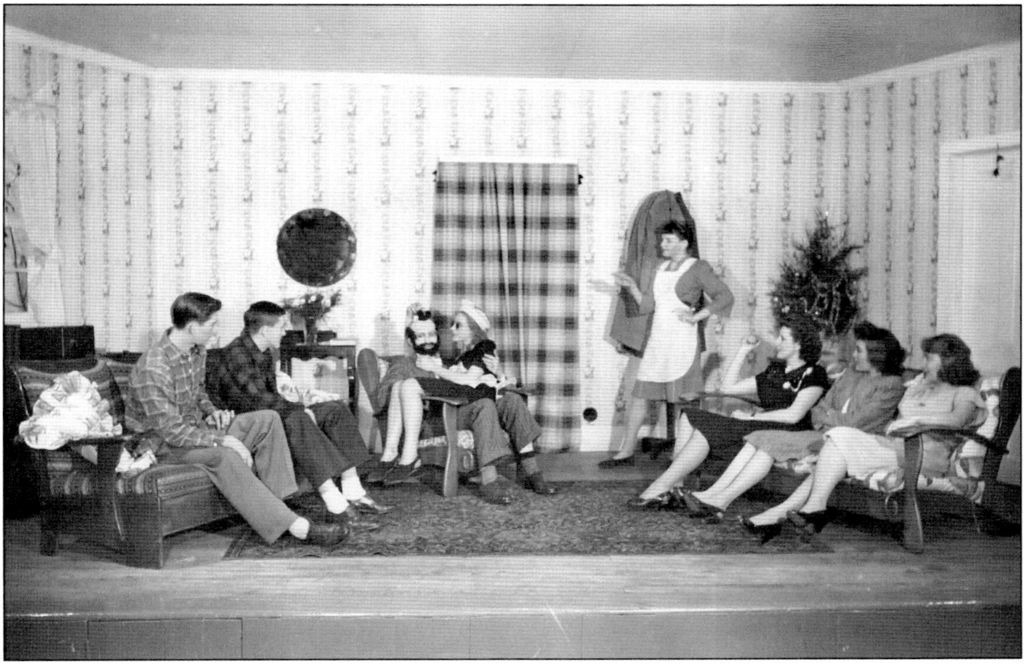

In the above image, the play *The Pest Guest* is being performed at the Green Barn in 1948 by, from left to right, Russell Sullivan, David Wheatley, Kenny Rice, Naomi Pohlmann Furlong, Shirley Rosenbaum, Dris Pohlmann Koch, Betty Cook, and Betty Adams Ellingsworth. The Green Barn was a derelict structure behind Hadley Pottery that was rehabilitated by Grace Immanuel United Church of Christ and the East End Civic Club to promote youth activities. In the photograph below, two ladies are helping with the clean-up effort. Furlong and Beverly Schmidt are sitting. (Both, courtesy of Grace Immanuel United Church of Christ.)

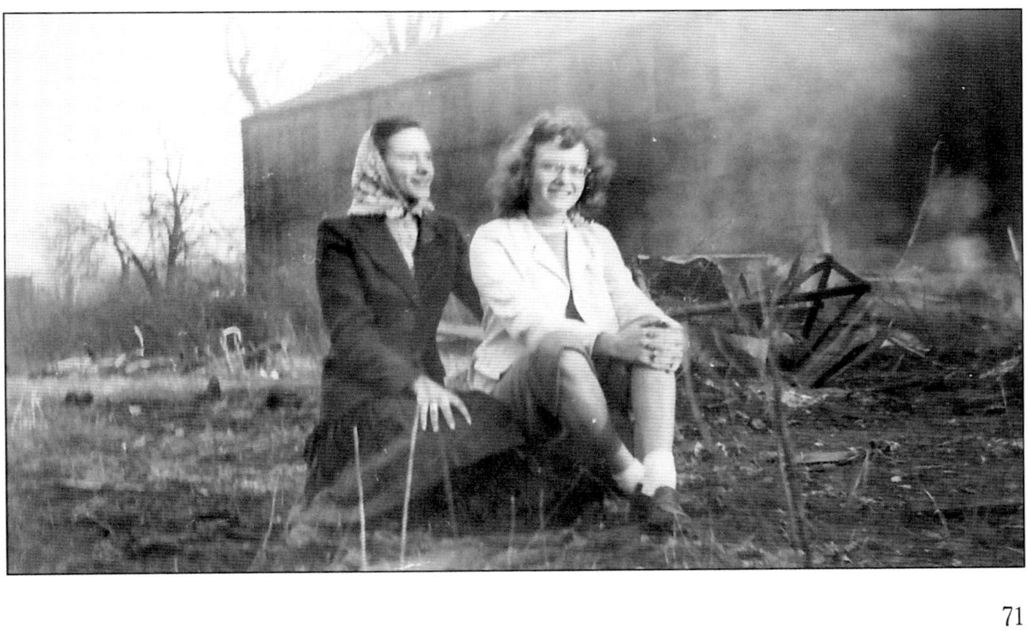

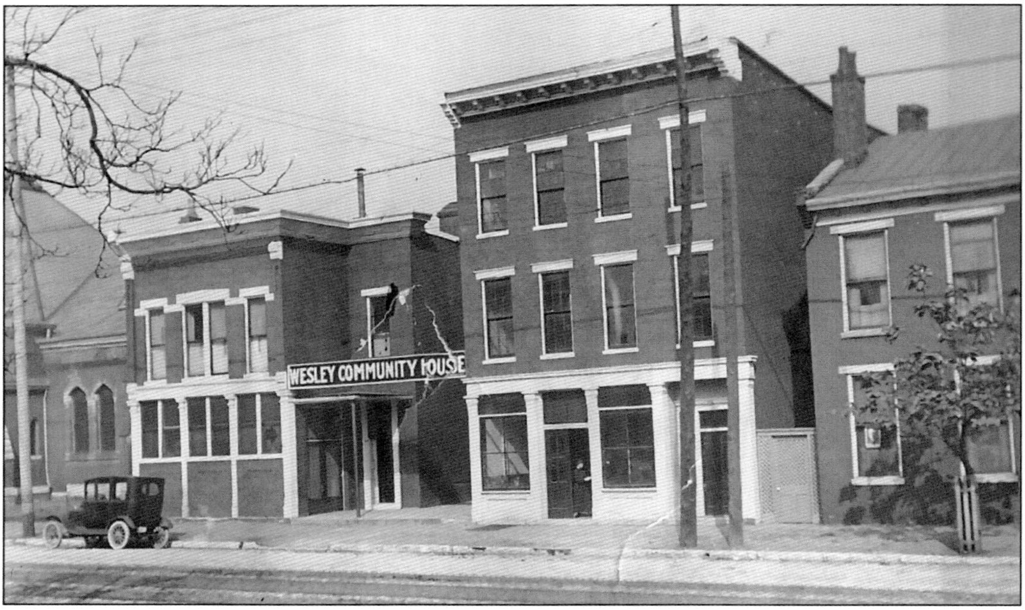

The Wesley House (above) began in 1903 at 834 East Jefferson Street as the Louisville Settlement Home, organized by the Methodist Episcopal Church South. Just five years later, it moved to 809 East Main Street and changed its name to the Wesley House in honor of John Wesley, founder of Methodism. Below, girls are learning housekeeping skills sometime between 1907 and 1925. (Both, courtesy of the Wesley House.)

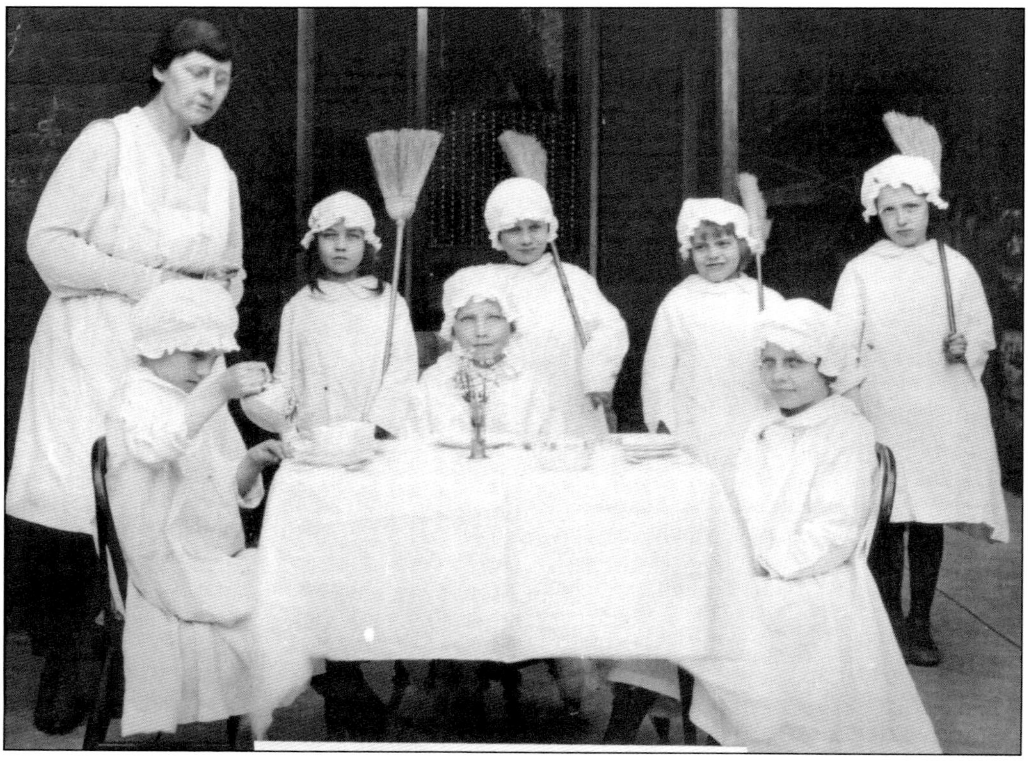

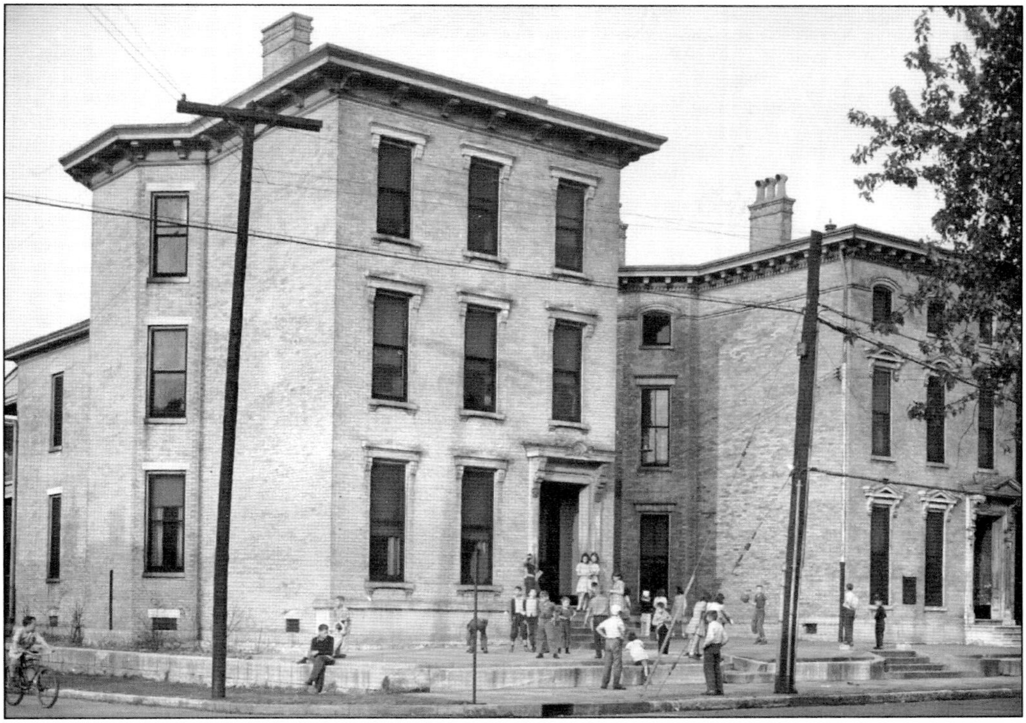

In 1925, Wesley House moved to its Butchertown location at 801–805 East Washington Street and added the gymnasium behind the building in 1928. Both buildings are former residences dating back to the 1800s. Former Louisville Water Company official William Ray lived in 805 East Washington Street and bought 801 for his son-in-law Robert Lavelle. Ray was rumored to have built the four houses immediately across the street for his nieces and nephews. Below is the interior of the library at Wesley House. (Both, courtesy of the Wesley House.)

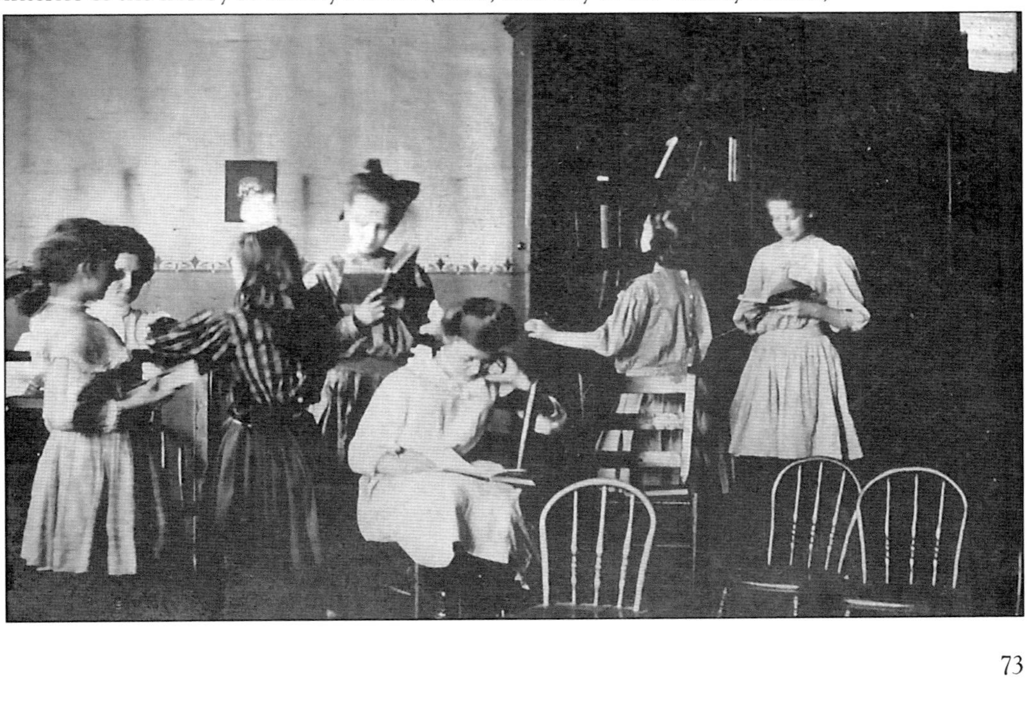

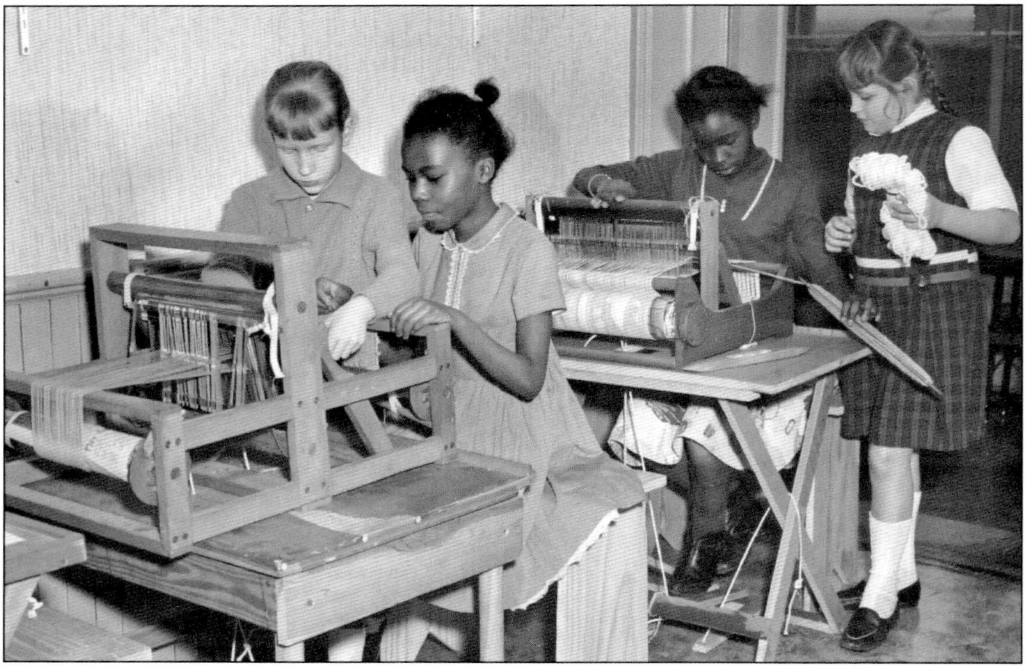

Above, children are learning crafts, such as weaving and painting from local teachers. Below, the gymnasium was a popular hangout and kept children out of trouble. This shows a number of members of all age groups skating across the Wesley House gymnasium in 1948. The Wesley House also sponsored basketball games with the East End Civic Club (now Boys and Girls Club) at 1519 Story Avenue. It was originally named the East End Optimist Club in 1950, as the organization attempted to deter problems with juveniles in the area by offering programs and strong leadership. (Both, courtesy of the Wesley House.)

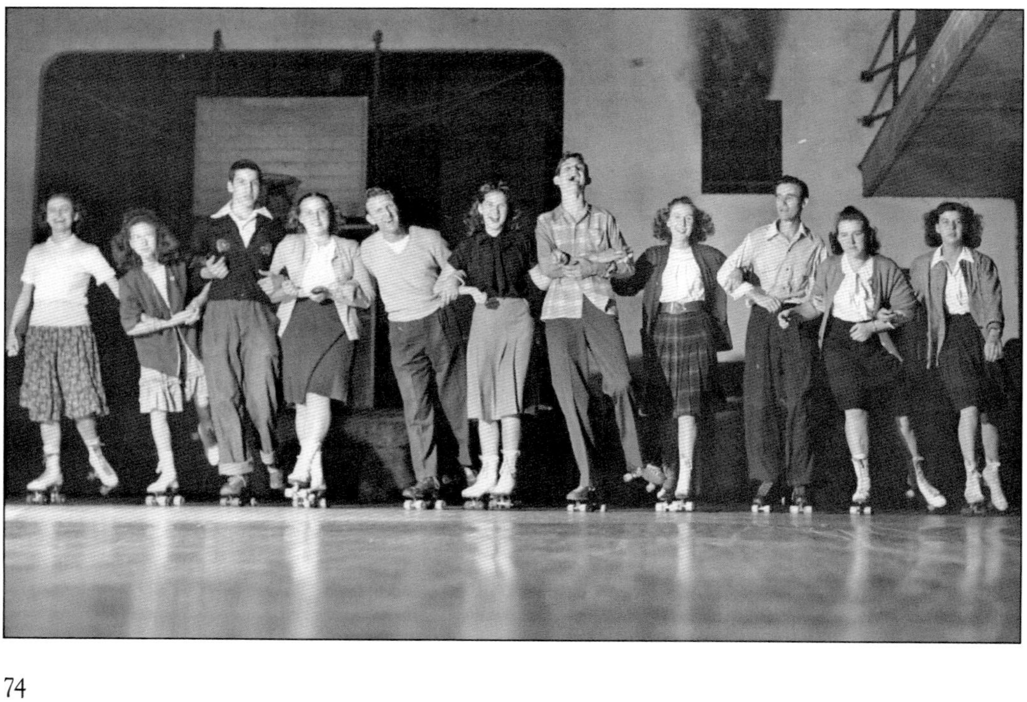

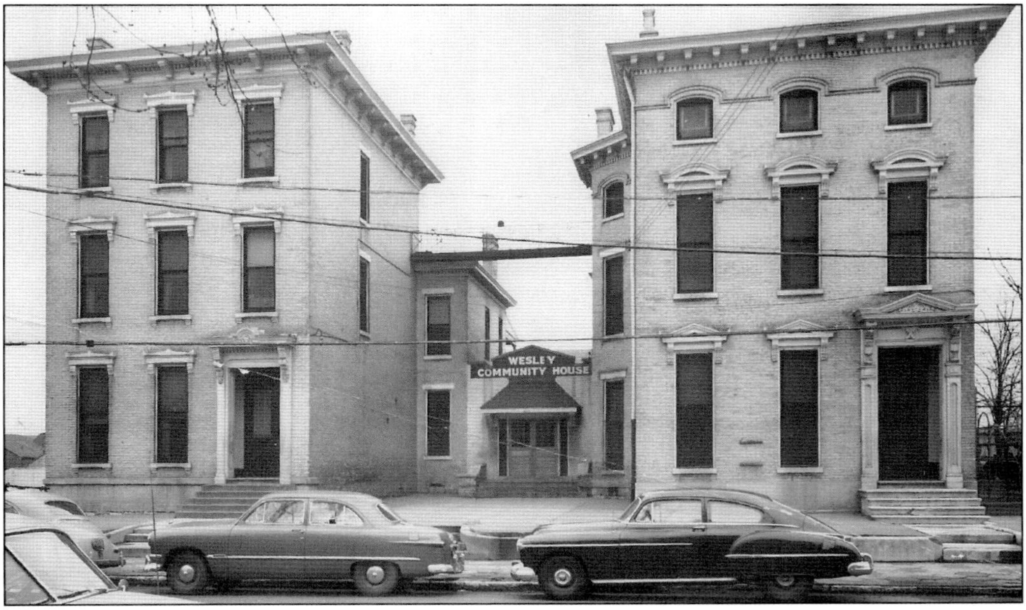

In 1972, a connector was added, linking the two buildings. Over the years, the programs offered by the Wesley House have changed somewhat, but its main goal continues to be teaching people to help themselves. Current programs include early childhood education, youth and family services, computer education, GED training, and English as a second language. (Courtesy of the Wesley House.)

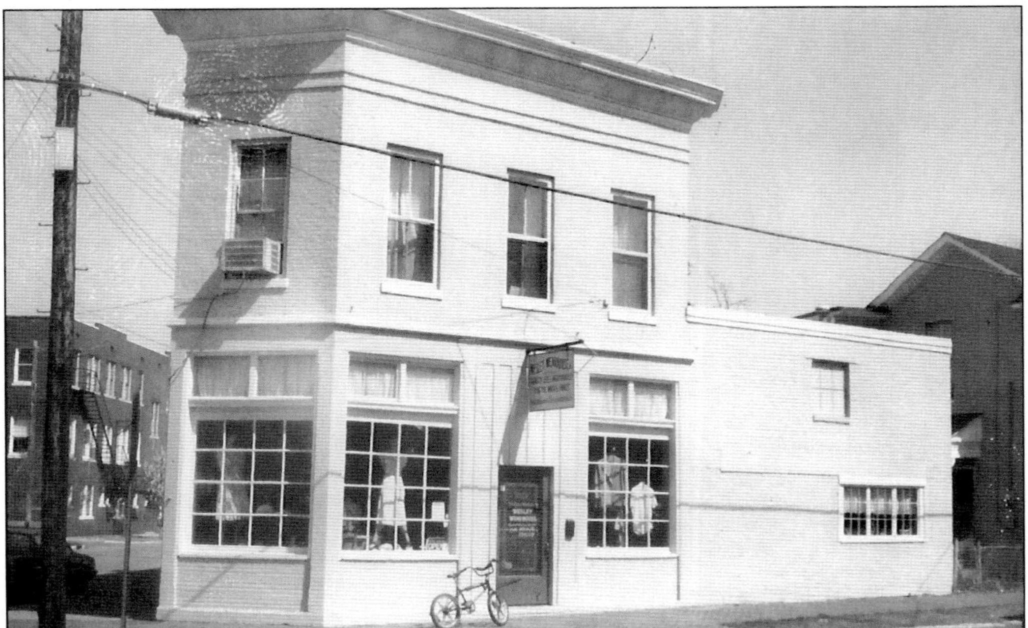

The Wesley Wear House, a clothing thrift store, was created to provide financial support to the Wesley House and is staffed by volunteers. It was originally located at 815 Washington Street before moving to 1001 Washington Street at the corner of Wenzel Street (pictured). In 2006, the store moved to 1501 Story Avenue. (Courtesy of the Wesley House.)

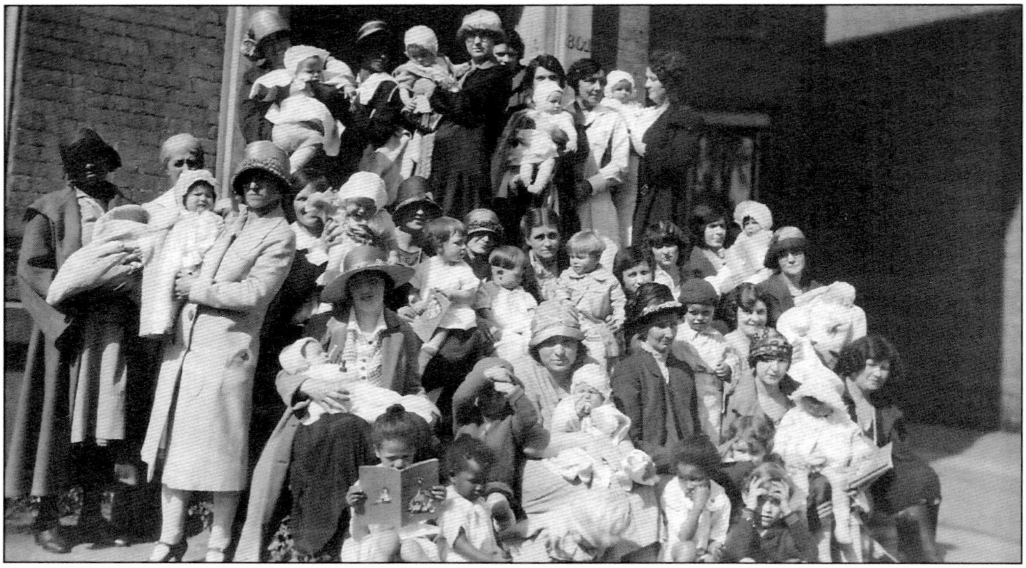

The Well Baby Clinic, also known as the Baby Milk Fund Association, was a way to provide health care to young mothers. The Wesley House had nurses visit in the 1930s to weigh babies, give inoculations, and refer more serious problems to a doctor. They came once a month to the Wesley House and charged modest fees, graduated by income. (Courtesy of the Wesley House.)

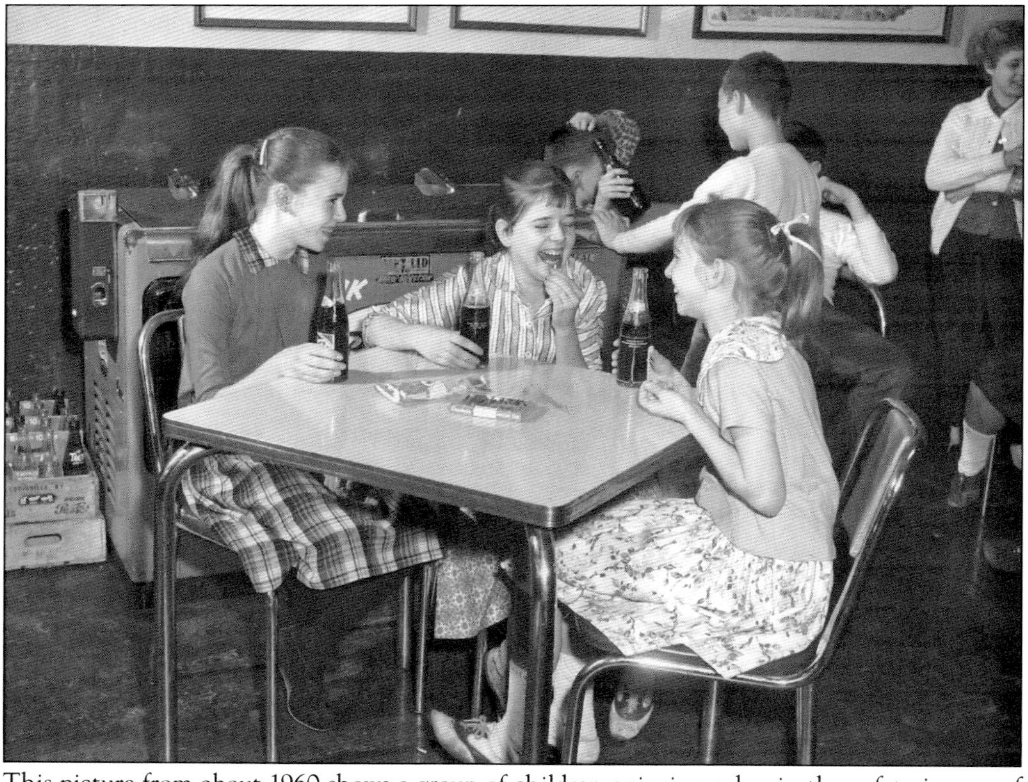

This picture from about 1960 shows a group of children enjoying cokes in the cafeteria area of the Wesley House. (Courtesy of the Wesley House.)

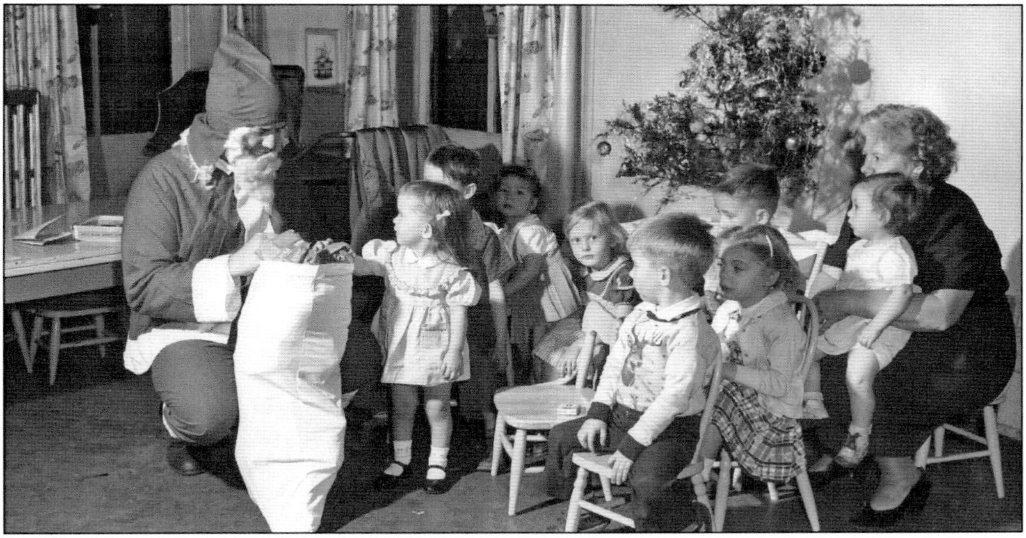

Santa coming to visit (above) was a treat, and children eagerly awaited presents. A puppet show in the Mother's Club Room in 1948 (below) was also entertaining for the many children involved at Wesley House. Members of the Mothers Club were integral to bringing attention to the problem of industrial zoning in Butchertown. Helen Carle and Jeanette Barnett organized the neighborhood and brought a strong turnout to the City County Planning and Zoning Commission meeting in 1966. By bringing in diverse members of the community from business owners to young homeowners, the group was able to get the Butchertown neighborhood rezoned from industrial to commercial and residential. (Both, courtesy of the Wesley House.)

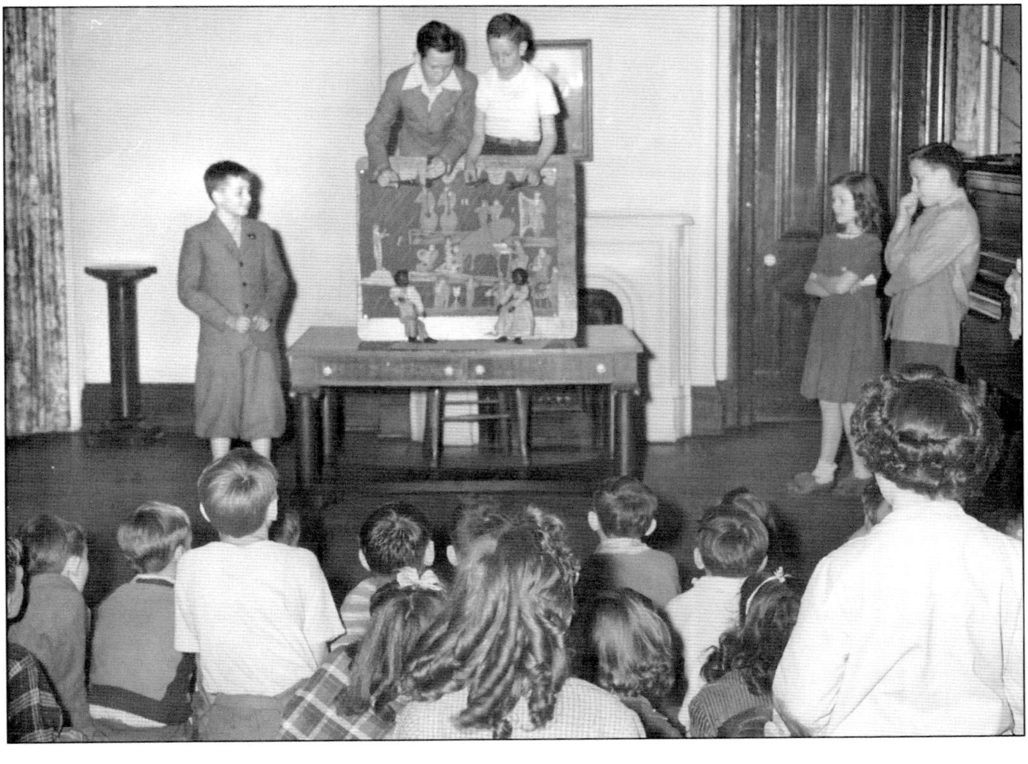

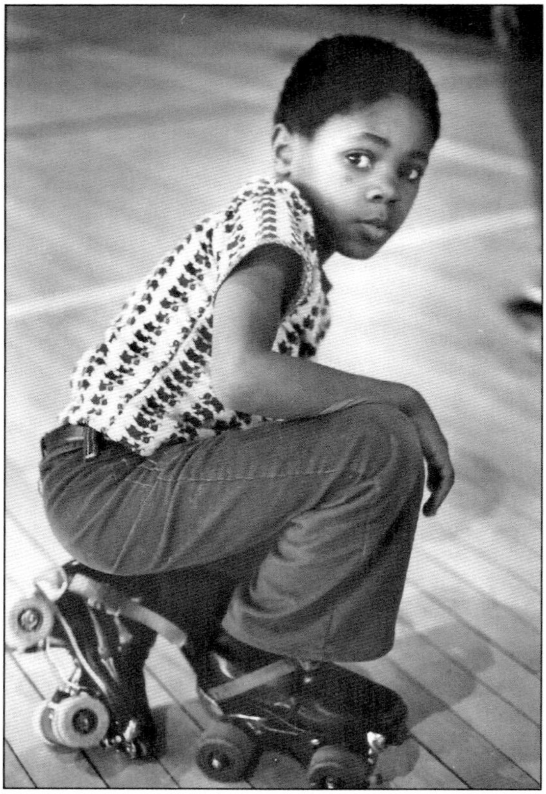

The young man above is learning to skate at Wesley House gymnasium. Many children came to the Wesley House after school. They were provided with a snack, cool, air-conditioned rooms, and help with homework. After homework was finished, youth participated in a wide variety of programs from basketball and skating to dancing and art projects. Below, looking southeast along the 800 block of Washington Street the street carousel in front of the Wesley House is seen. Youth activities were free or very low cost, and many different programs were offered. (Both, courtesy of the Wesley House.)

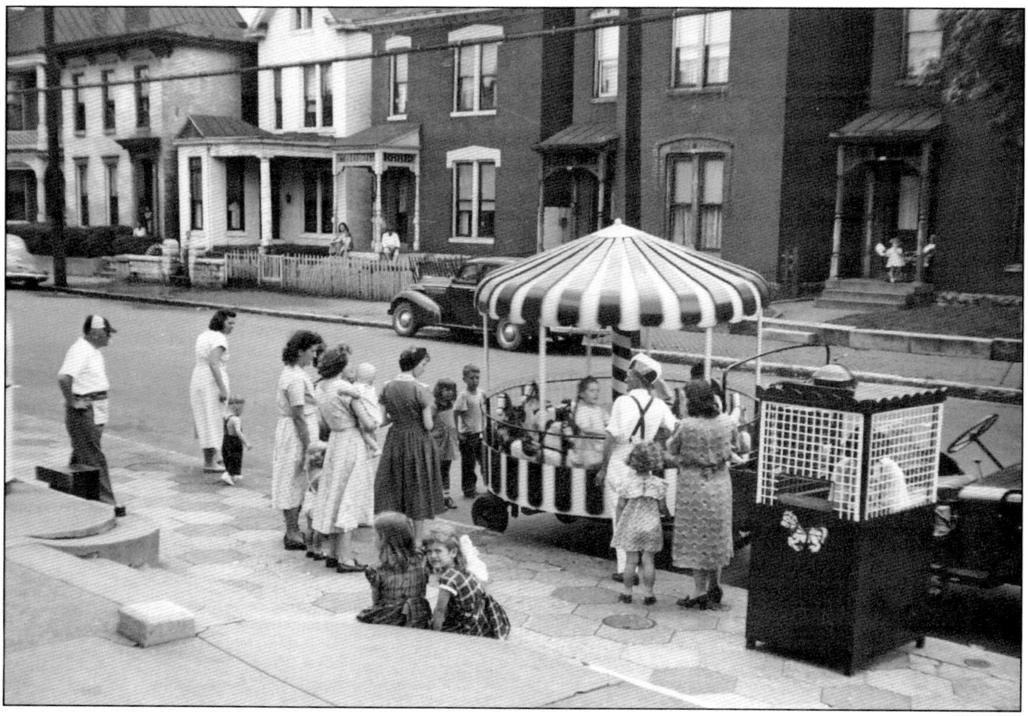

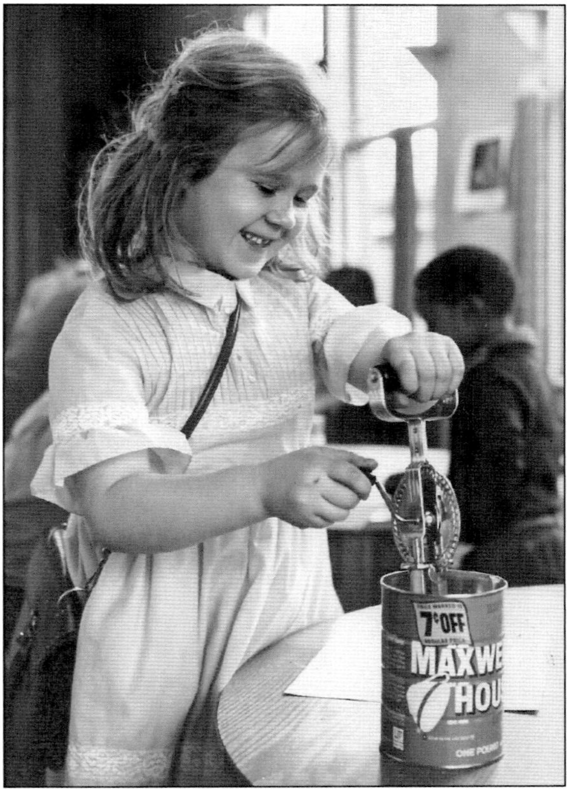

Over the years, programs at the Wesley House have included cooking classes and sewing clubs. Youthful members of Wesley House dressed up for an event planned there. Until 1991, the organization focused more on providing recreational events for youth before shifting to services for at-risk youth. It provides job readiness skills in computer training for single-female heads of households. In 2006, Wesley House moved to 5114 Preston Highway and sold 801–805 East Washington Street, which are being made into condominiums in 2009. (Both, courtesy of the Wesley House.)

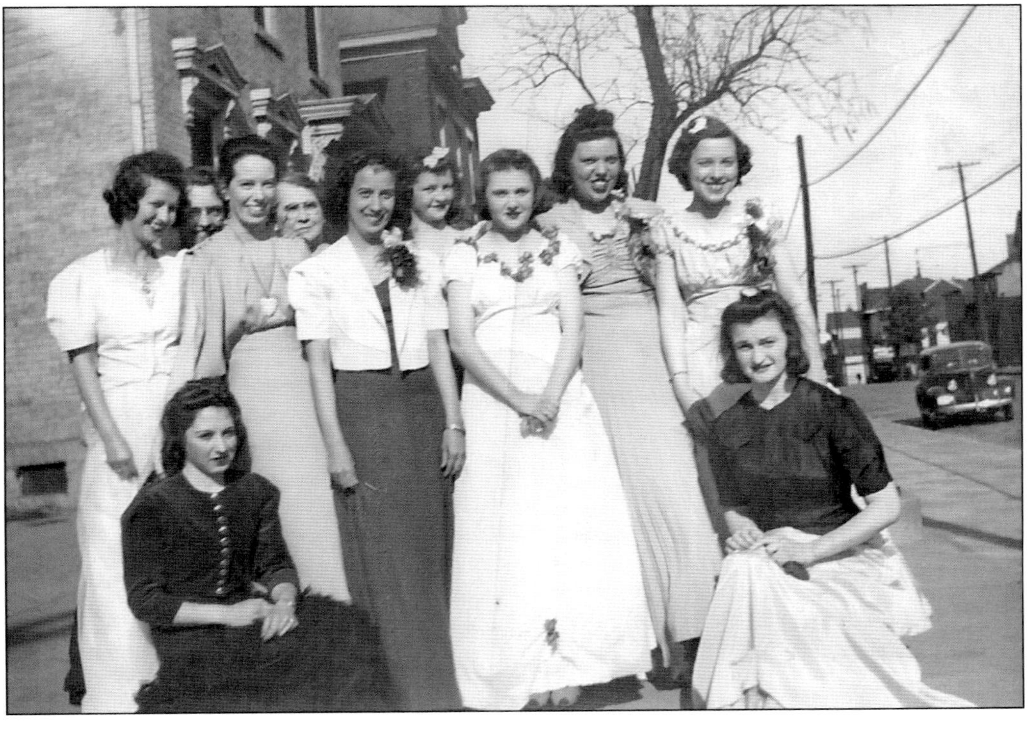

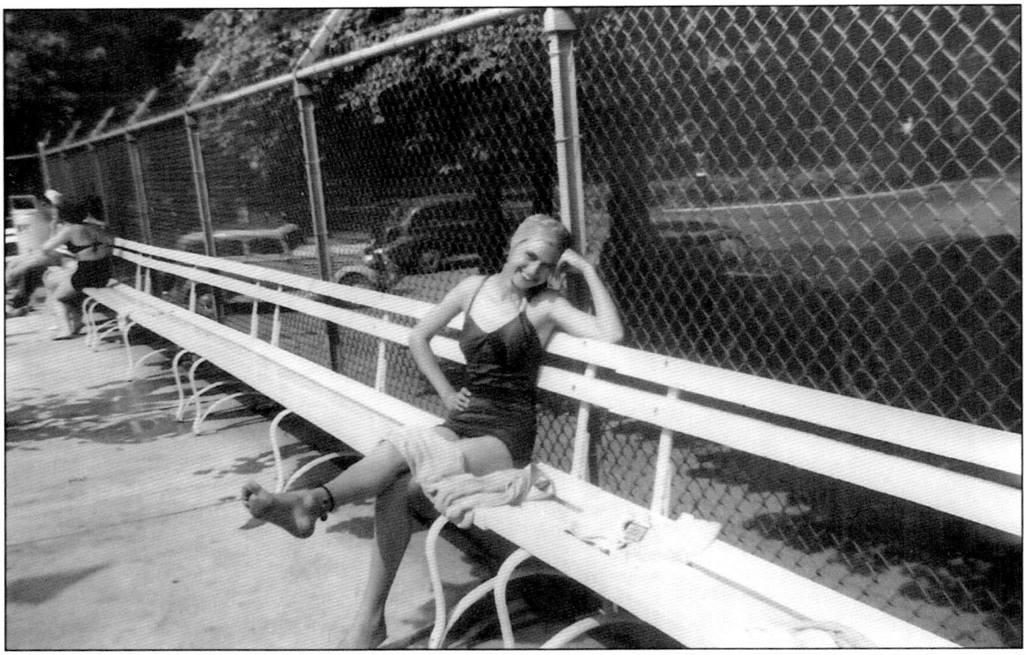

Rosemary Gatson enjoyed cooling off at nearby pools in the 1940s. (Courtesy of Rosemary Gatson.)

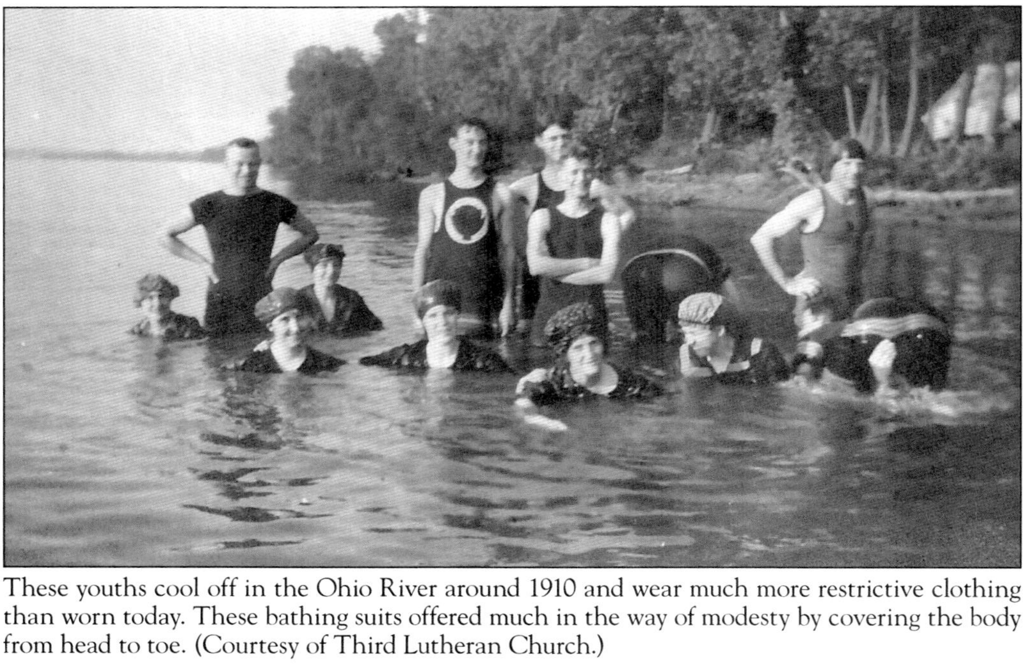

These youths cool off in the Ohio River around 1910 and wear much more restrictive clothing than worn today. These bathing suits offered much in the way of modesty by covering the body from head to toe. (Courtesy of Third Lutheran Church.)

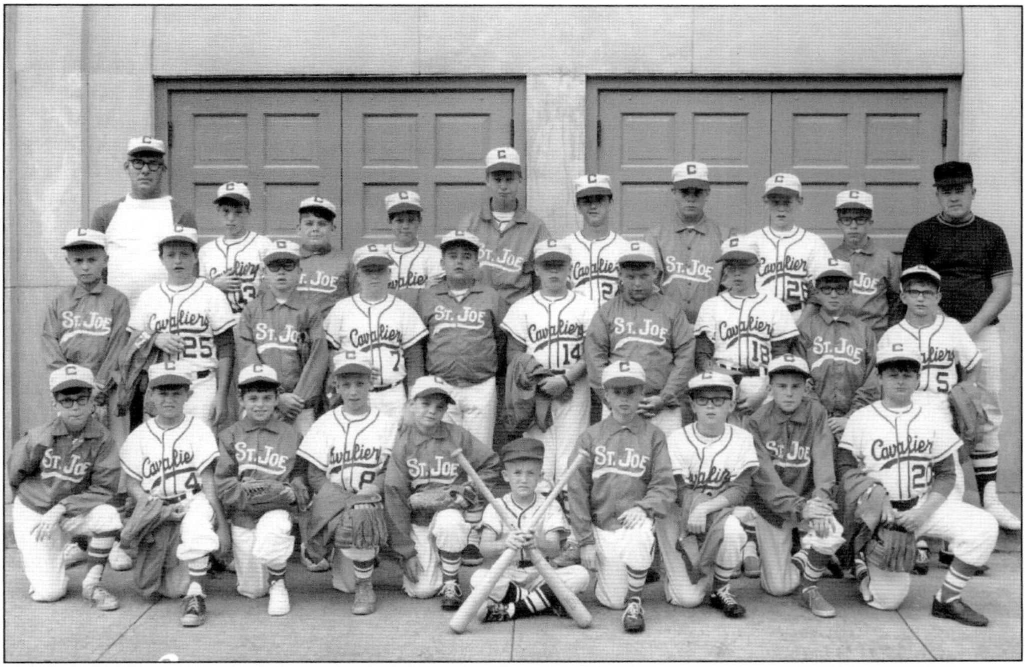

Members of St. Joseph's baseball team are in front of St. Joseph's Catholic Church cafeteria. In the old days, residents flocked to watch games at the Morning Star baseball diamond behind Oertel's Brewery, which had bleachers and a referee. One of the teams that played there was called the Bloomer Girls. (Courtesy of R. Dale McCall, the Vernon Club.)

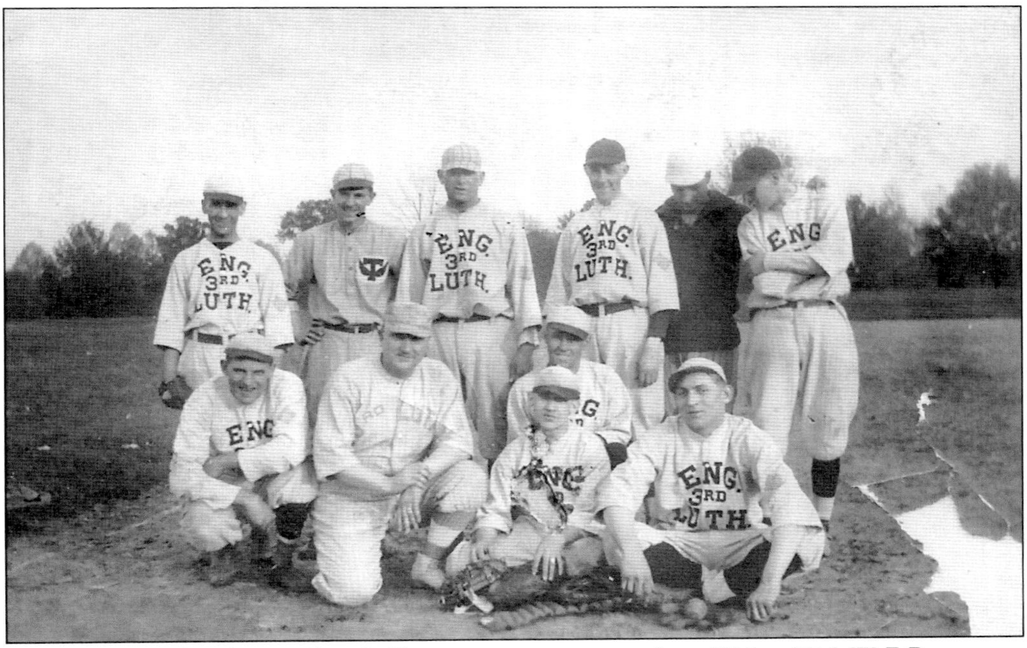

This is the Third Lutheran Church Champions team picture from 1915 or 1916. W. F. Rogers was manager and Eddie Kinker, Chester Smith, and Alfred Layer were coaches. (Courtesy of Third Lutheran Church.)

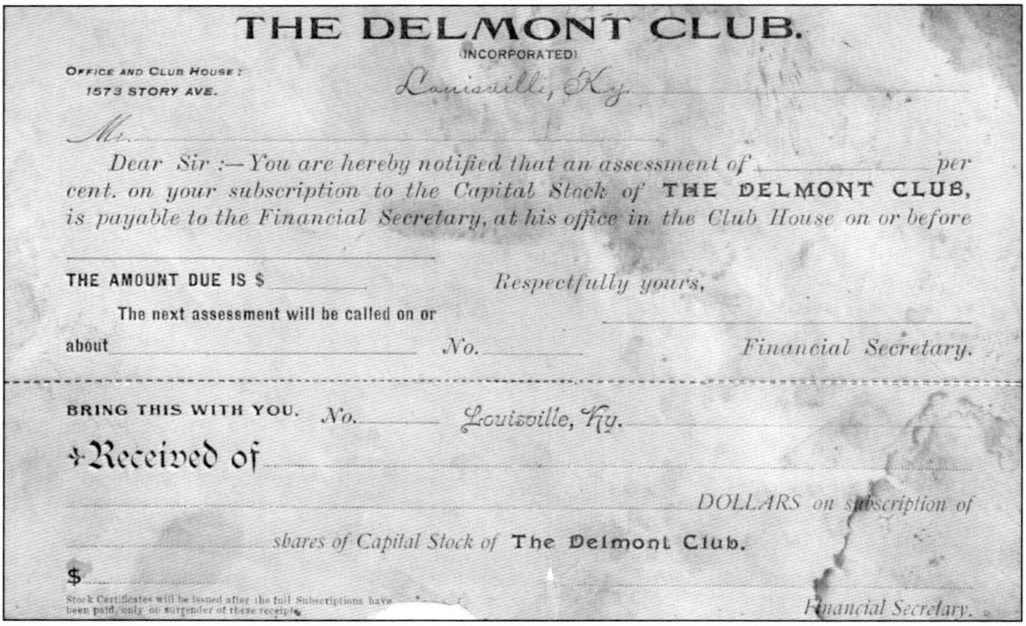

THE DELMONT CLUB.
(INCORPORATED)

OFFICE AND CLUB HOUSE:
1573 STORY AVE.

Louisville, Ky.

Mr.

Dear Sir :—You are hereby notified that an assessment of ______ *per cent. on your subscription to the Capital Stock of* THE DELMONT CLUB, *is payable to the Financial Secretary, at his office in the Club House on or before*

THE AMOUNT DUE IS $ ______ *Respectfully yours,*

The next assessment will be called on or about ______ *No.* ______ *Financial Secretary.*

BRING THIS WITH YOU. *No.* ______ *Louisville, Ky.*

Received of ______

______ *DOLLARS on subscription of*

______ *shares of Capital Stock of* The Delmont Club.

$ ______

Stock Certificates will be issued after the full Subscriptions have been paid, only on surrender of these receipts.

Financial Secretary.

Original stock from the Delmont Club, now Vernon Lanes, is seen here around 1900. The Delmont Club was organized in the 1890s to promote sociability and recreation and was originally located at 1618 Story Avenue. As the club grew, it required more space and relocated to 1575 Story Avenue, originally the residence of prominent butcher Henry Conrad. When membership declined during World War I and repairs were needed for the building, the club was sold in 1918 to St. Joseph's Catholic Church. In 1936, the church also acquired the property to the immediate west, the residence of Jacob Krauth, also a butcher, and cleared it for a picnic place and parking lot. In 1944, the old two-story frame structure behind the brick residence was torn down and replaced by a new fireproof clubhouse. (Courtesy of R. Dale McCall, the Vernon Club.)

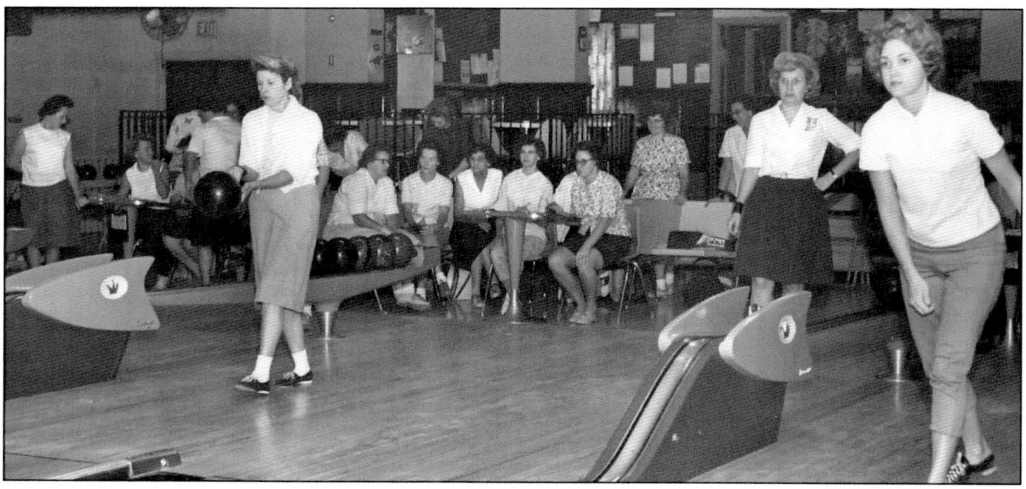

Members of St. Joseph's Catholic Church are enjoying the Vernon Club's eight bowling lanes around 1960. According to old church minutes, bowling has long been a favorite pastime. In 1914, there were four bowling teams called the Owls, Eagles, Quails, and Nightingales; and in 1915, the Jewels, Pearls, Diamonds, Opals, and Emeralds played against one another. (Courtesy of St. Joseph's Catholic Church.)

Above is Vernon Lanes as it looked in the 1930s. After buying the Delmont Club, St. Joseph's Catholic Church decided to name it the Vernon Club in honor of Mount Vernon, Virginia, the birthplace of Pres. George Washington. The church intended the Vernon Club to be a civic center for residents of the east end and encouraged activities and gathering there. Many residents have fond memories of wedding receptions, bowling, and celebrations that were held there. During the 1937 flood, close to 50 Butchertown families took refuge in the building. Bill Kimpflein remembers working behind the lanes setting bowling pins, a way of engaging youth and providing them with a little pocket change. Below, members of the St. Joseph's Catholic Church Dramatic Club from between 1898 and 1904 are pictured. From left to right are (first row) Louis Gnau, William Woodsmall, Robert Clark, and Frank Bader; (second row) William Stauble, Raphael Liebert, Frank Schweis, Jacob Steurer, William Schmidt, Frank Latch, and Albert Gnau; (third row) Al Doerflinger, Joseph Lichtefeld, Charles Kircher, Albert Schmitt, Fr. Prosper Stemann (O. F. M.), Joseph Schmitt, Joseph Hillerich, and Fred Haas. (Above, courtesy of St. Joseph's Catholic Church; below, courtesy of the Kimpflein family.)

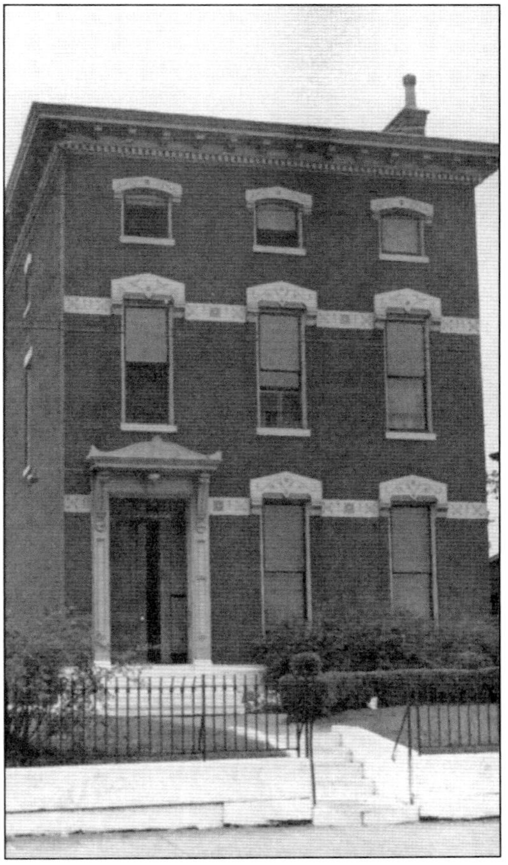

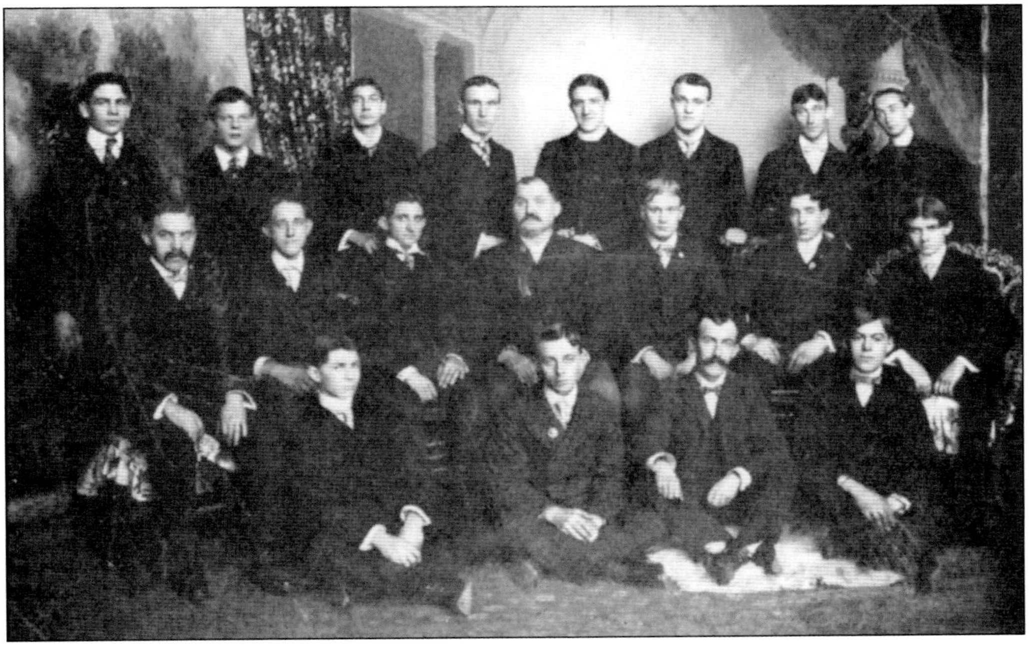

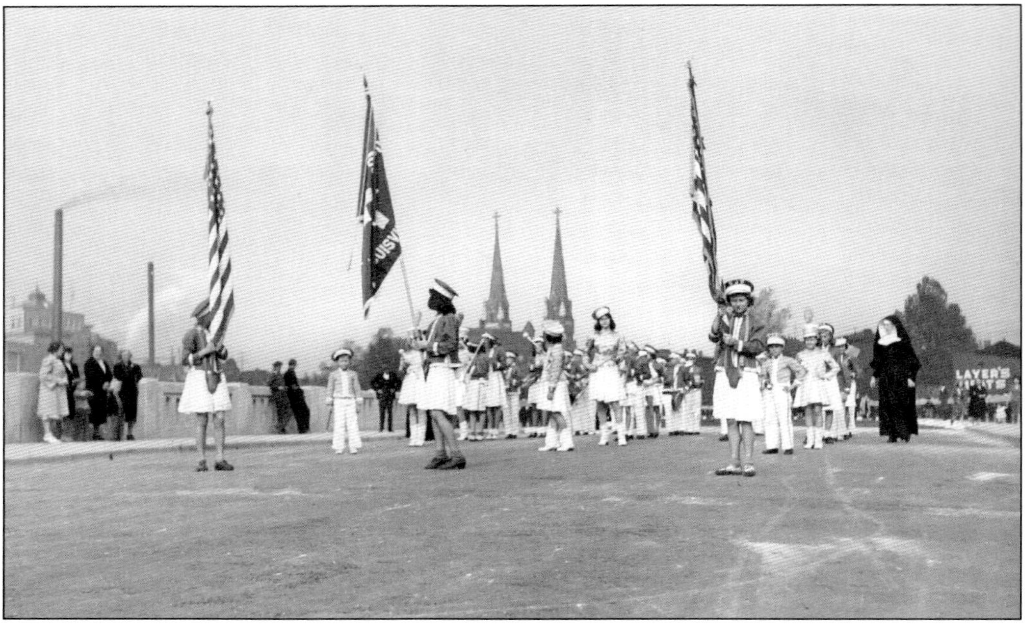

On October 16, 1942, the Spring Street bridge was officially dedicated. Previously residents used an old wooden footbridge across Morning Star Valley behind Oertel's Brewery. It was torn down in 1933 and 1934, and a new link was needed between Story Avenue and Mellwood Avenue. The new bridge was built one foot higher than the flood heights reached during 1937. Organized in October 1939, the St. Joseph's School Band had 36 members and played at church celebrations. The band poses on the steps of the church, showing off their uniforms. Below, members of the band march across the new bridge. In the distance are the St. Joseph's Catholic Church spires, and to the right is a sign for Layer's Meats on the back of a building. (Both, courtesy of St. Joseph's Catholic Church.)

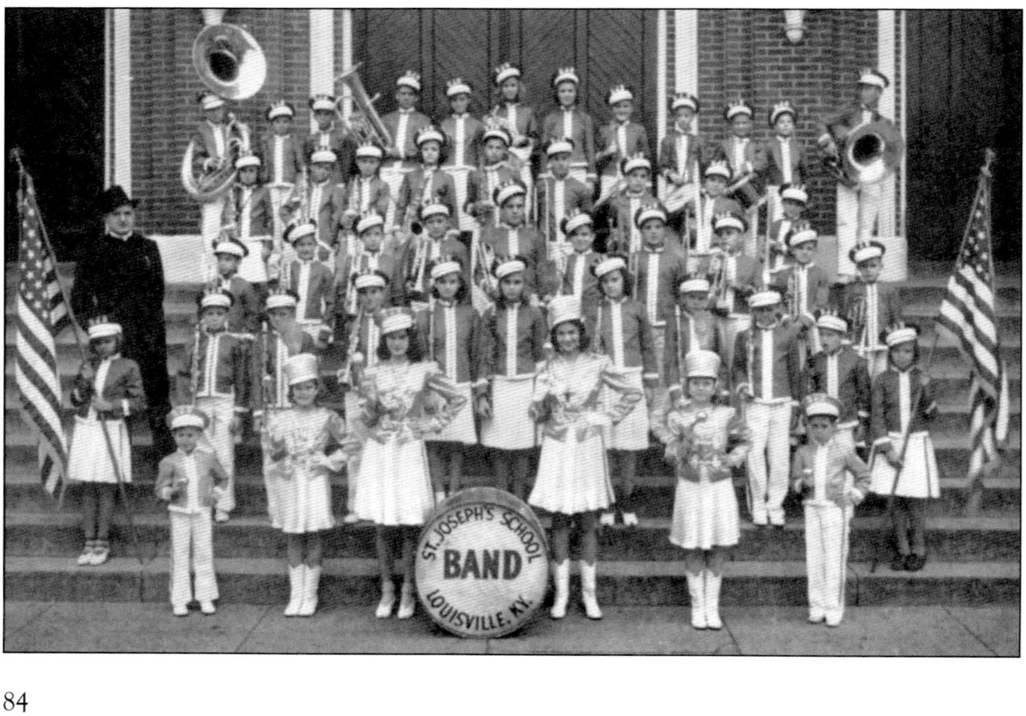

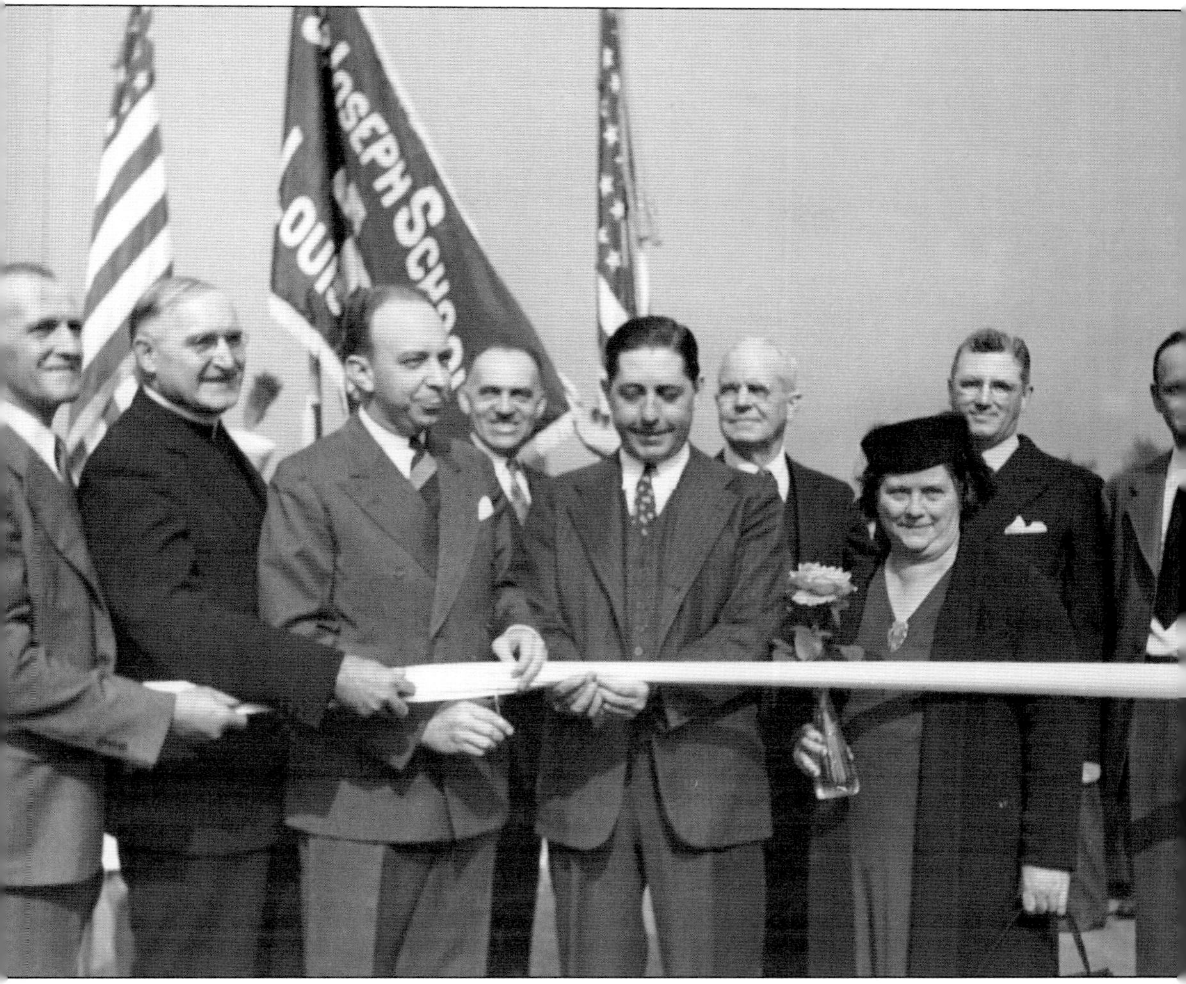

From left to right, Charles Schmetzer (East End Civic Club), Rev. Damien Sander, Mayor Wyatt, Ernest Schimpler, State Rep. Robert E. Berry, Mrs. Benjamin L. Williangham, George Bickel, and Clifford Hall are cutting the ribbon for the new Spring Street bridge. (Courtesy of St. Joseph's Catholic Church.)

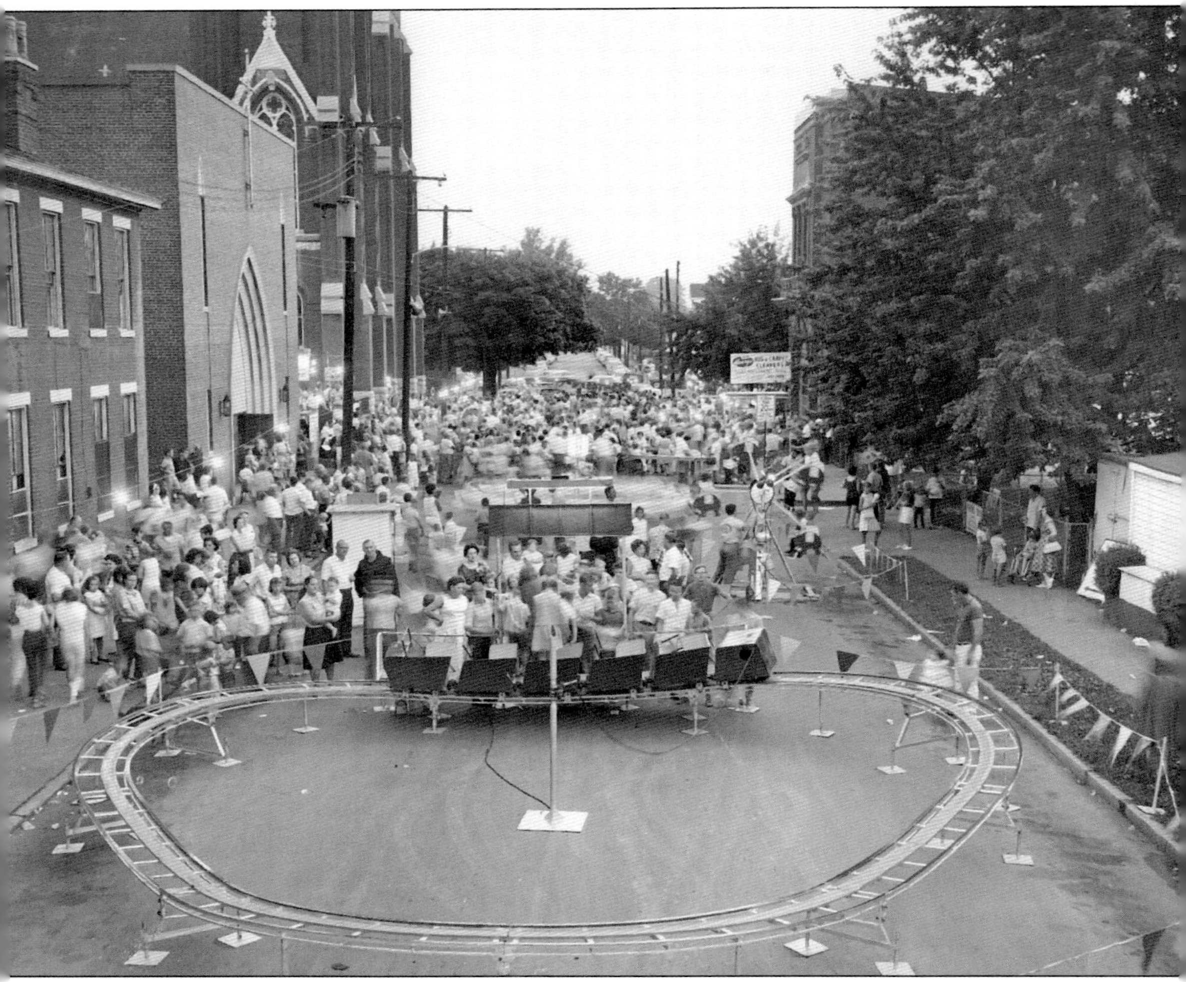

In 1966, St. Joseph's Catholic Church celebrated its 100th anniversary with three days of festivities along Washington Street. The play *One Hundred Years* was performed by parish youth, and a Swiss orchestra provided music for the festivities. The neighborhood turned out for a miniature roller coaster and other entertainment. (Courtesy of St. Joseph's Catholic Church.)

Five

People and Places around the Neighborhood

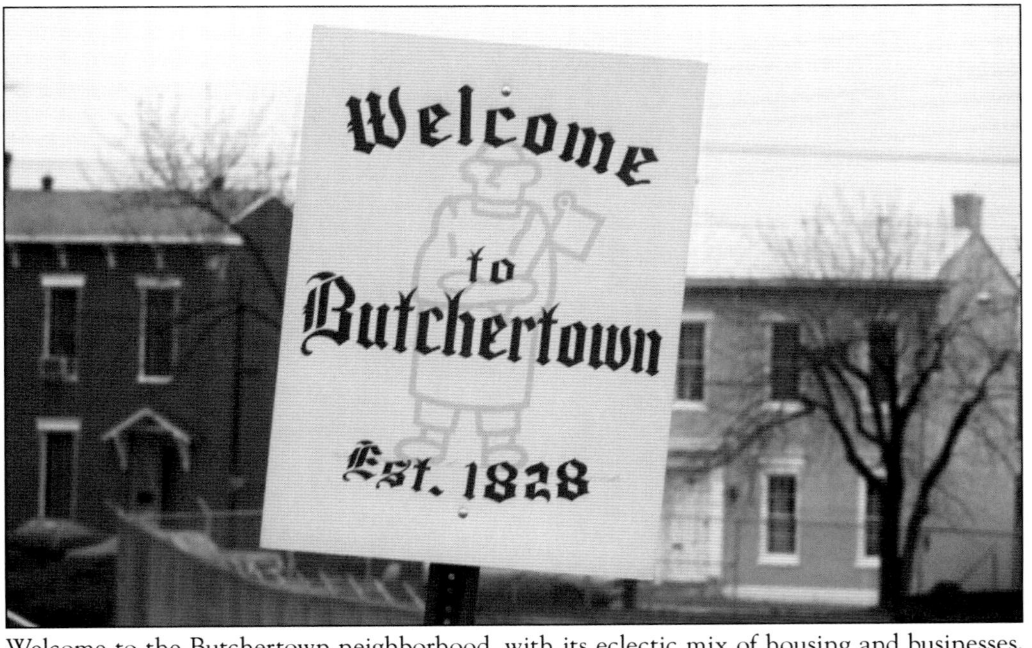

Welcome to the Butchertown neighborhood, with its eclectic mix of housing and businesses, surprises, and interesting details that can be found hidden between houses, along the sidewalk, and in people's backyards. Walkers should pay attention to the sidewalk in front of Hadley Pottery; many round ceramic inserts featuring Mary Alice Hadley's distinctive designs are in the sidewalk around the building. (Courtesy of John Beckman.)

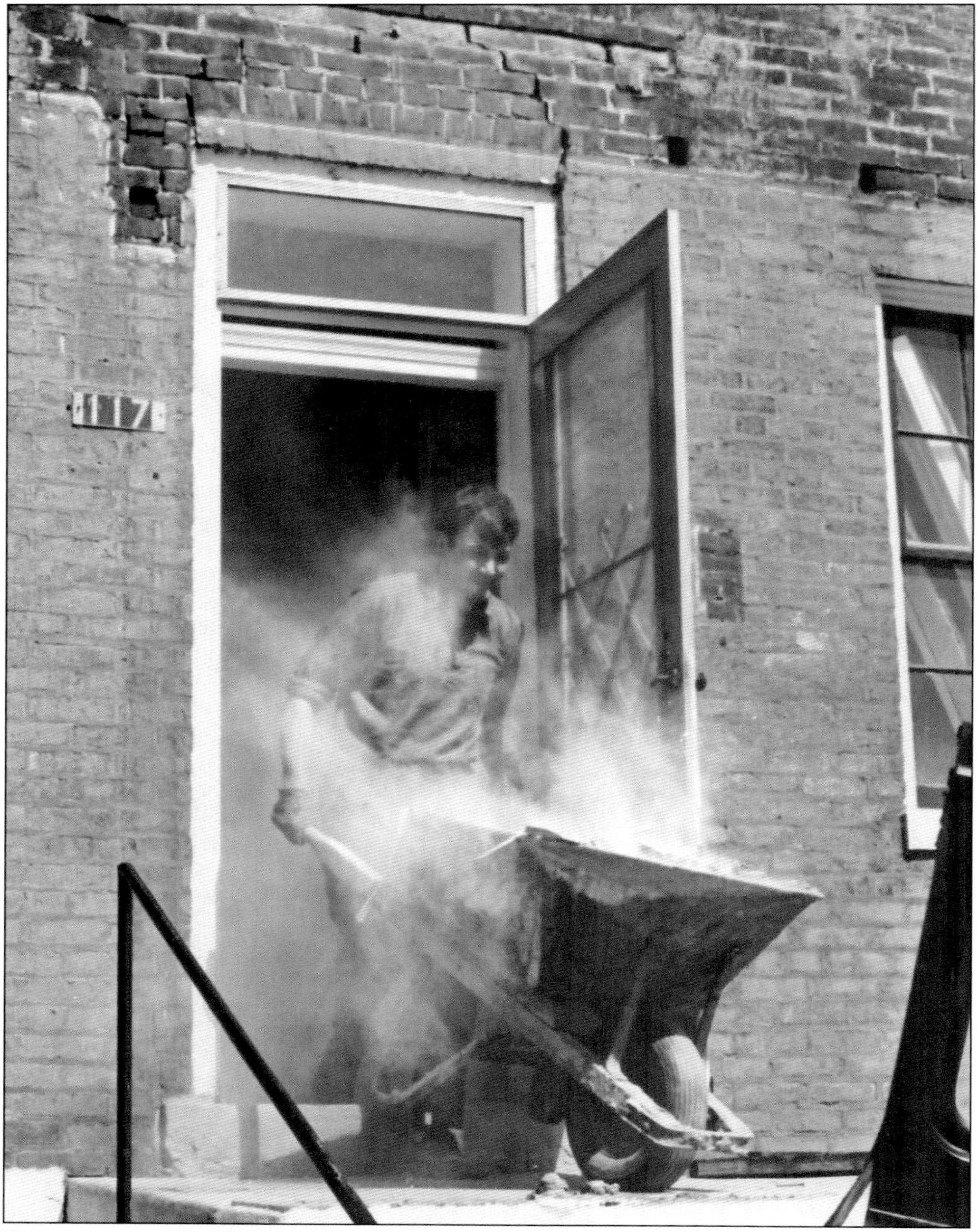

Renovations at 117 Adams Street show the hard work needed to restore historic homes such as this. Many times structures are torn down to their frames before interiors are renovated. A park was named in honor of the third president of Butchertown, Inc. and worker at the Thomas Edison House, Ginny Reichert. She was the sister of Tom and Mary Stewart Reichert, the owners of this home. (Courtesy of Leslie Tichenor.)

Cynically nicknamed "Our Lady of Junkyards," in the 1960s, Butchertown was a mix of deteriorating homes and junkyards that dotted the devastated land on North Adams Street. Residents were shocked to discover that the whole area had been zoned industrial in 1931, and therefore residential use was a nonconforming use. That meant that they could not get loans to improve their properties, get mortgages for interested new homeowners, or rebuild if their houses burned down. (Courtesy of Leslie Tichenor.)

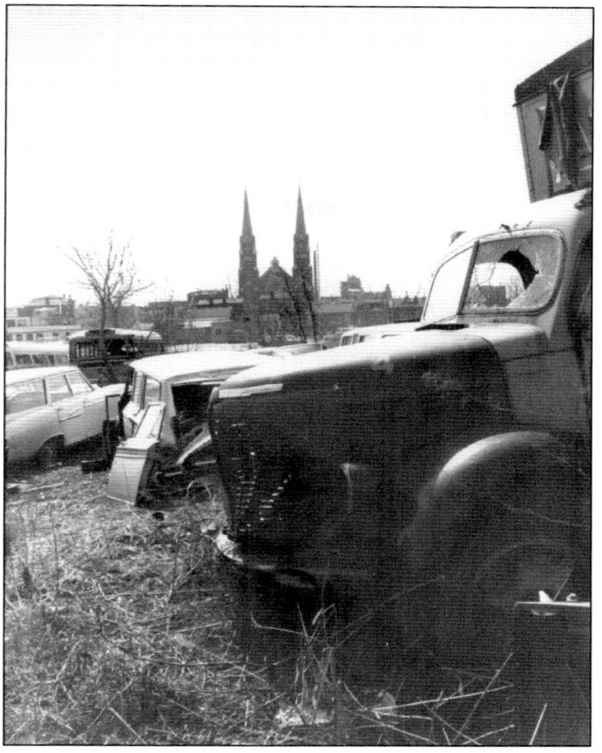

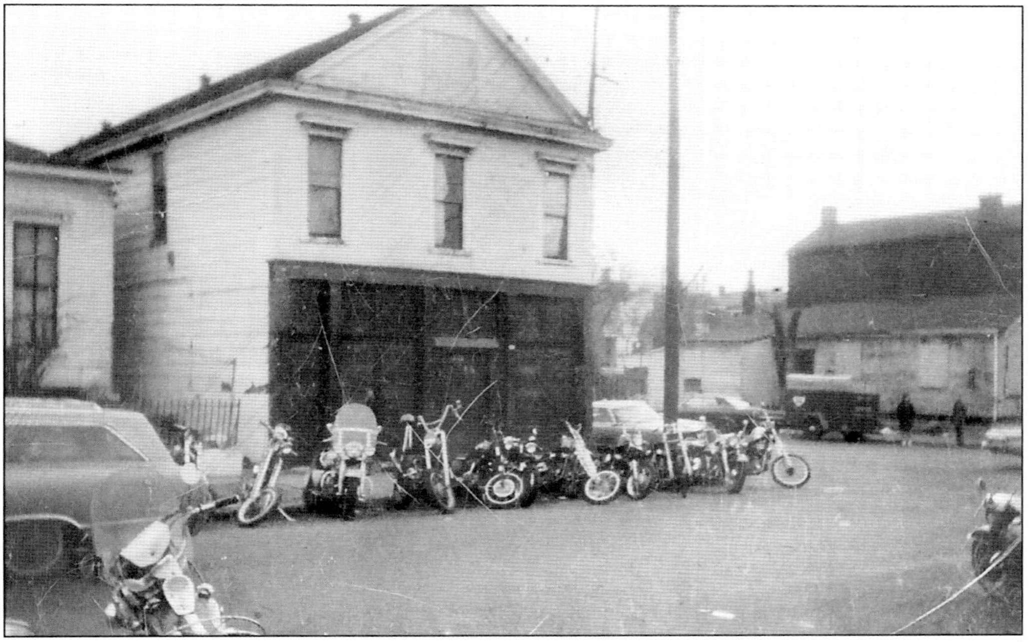

The motorcycle gang the Outlaws moved into the 900 block of Franklin Street in the 1970s and terrified the neighbors. When the mother of a motorcycle gang member died, neighbors elected Jeanette Barnett of the Wesley House to approach the Outlaws's house with the news. (Courtesy of Jeanette Barnett.)

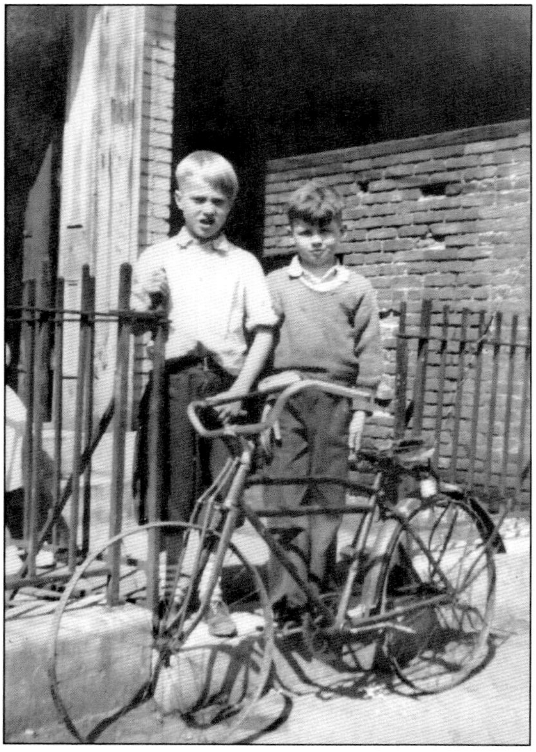

Ollie Bratcher (left) and David Byrd are seen on Franklin Street in 1937. During those years, families had little money, and kids amused themselves with games and programs offered at the Wesley House. Since gasoline was rationed and few people owned vehicles, it was safe to play in the streets without worrying about being hit by a car. (Courtesy of Ethel Stoke.)

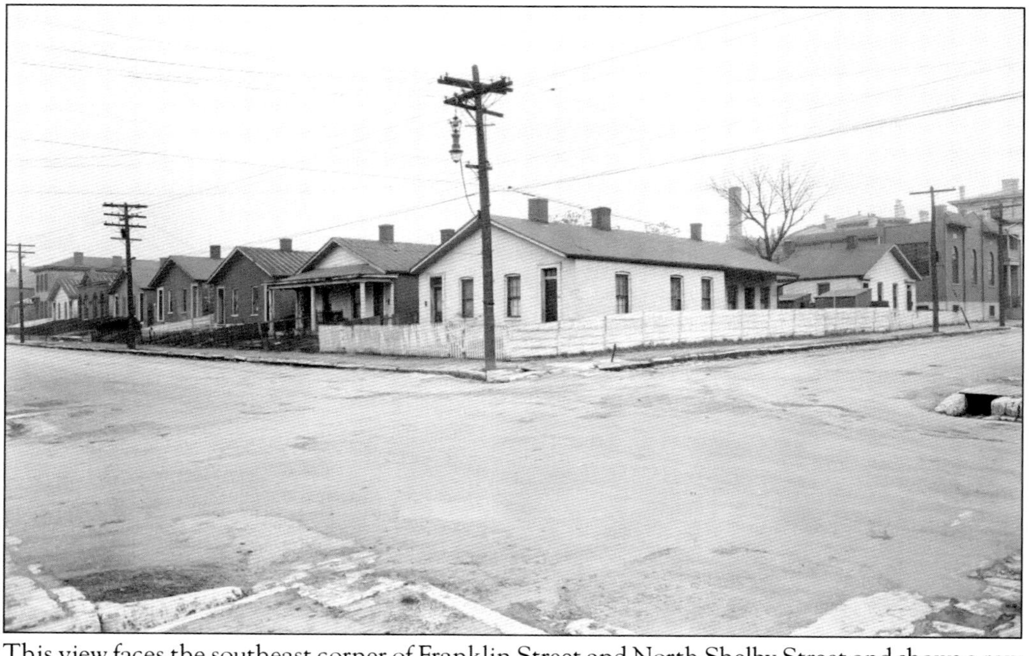

This view faces the southeast corner of Franklin Street and North Shelby Street and shows a row of sturdy duplex shotgun homes. While *duplex* has various definitions, in this case it refers to side-by-side shotgun homes with separate ownership that share a common wall. This lot later became Wesley Community Park. (Courtesy of the University of Louisville Photographic Archives.)

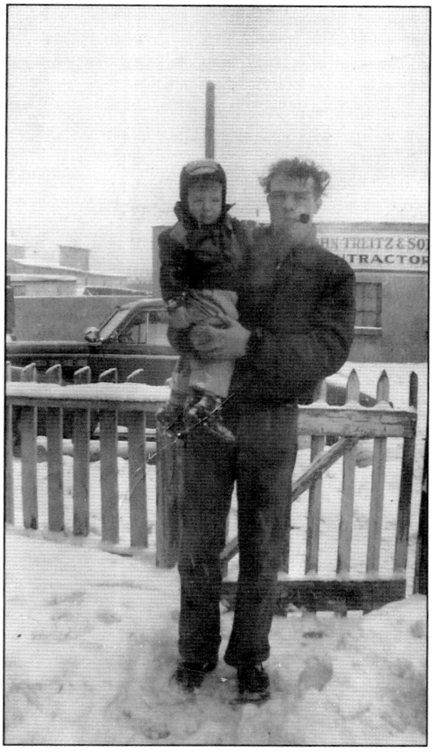

At right, Robert Hoke is holding his son Bobby Jr. in the 1950s on the corner of Franklin and Shelby Streets. In the background is Treitz and Sons, a family construction business. Below, Margaret Hoke is at the intersection of Franklin and North Shelby Streets in the 1950s. Down the hill is Vendome Copper and Brass Works, a company operating in Louisville for over 100 years, which made items such as kettles for distillers and breweries. (Both, courtesy of Connie Pratt.)

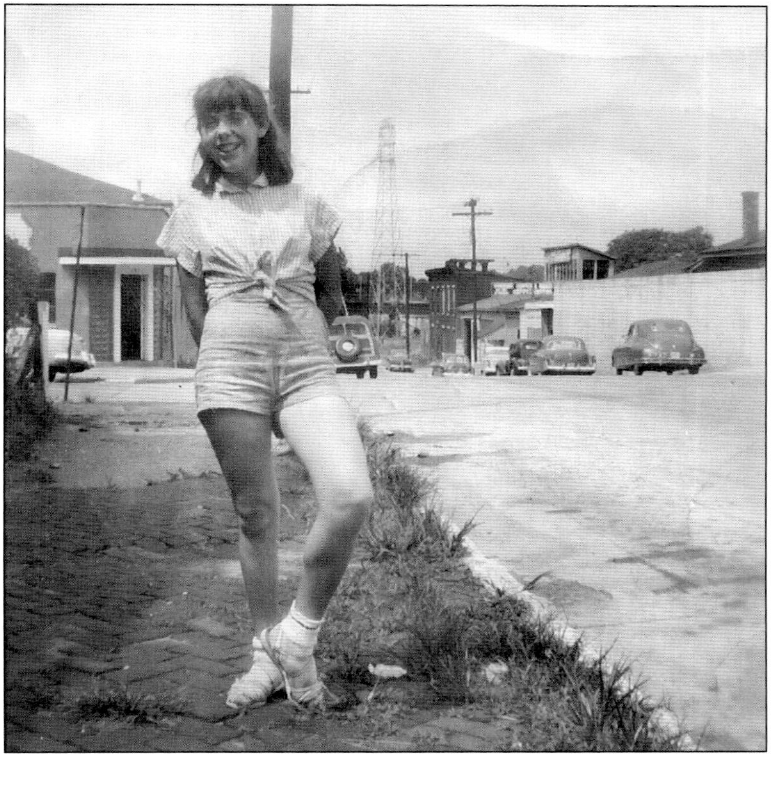

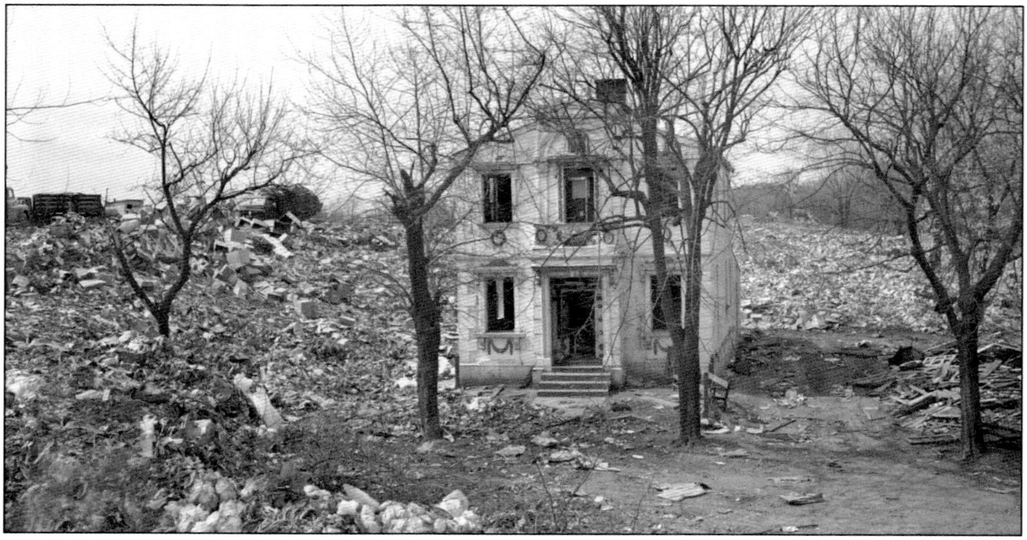

Devastated by the 1937 flood, what is known as the Heigold House became surrounded by the local dump. Formerly located at 264 Marion Street, the house was built in 1853 by Christian Heigold, a German immigrant who fled the 1848 revolutions in Germany. To show his loyalty to his new country, Heigold carved stone busts of Pres. George Washington to represent freedom and Pres. James Buchanan to signify the champion of immigrants, characters depicting Liberty holding a shield and Justice holding scales, as well as patriotic inscriptions into the facade of his house. When the city sought to expand the local dump in 1955, preservationists were able to get the house moved next to the Paget House at 1562 Fulton Street until a permanent home could be found. It was recently placed in the median in Ohio Street to serve as an entrance to the neighborhood. (Above, courtesy of University of Louisville Photographic Archives; below, courtesy of Elizabeth Jones, NRHP.)

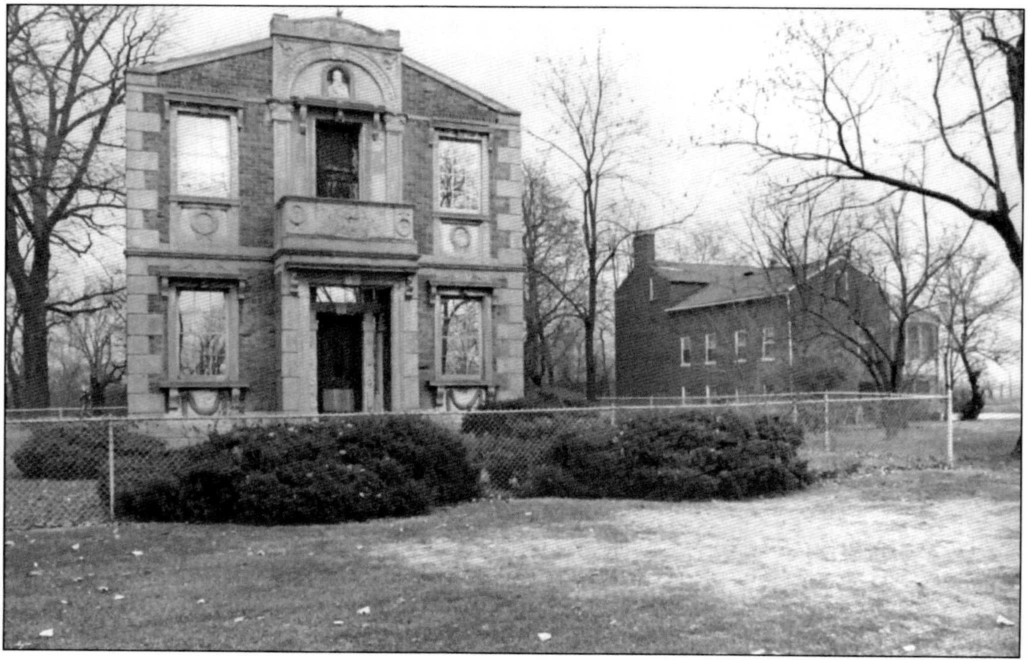

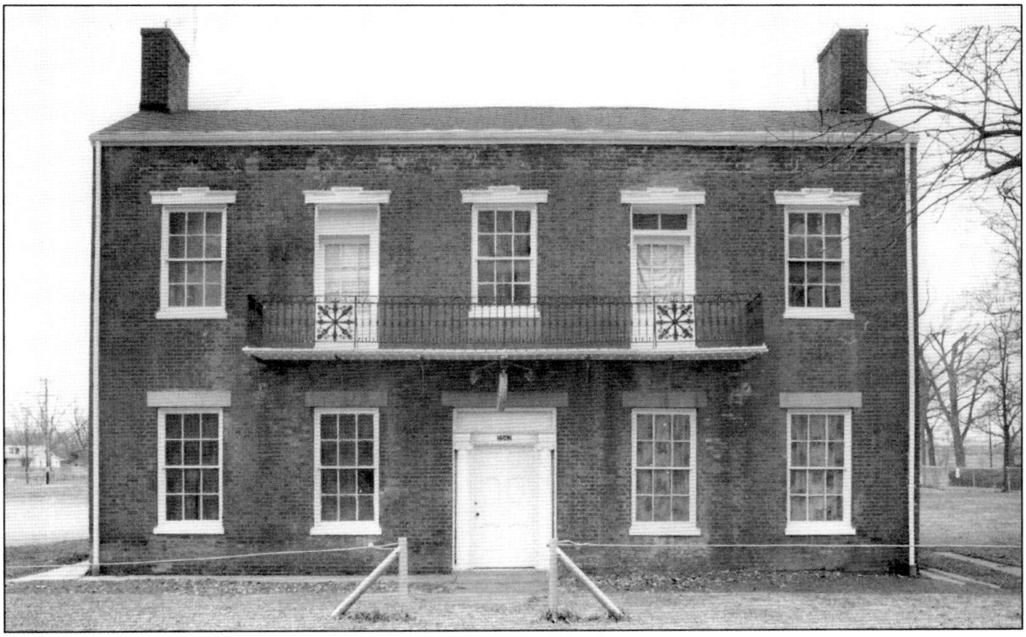

The Paget House is a stunning two-story structure so well built that it survived being completely submerged in both the 1937 and the 1945 flood without any structural damage. Originally built in the 1800s, it was named the Paget house after Margaret Paget, a descendent of Washington, bought it from its original owners in 1838. The balcony in front faced the river and featured a decorative wheel motif, replicating a steamboat wheel in its iron balustrade. (Both, courtesy of Elizabeth Jones, NRHP.)

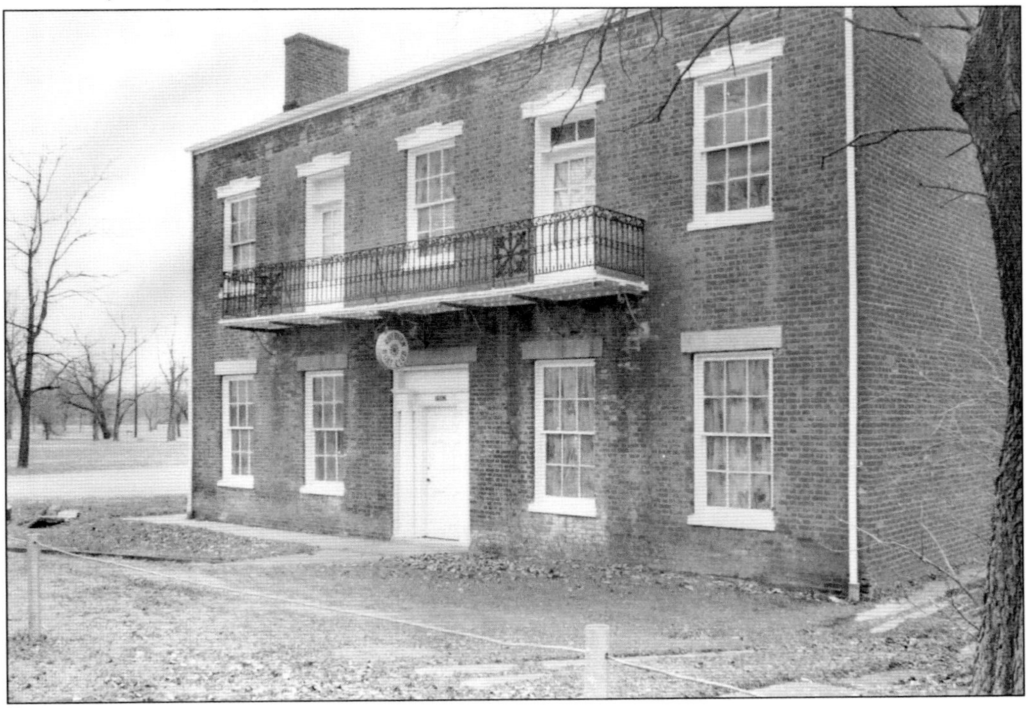

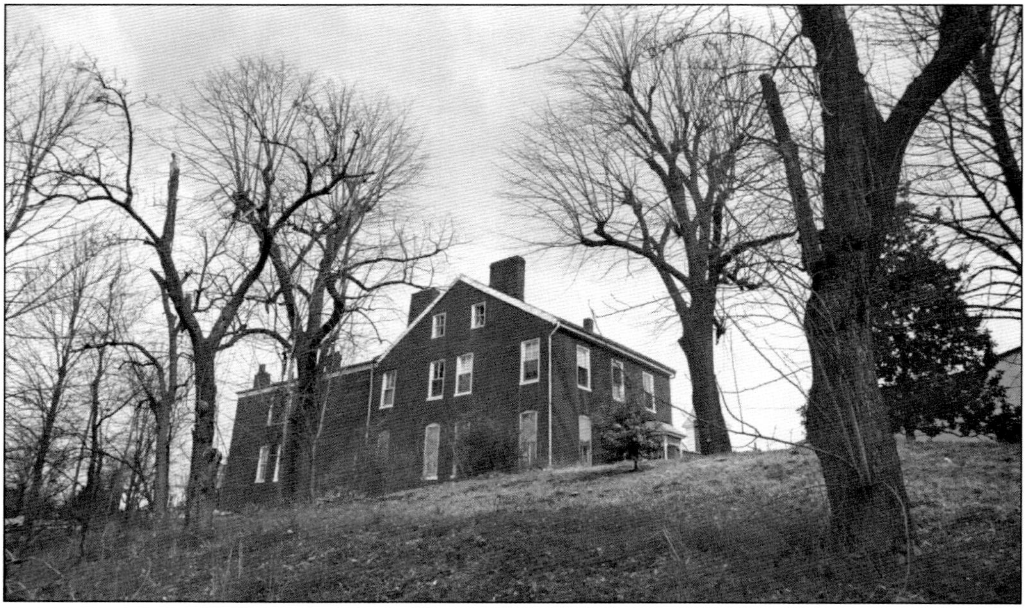

Col. Frederick Geiger settled in Louisville around 1795. The Geiger family owned a ferry service across the Ohio River to Jeffersonville and a gristmill on the river. In 1797, Geiger bought this 21-room farmhouse located at 1607 Frankfort Avenue from Henry Fait, who started constructing it in 1794 and owned two mills on Beargrass Creek. Before leaving for the battle of Tippecanoe in 1811, Geiger's troops camped in an apple orchard on his farm. (Courtesy of John Beckman.)

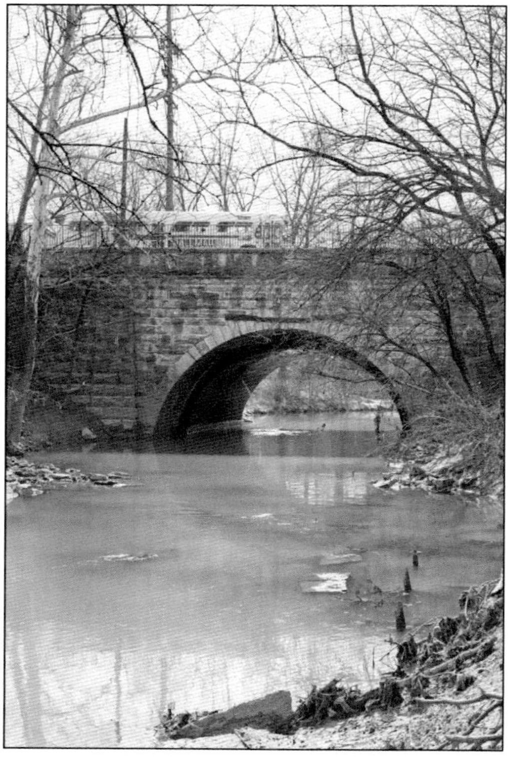

This is a view of the Frankfort Avenue bridge over Beargrass Creek. Embedded in the bank of the creek for 30 years was a 1970s-era Volkswagen Beetle that was removed in 2008 by MSD (Metropolitan Sewer District). The car body will be refashioned into a bench by local metal worker Greg Kaviar, and the steering wheel will be repurposed as an award to honor an individual or group that helps maintain and improve Beargrass Creek. (Courtesy of John Beckman.)

Here is the intersection of Blue Horse Avenue and Frankfort Avenue just north of the bridge crossing Beargrass Creek. Formerly Rehm Street, it was renamed in honor of Mary Alice Hadley's whimsical blue horse design. One resident on Blue Horse Avenue remembers his father buying the Hadley's old boat and living in it on the street while building a house using demolition materials in the 1940s. (Courtesy of John Beckman.)

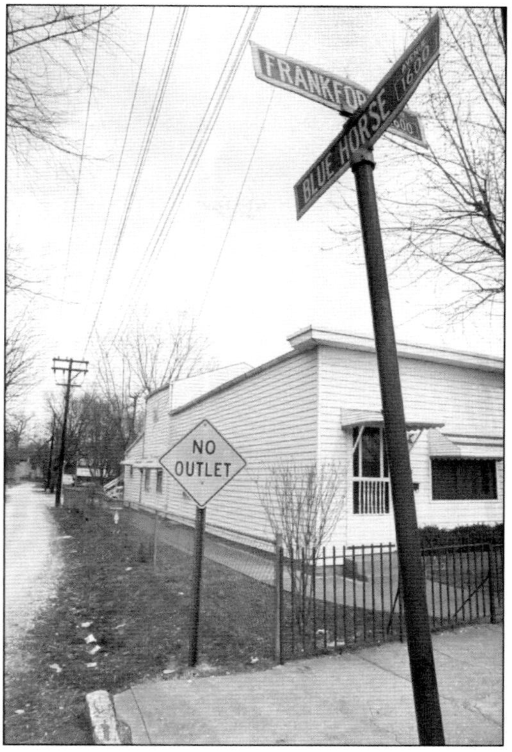

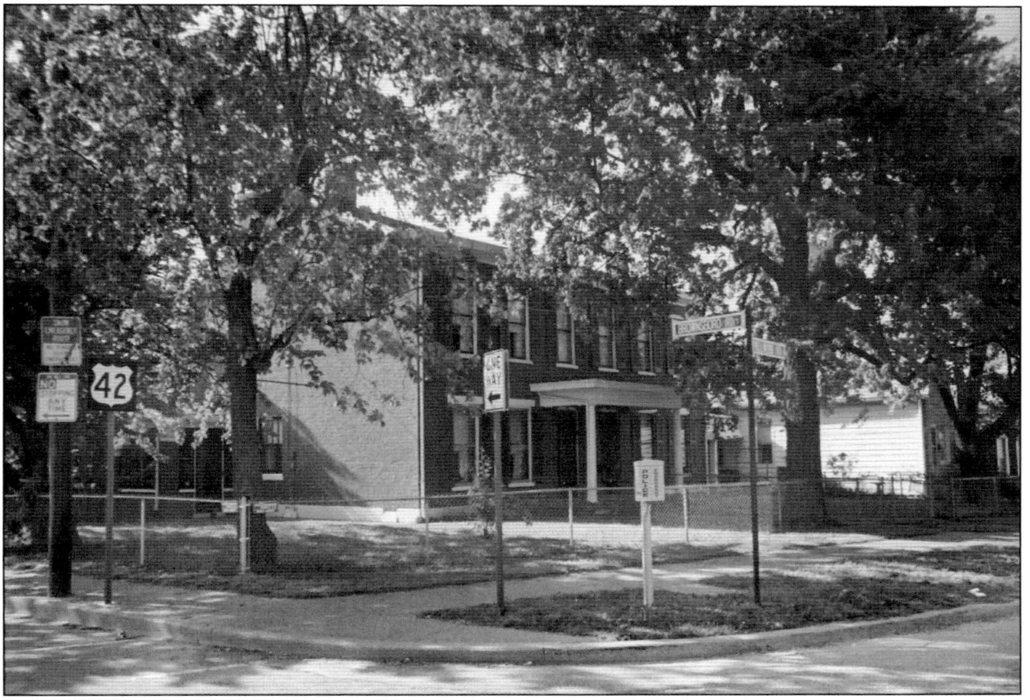

This image shows the intersection of Mellwood Avenue and Brownsboro Road in 1975. The house was converted into L&N, a popular local restaurant. (Courtesy of Mark Thompson, NRHP.)

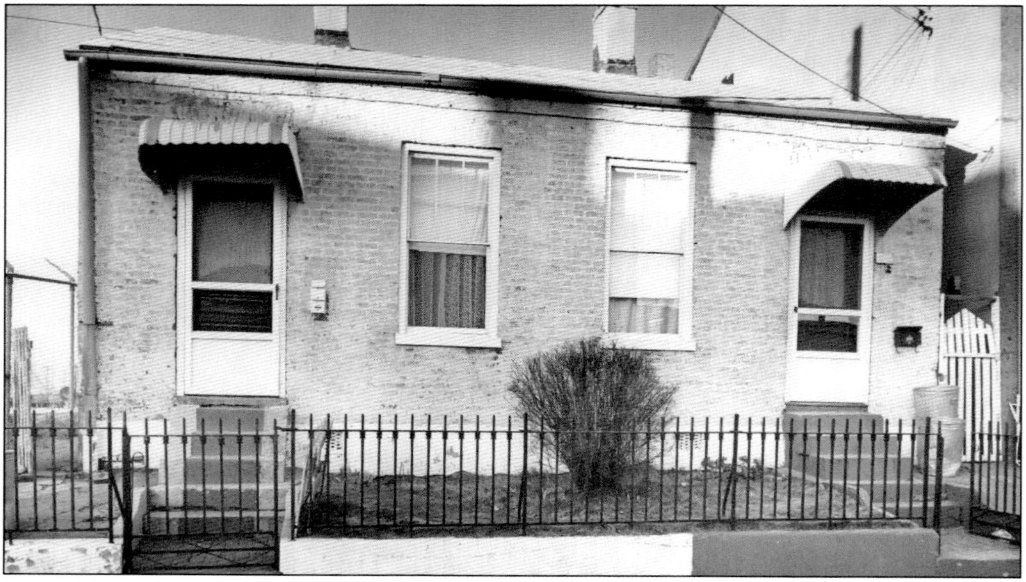

In 1972, the Edison House Corporation bought the cottage at 729 East Washington Street, where Thomas Edison lived while he worked as a telegraph operator for Western Union on Second and West Main Streets in Louisville from 1866 to 1868. Built in 1850, the shotgun home needed a lot of work when it was bought. Butchertown, Inc. raised enough money to restore it and created a museum showcasing Edison's inventions and life. (Courtesy of Leslie Tichenor.)

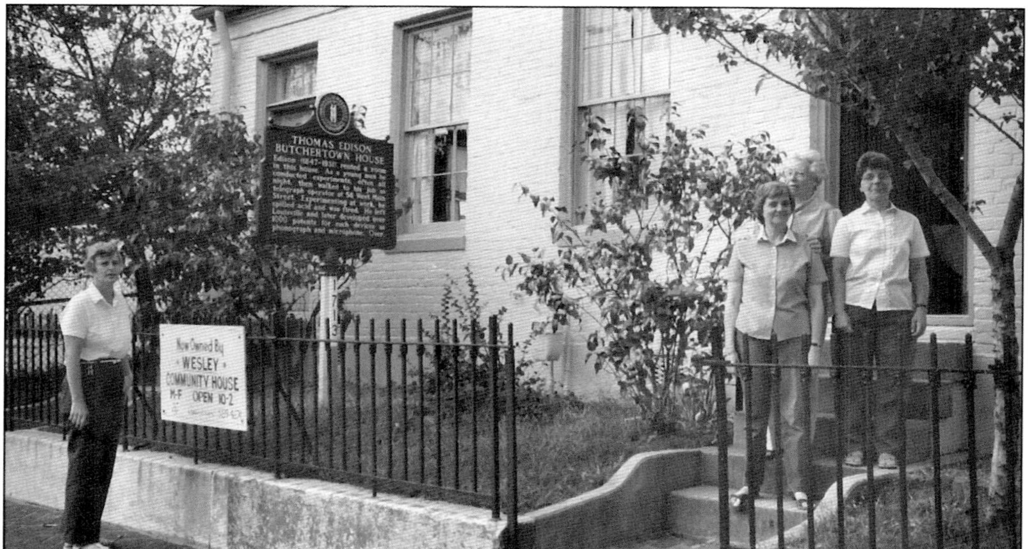

The museum showcases the life of prolific inventor Edison, who received 1,093 patents in his lifetime. From making improvements to telegraphs and telephones to designing the first indoor lighting system, Edison constantly was thinking of ways to make life easier. In fact, he was fired from his job as a telegraph operator in Louisville for ruining his boss's rug while experimenting with sulfuric acid. Pictured are, from left to right, June Fischer and Helen Mandelbaum, both former directors of Wesley House, visiting the museum with Muriel Williamson and Kay Stoke. (Courtesy of Ethel Stoke.)

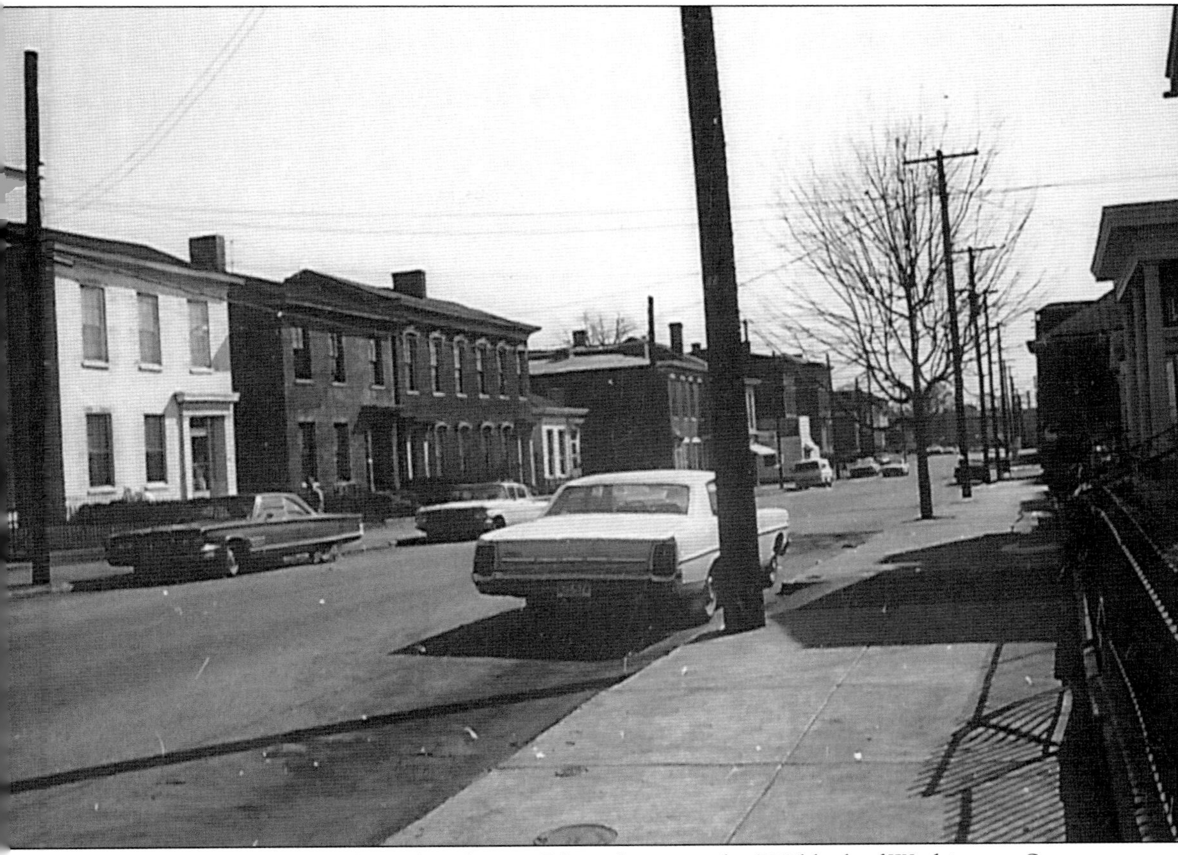

The view above looks east from the Thomas Edison house in the 700 block of Washington Street in the late 1960s. The view below looks east in the 800 block of Washington Street and shows the lack of trees. When the Tichenor family moved to Butchertown, they rented a concrete saw and cut holes in the sidewalk in front of their store to plant trees. The first two plantings did not take, but the third prospered. (Courtesy of Leslie Tichenor.)

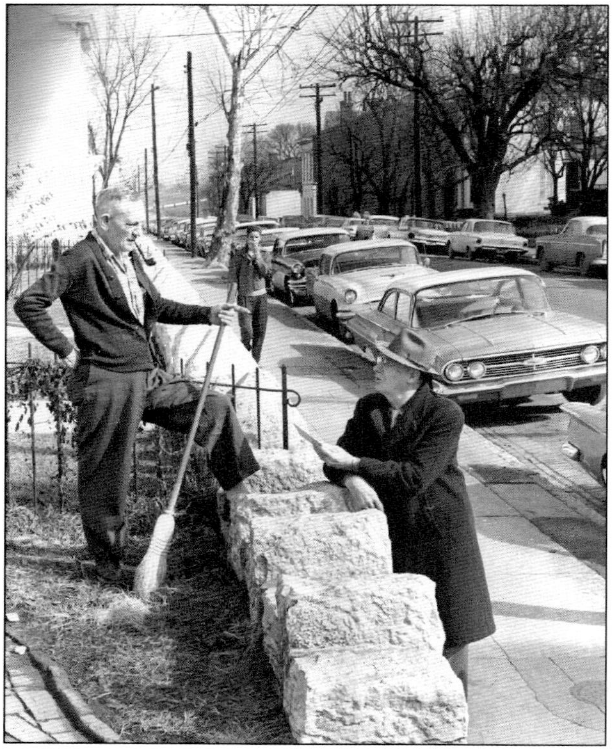

Walter Mattern is taking a break from tidying up to speak with his neighbor in the 1600 block of Story Avenue. Story Avenue is a two-way street, and cars are parked in both directions. The Last Chance Tavern can be seen in the distance. In 1961, twenty-three homeowners received the first City Beautiful commission's citation in recognition of the neighborhood's work in remodeling and maintaining the 1600 block of Story Avenue. (Courtesy of Louis Moseson.)

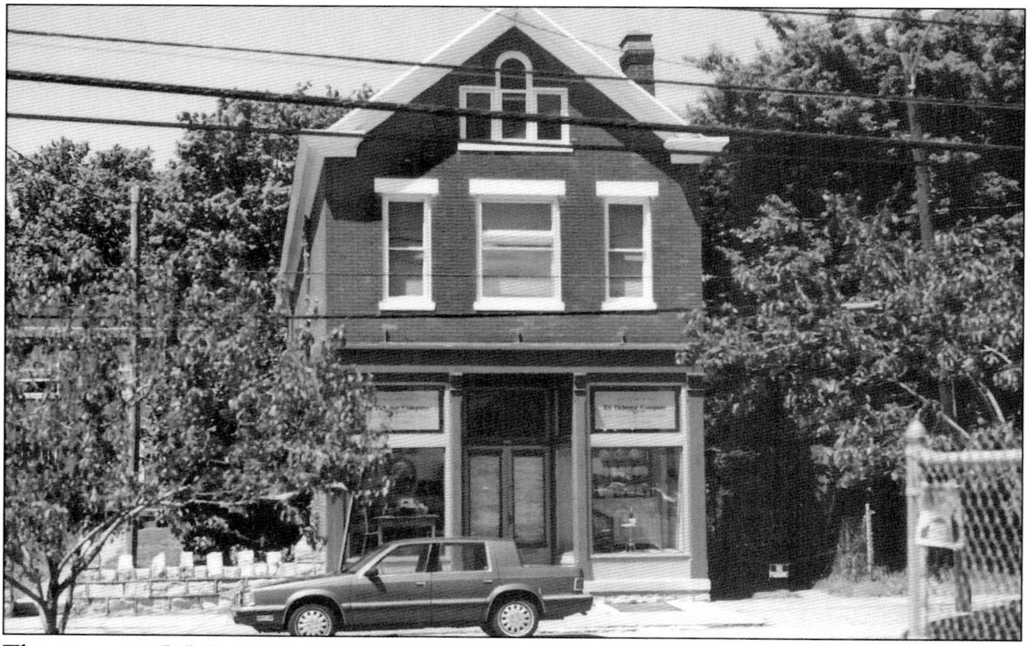

This store at 1515 Story Avenue used to be Theresa Georgel's dry goods and notions store. She and her husband moved to Louisville in 1892 and passed her memories of Butchertown—the days of wagons rolling past and getting water from the pump at the corner of Ohio Street and Story Avenue—on to the next generation of residents. (Courtesy of Leslie Tichenor.)

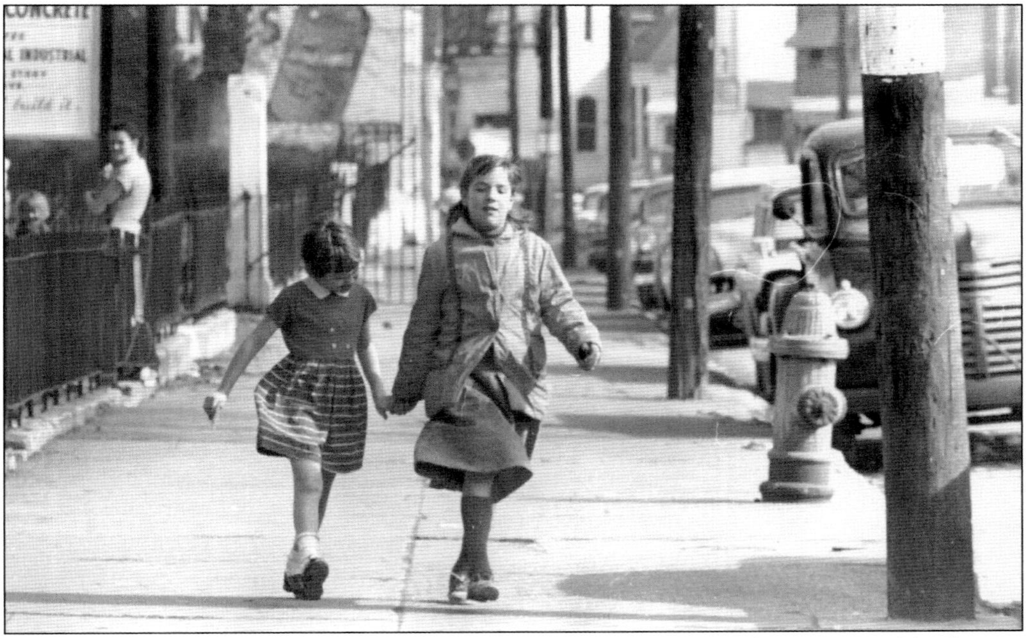

Taken in 1965, this shows two girls skipping along Story Avenue, the main road leading to downtown from the east. Already considered an old neighborhood in the 1890s, the waves of immigrants between 1890 and the 1920s increased the number of houses in the area. (Courtesy of Louis Moseson.)

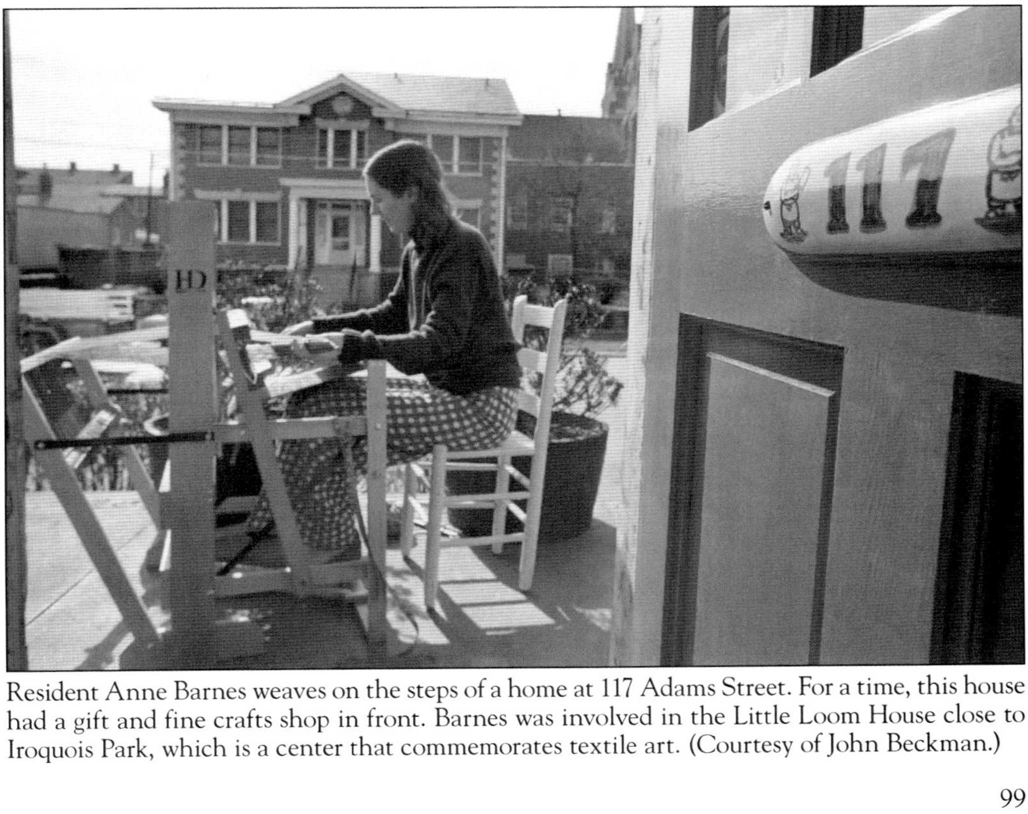

Resident Anne Barnes weaves on the steps of a home at 117 Adams Street. For a time, this house had a gift and fine crafts shop in front. Barnes was involved in the Little Loom House close to Iroquois Park, which is a center that commemorates textile art. (Courtesy of John Beckman.)

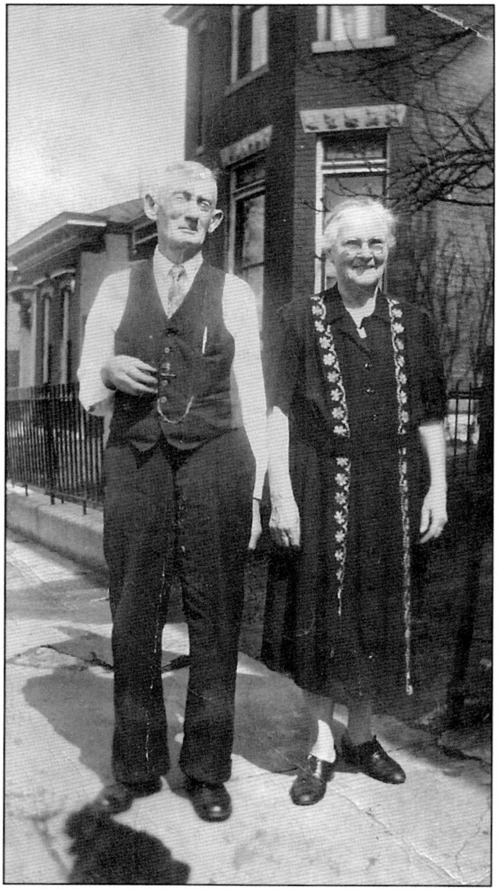

Mr. and Mrs. Bottorf, the grandparents of Eddie Mattern, are seen on Story Avenue in the 1930s or 1940s. As early as the 1890s, homeowners in Butchertown had moved to other parts of the city of Louisville and rented out their homes. As a result of deteriorating housing stock, the smells of the meatpacking operations and the city and private dump to the north, rent in Butchertown became very cheap. (Courtesy of Eddie Mattern.)

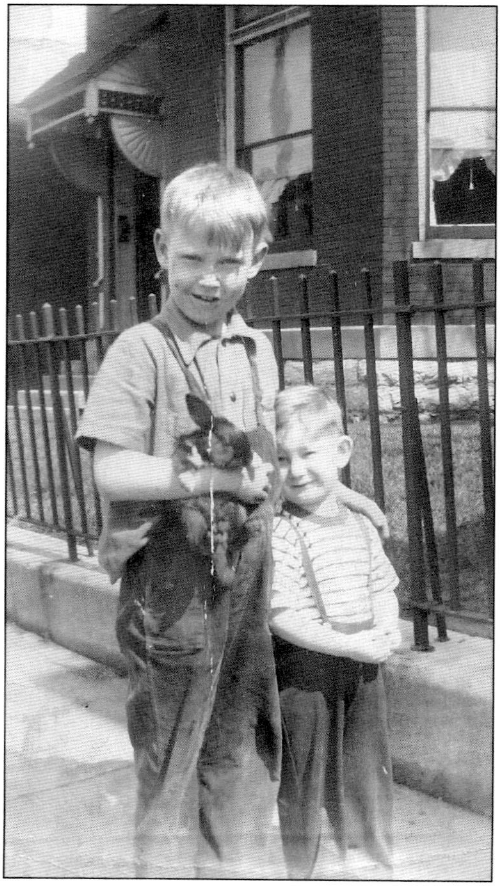

Owning a childhood pet, such as the rabbit that Mattern (right) and his brother are pictured carrying along Story Avenue, was a rite of passage. Notice the ornate porch in the background with its spindles and carved sides. (Courtesy of Eddie Mattern.)

Eddie Mattern, Venita Brown, and Mildred Mattern are next to the Last Chance Tavern in the 1950s. (Courtesy of Eddie Mattern.)

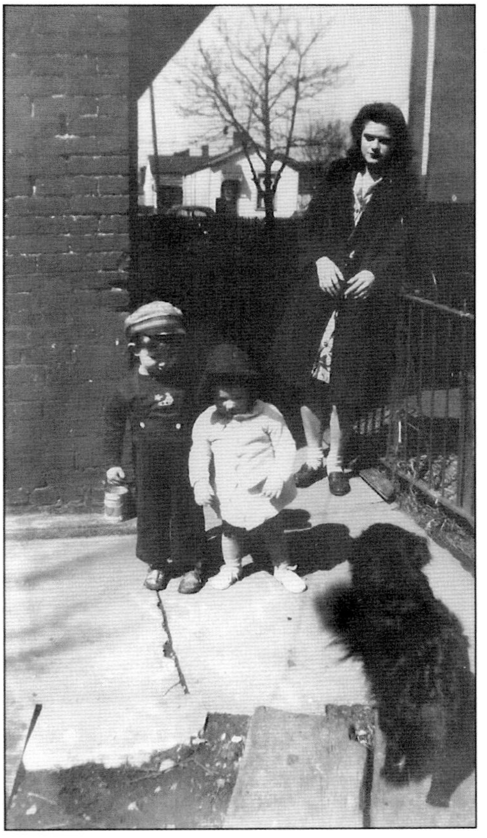

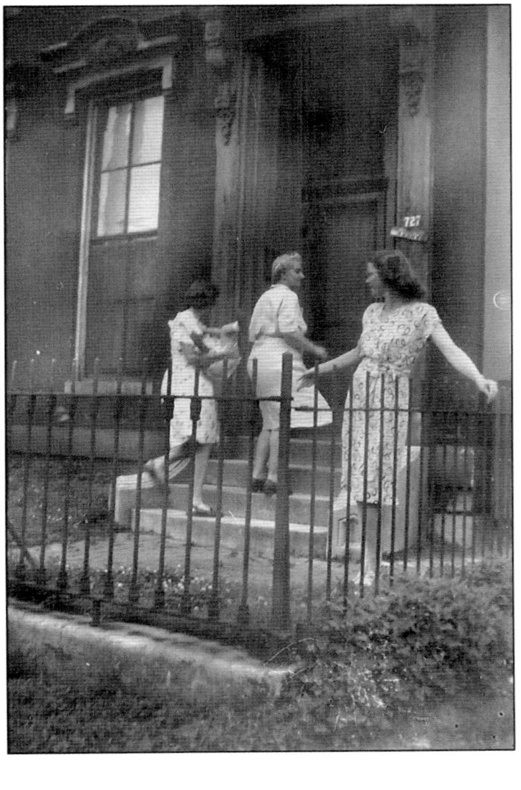

Pictured is 727 Washington Street, the home next to the Edison house in the late 1930s or early 1940s. At that time, rent in Butchertown was as little as $3 or $4 a month, and the iceman would move one to a new apartment for $1. Thrifty residents would venture to the hay market at closing and snap up damaged fruits to can or make into preserves. (Courtesy of Ethel Stoke.)

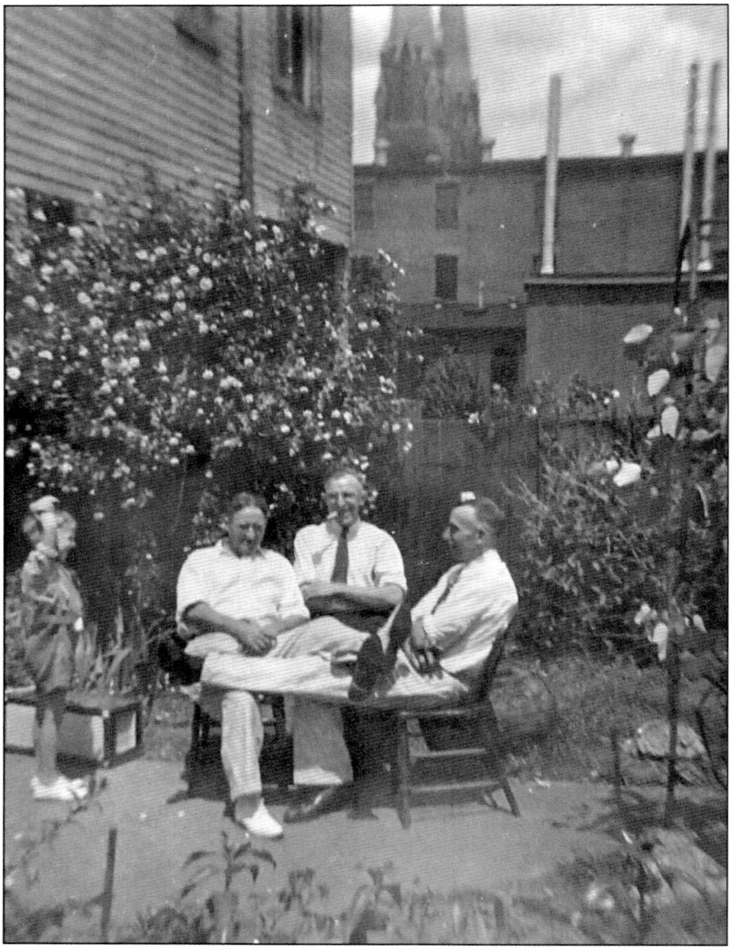

At left, from left to right, William McClain, Joe Wiggins, and Zack ? take a well-earned break from their workweek in a backyard in the 1930s. Daughter Bernice tries to catch her father's and uncle's attention. Many backyards in Butchertown have an area of sinking ground where an outhouse was located. Below, a hot day in the park in the 1920s is helped by ice cold drinks, a treat at any time. Pictured are Bernice, Mary, Helen, and Raphael. (Both, courtesy of the Kimpflein family.)

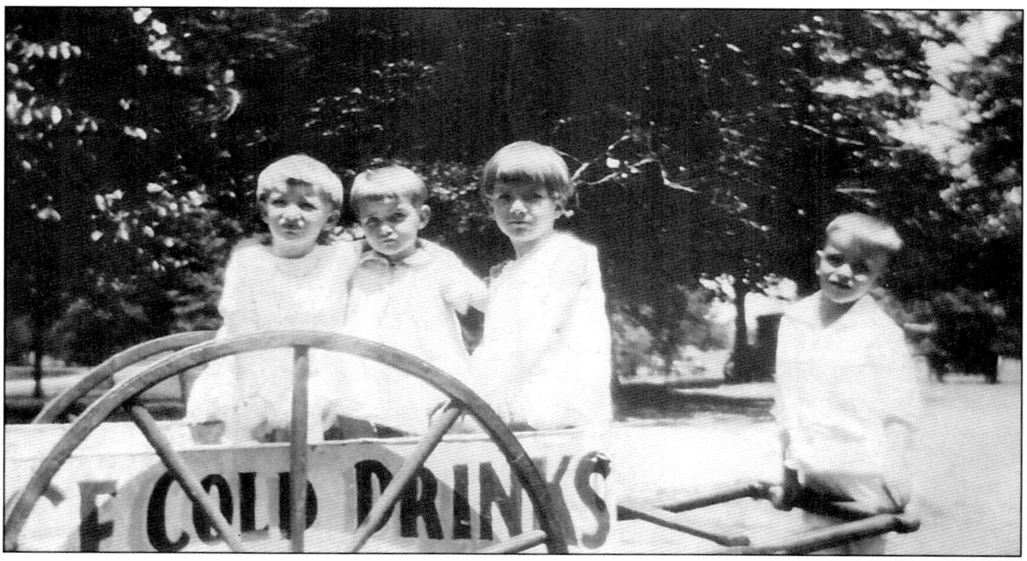

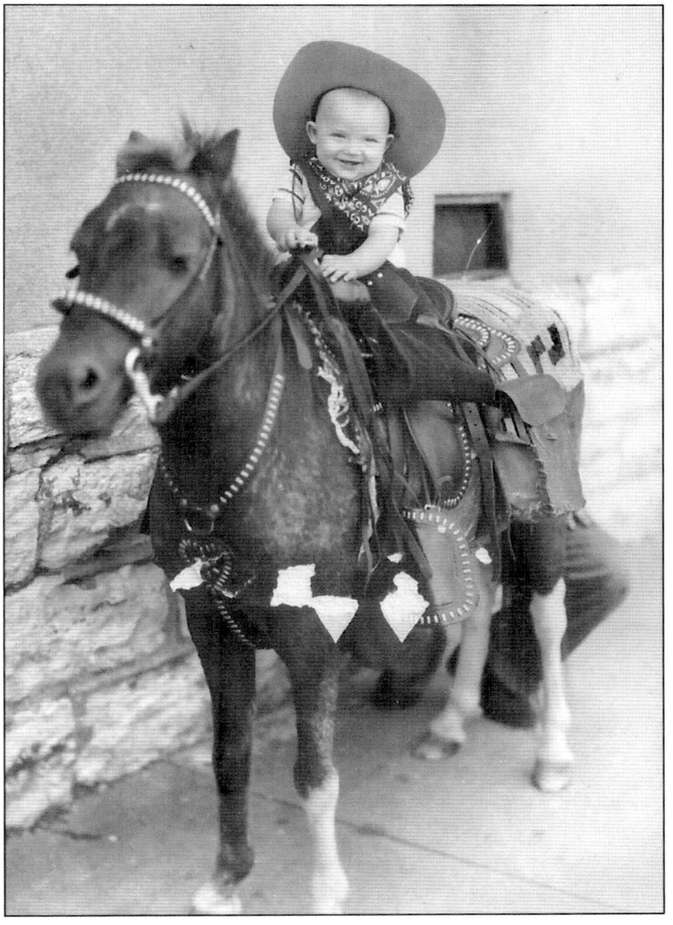

Getting their picture made with a traveling photographer's horse and cowboy hat was the highlight of many a child's year. Pictured is Bill Kimpflein next to the Hellmueller's bakery building in 1953. He remembers getting "hot-cross-buns" for 5¢ at the bakery and running home with them while they were still piping hot. Below, Helen McClain, Mary Liebert, and Bernice Wiggins show off their matching dolls in the backyard around 1920. (Both, courtesy of the Kimpflein family.)

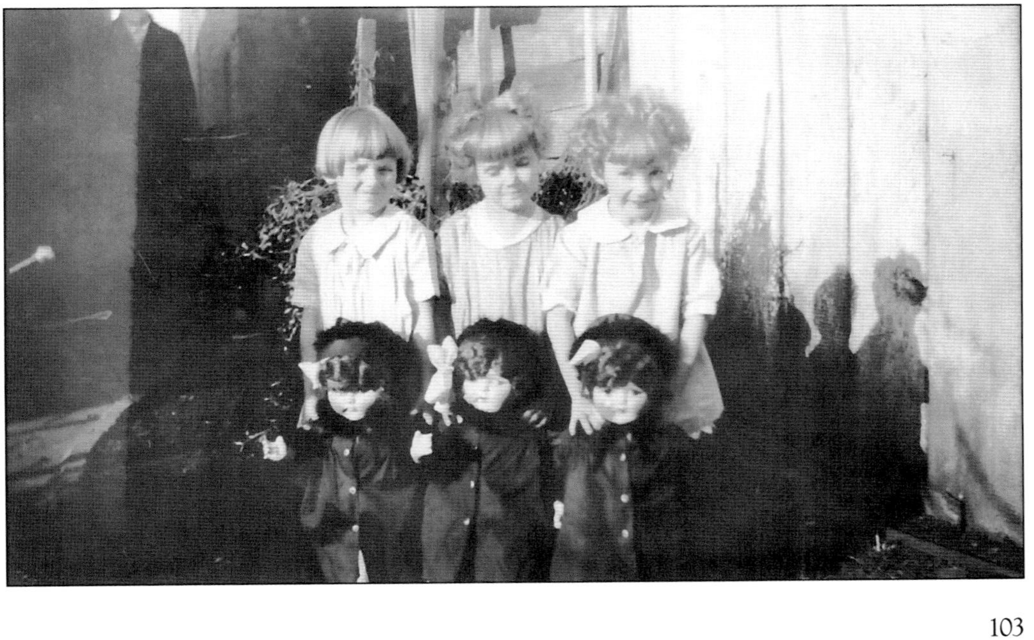

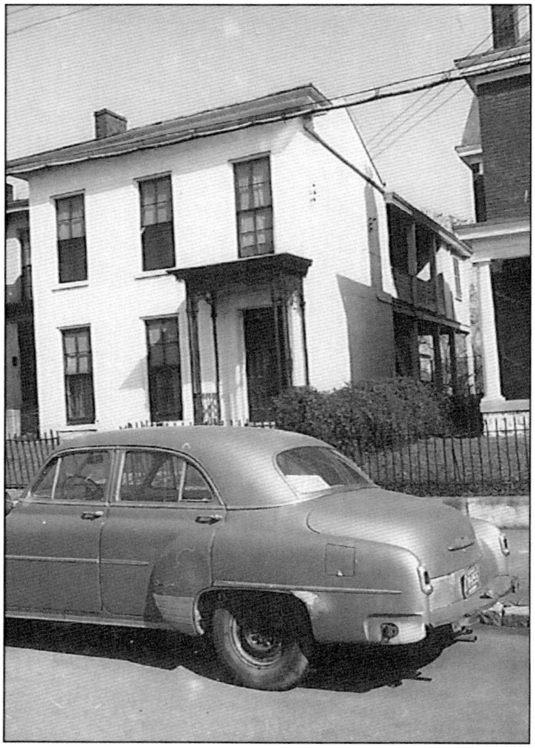

This is a two-story house at 815 East Washington Street. The front door has two teardrop-shaped glass windows and a smoothly flowing stairway on the side porch. It was owned by Alberta and Bessie Honnecker, sisters whose parents purchased the already old house in 1888. Until the 1970s, the sisters had the original horsehair furniture, no plumbing or electricity, and still used the gas jets protruding from the wall for lighting. This house was painted by members of Butchertown, Inc. as one of the neighborhood beatification projects. (Courtesy of Leslie Tichenor.)

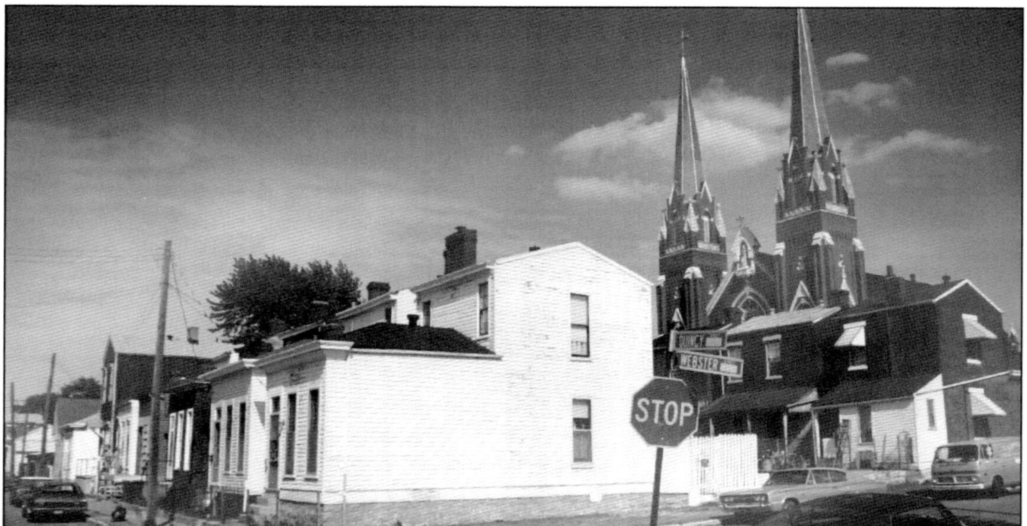

This image shows camelback homes on Quincy Street at Webster Street looking southeast with St. Joseph's Catholic Church in the background. Many homes in this block of Washington and Quincy Streets are camelback shotguns, which were built as a way for homeowners to add extra living space to their homes. The home on the far right is 1401 Washington Street and was built between 1889 and 1891. Known as the Kuntz shotgun house, it is typical to camelback shotgun homes; it has three rooms back to back and a forth built over the rear, forming the camelback. (Courtesy of Mark Thompson, NRHP.)

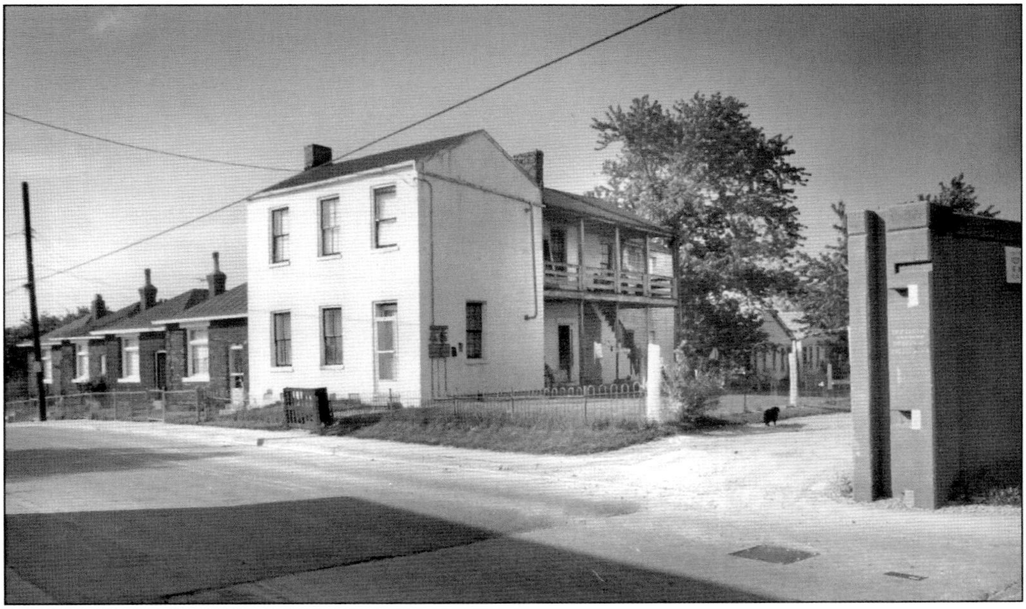

Here is a view of the 200 block of Ohio Street through the flood wall, showing several shotgun homes and a fine two-story brick house with a gallery and exterior stair. That building has a deceiving front door—it is painted on the bricked-up former entrance. Ohio Street used to be known as Pork House Alley, on account of the many pork houses in the vicinity. (Courtesy of Mark Thompson, NRHP.)

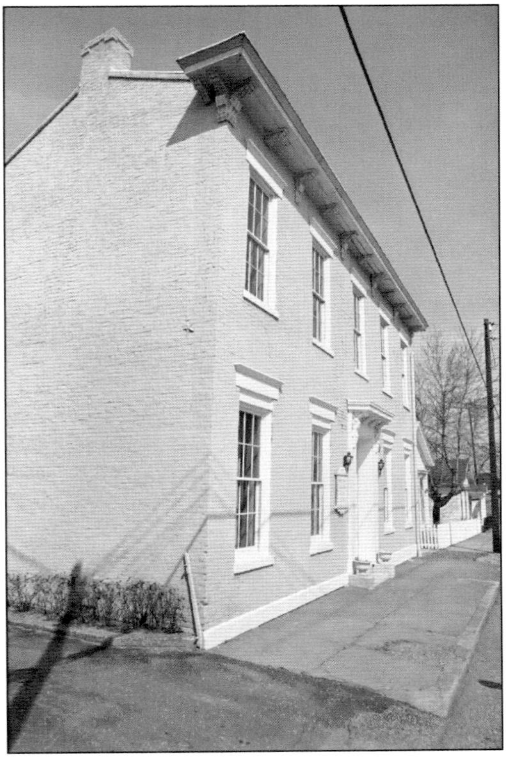

This view of the 1600 block of Story Avenue looking east at the earthen flood wall shows where it curves into Brownsboro Road. The Metzgers Verein, German for butcher's society, used Ehrmanns Halle at 1663 Story Avenue for their meetings in 1869 and sponsored annual parades and picnics. The first president was John M. Letterle, a butcher and city councilman. (Courtesy of John Beckman.)

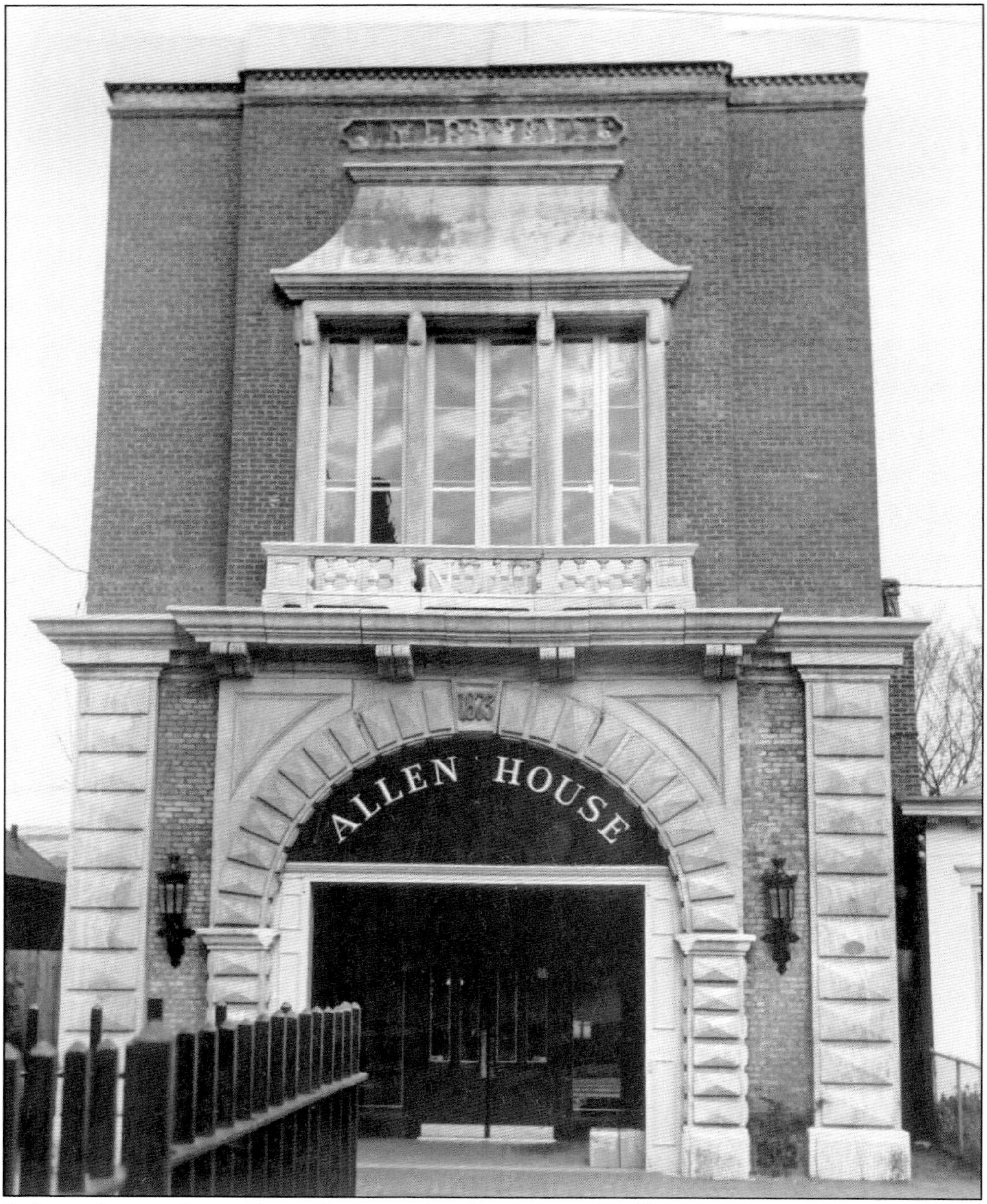

Fighting fires on the outskirts of town in the 1800s required well water and a bucket brigade until the nearest fire engine could arrive. Sen. John M. Letterle was influential in the building of the fire station, which opened in 1874. One of the oldest standing firehouses in Louisville, it was in operation until 1925. The building has since housed the Moseley Feed Manufacturing Company, the Humphrey Candy Company, Henry's Rug Cleaning, and the Allen House Antique Shop. It was converted into a residence in 2003. (Courtesy of Mark Thompson, NRHP.)

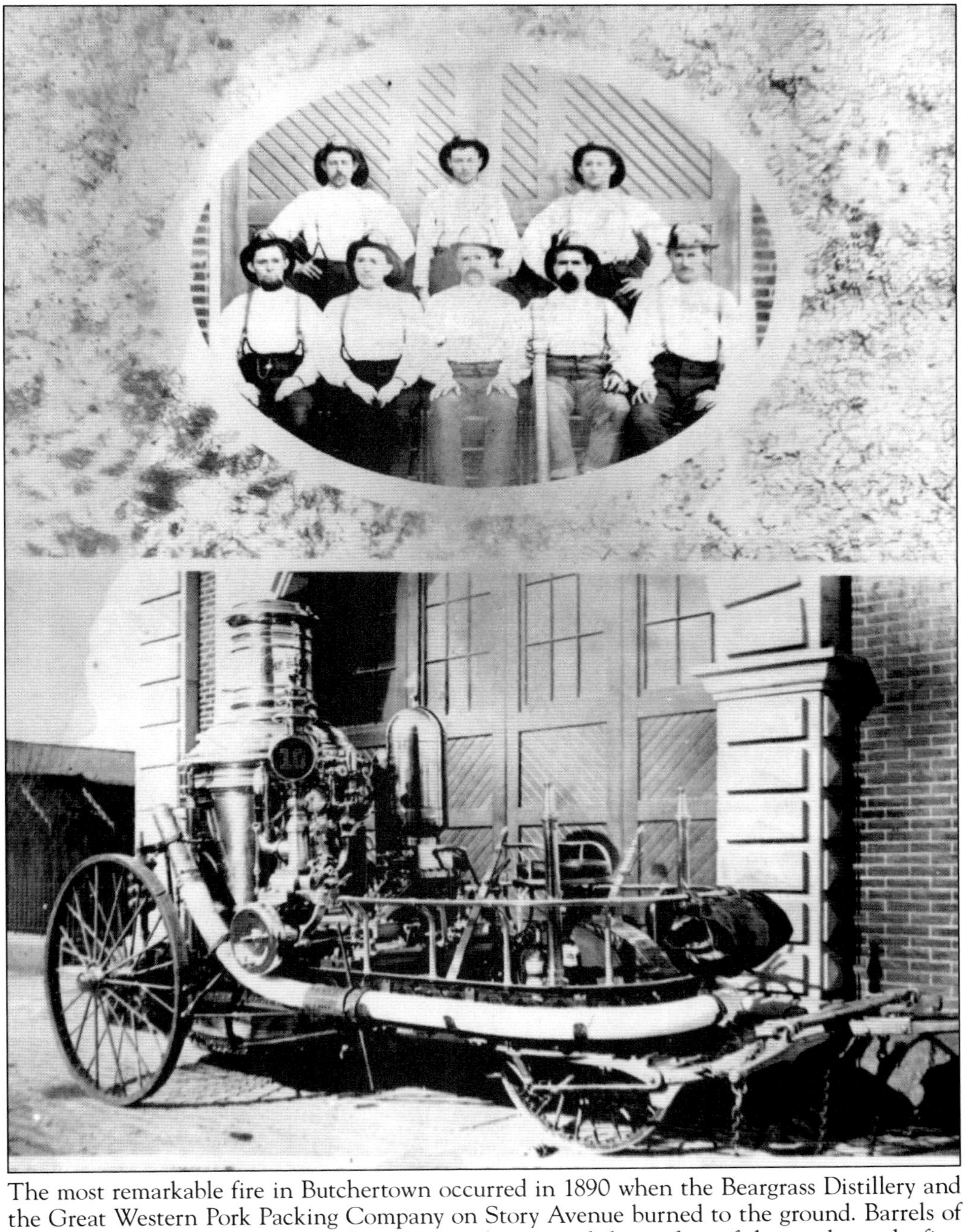

The most remarkable fire in Butchertown occurred in 1890 when the Beargrass Distillery and the Great Western Pork Packing Company on Story Avenue burned to the ground. Barrels of burning, exploding whiskey were launched in the air, and the surface of the creek caught fire. There is still scarring from hoofs on the wooden floor and a marker showing the height of the 1937 flood in the doorway. (Courtesy of Mac and Catherine Willett.)

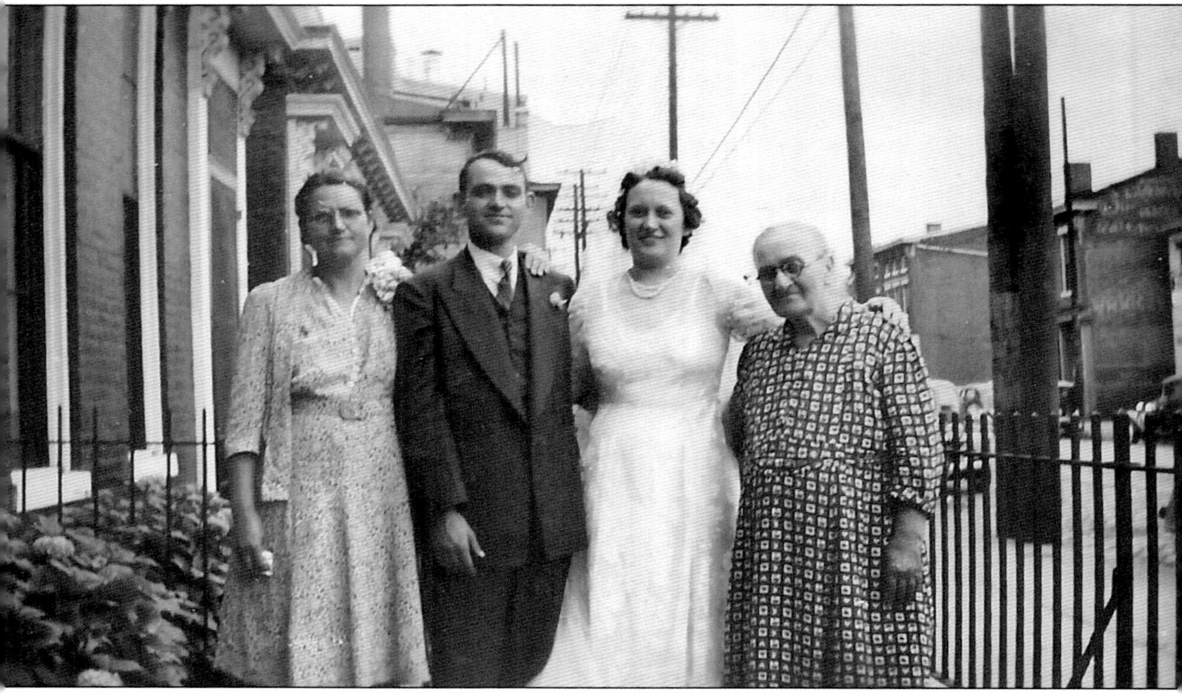

From left to right, Mrs. Ottersbach, Freddie, Bea, and Grandma Preher are in Butchertown. With the success of a zoning change in 1966, Butchertown, Inc., a for-profit corporation, was launched at $10 a share. The purpose of the corporation was to buy and rehabilitate homes in the neighborhood to maintain cohesion. (Courtesy of the Kimpflein family.)

This image shows Mrs. Preher and her daughter holding a large catfish in the 1930s. With the close proximity of the river, many residents went to the Louisville Municipal Harbor. The harbor, closed in 2005, was thought to be one of the oldest continuously operating municipal harbors on the Ohio River and among the oldest surviving inland recreational harbors in the entire country. (Courtesy of the Kimpflein family.)

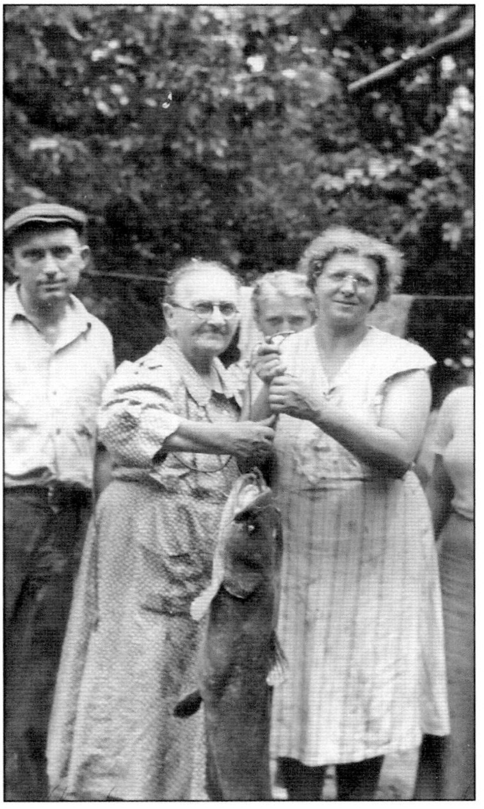

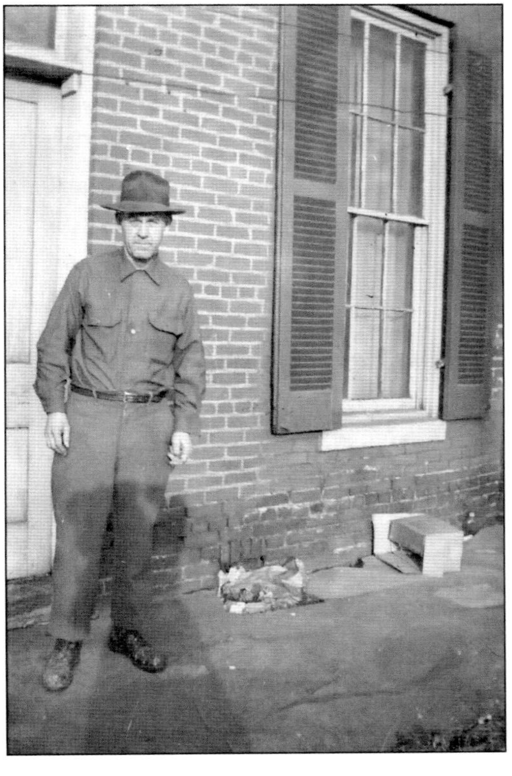

Charles Hoke was a neighborhood handyman and did tuck pointing on stonework and painted houses and shutters. He brought the shutters home and his children helped scrape off the old paint and apply the new. Later Butchertown, Inc. began organizing neighborhood improvement projects by painting houses with donated paint for those that were unable to do so themselves. (Courtesy of Connie Pratt.)

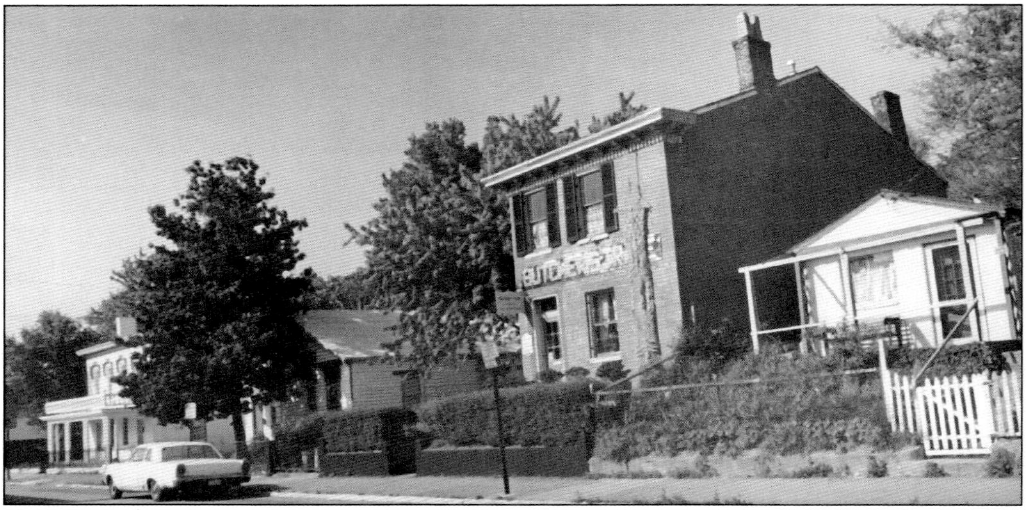

The Letterle-Rehm house at 129 North Adams Street (on the far left) was built in 1840 by John M. Letterle. An active member of the community, he organized the Butchers Union No. 1 in 1869, was an alderman in Louisville from 1869 to 1878, and was the Democratic representative from the fifth district in the state legislature. The porch pictured was later removed, and molds were made to match the curved hoods of the bottom windows with the top. Looking at the building from the side, it appears that the ornate facade was attached to add sophistication to a much simpler original home. (Courtesy of Mark Thompson, NRHP.)

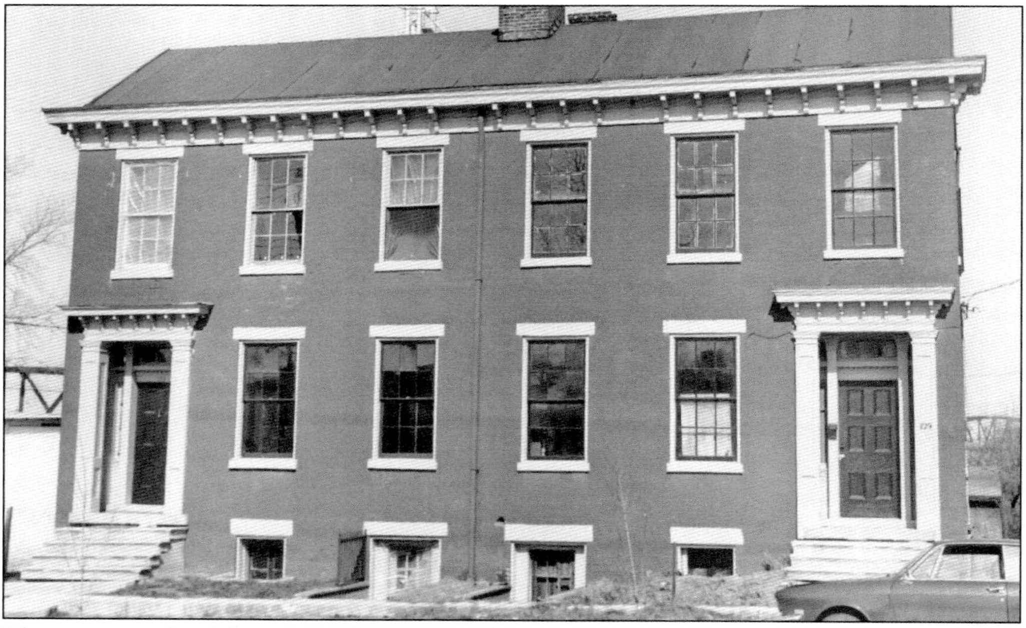

This two-story brick home at 727–729 Franklin Street is an example of an early housing style with its simple lines and shared fireplace. The property line ran through the middle of the house. During the 1930s, it was used as apartments, and Ethel Stoke remembers her mother chatting through the bathroom medicine cabinet and dividing wall with the neighbor because the cabinets in the apartments were back to back. It is now the offices of Vendome Copper and Brass Works. (Courtesy of Bob Hutchinson, NRHP.)

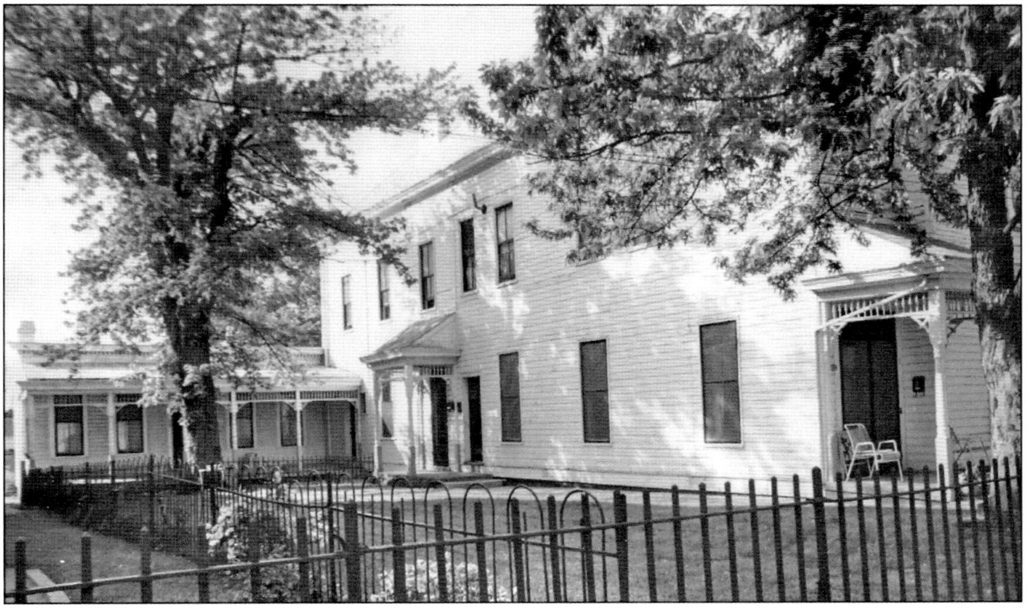

This view shows the side of the Edward Stoecker House at 1633 Story Avenue. This house is an example of adding onto a small home as income improves or a family grows. It was originally a three-room dwelling and is shown with an ell addition to the side. Lost Alley, off Ohio Street and parallel to Story Avenue, was renamed Stoecker Avenue and was the location of the C. Stoecker Tannery. (Courtesy of Mark Thompson, NRHP.)

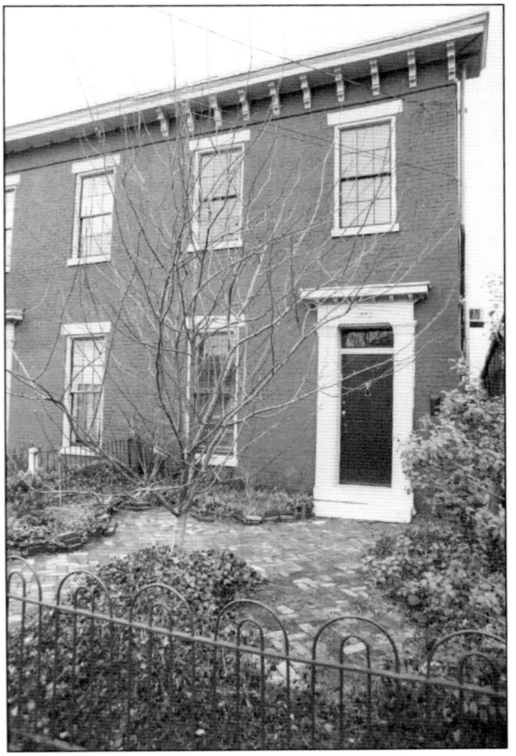

Here is 811 Franklin Street. This elegantly refurbished house was the third of several Butchertown residences that neighborhood advocate Jim Segrest refinished. Segrest worked for Louisville Planning and Zoning in 1966 and created the Butchertown Neighborhood Plan with neighbors. (Courtesy of John Beckman.)

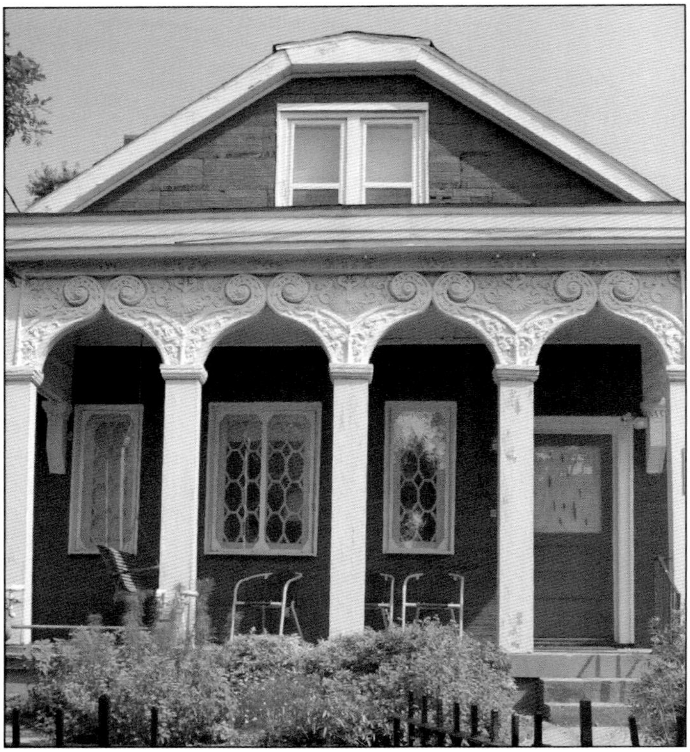

The small cottage (at right) at 909 East Washington Street features a surprisingly ornate porch with columns in the Venetian Gothic style. This is an example of the architectural diversity in Butchertown; while homes share similarly small front yards, they have varied architectural styles. A handsome two-story Italianate-style house may be built next to a wooden-frame shotgun home with Eastlake Victorian details. Below, an amusing house at 1313 East Washington Street attracts stares for the mounted bull's head on the gable. The owners bought the head in Paris and brought it back because it reminded them of the area. (Both, courtesy of author's collection.)

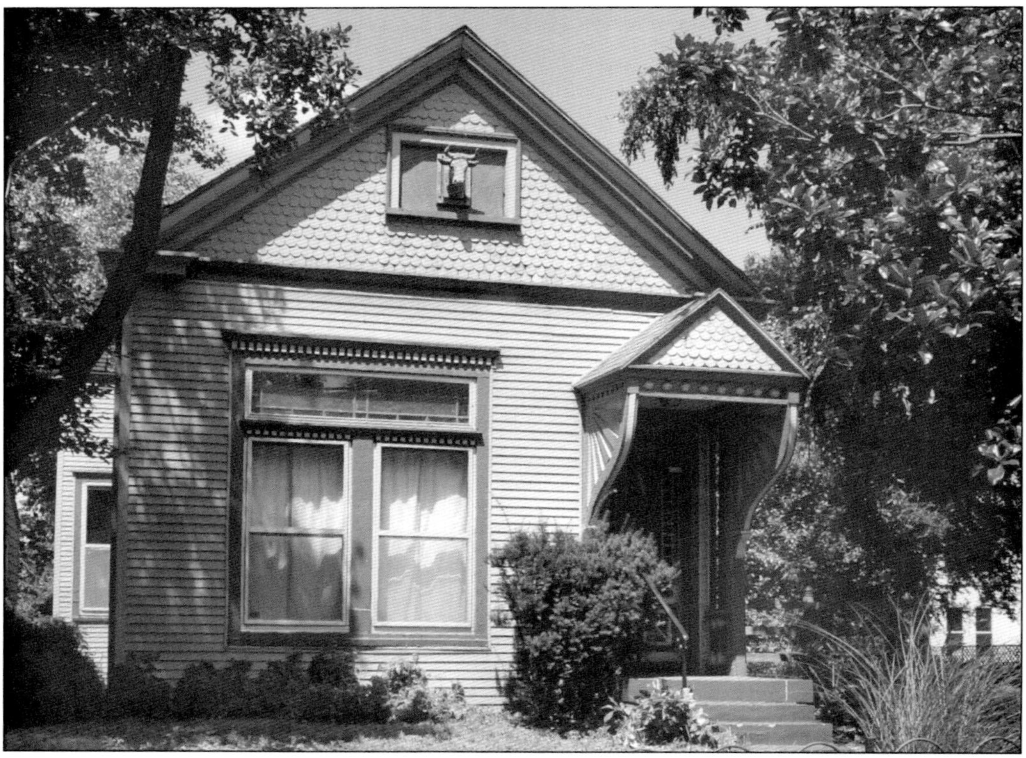

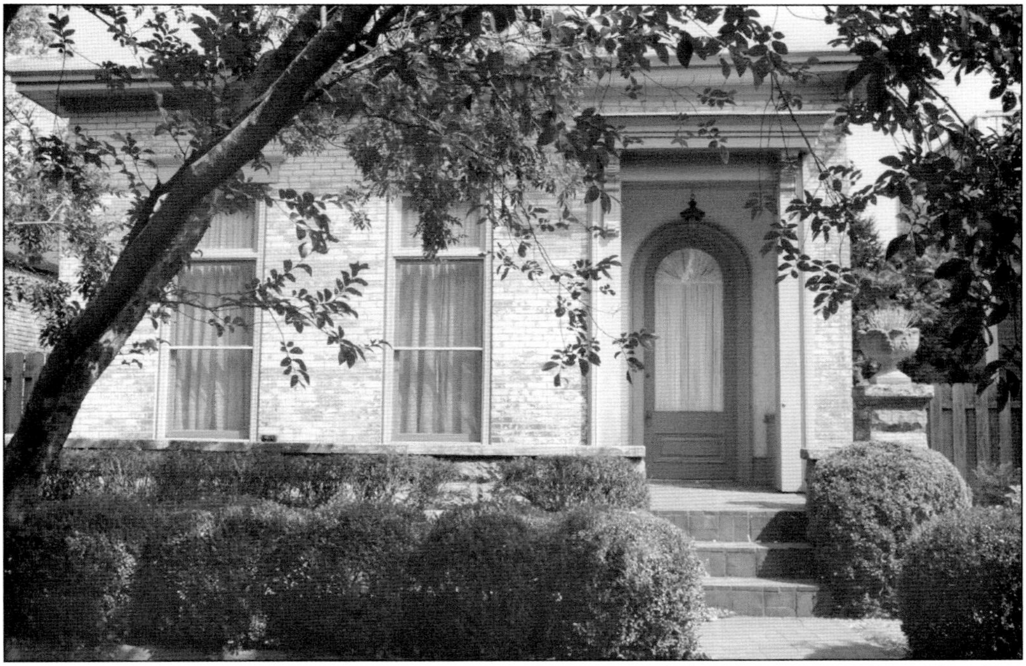

This residence at 925 Franklin Street boasts a Mediterranean feel with its orange door, blue door frame, and yellow recessed entryway. The simple landscaping adds to its appeal. (Courtesy of author's collection.)

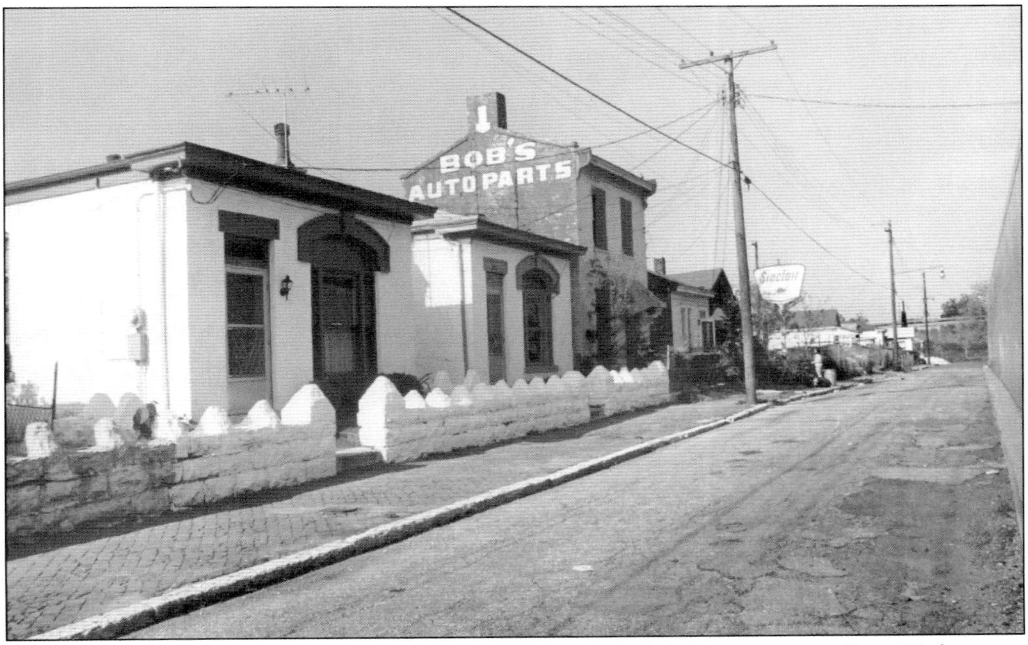

A hand-painted sign points the way to Bob Collett's automobile parts store on East Washington Street, formerly Maiden Lane, in 1975. His popular sales slogan was, "Don't get robbed, call Bob!" Maiden Lane used to run between Adam and Ohio Streets, and Henry Conrad and Jacob Krauth's slaughterhouse was located on this street. (Courtesy of Mark Thompson, NRHP.)

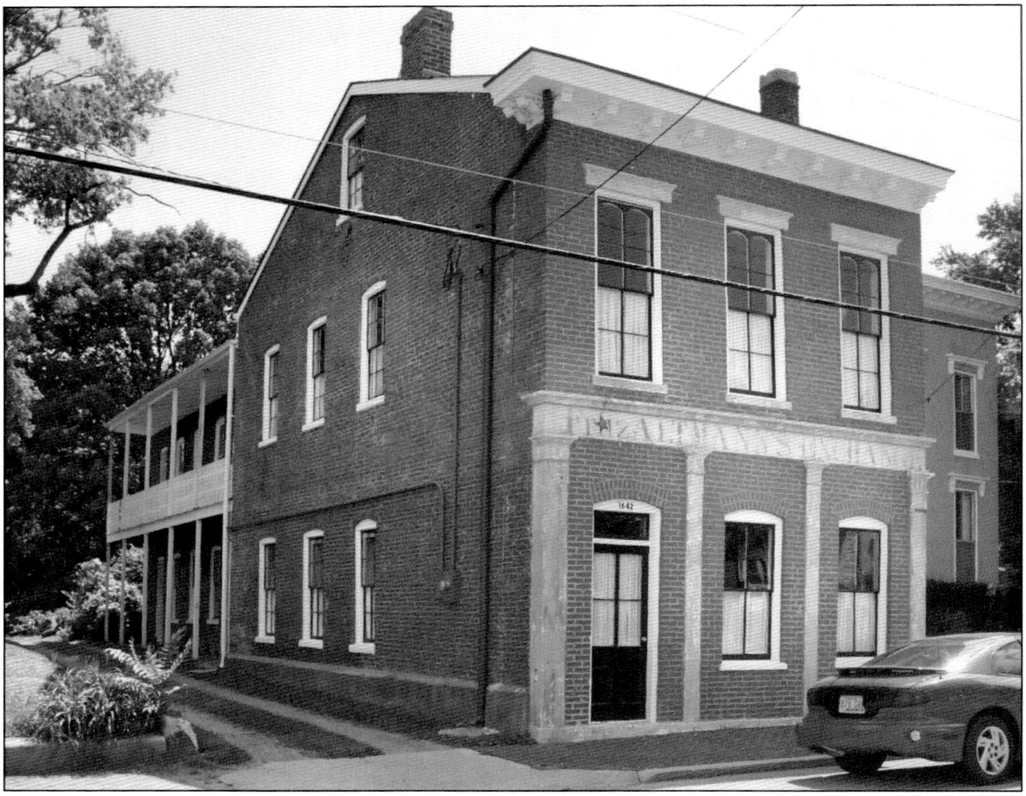

This picture shows the Last Chance Tavern at 1642 Story Avenue with the Hadley house at 1638 Story Avenue to the right. The Hadley house is a large, brick Italianate-style house with a heavy cornice and intricate door and window trim. The tavern was converted into a residence in 1904; it is presumed that the front porch was bricked up at that time. (Courtesy of author's collection.)

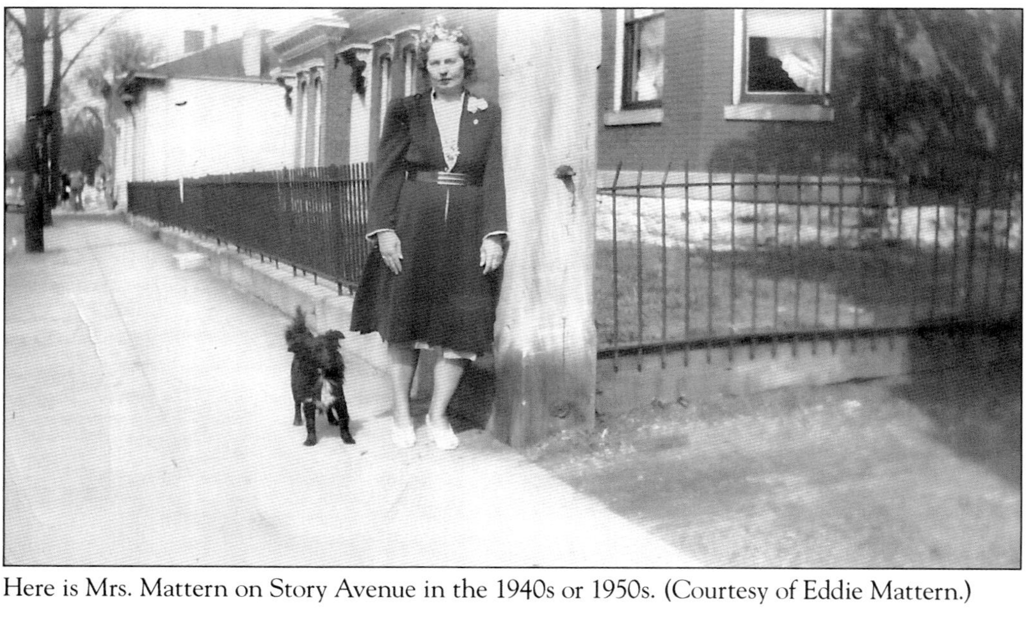

Here is Mrs. Mattern on Story Avenue in the 1940s or 1950s. (Courtesy of Eddie Mattern.)

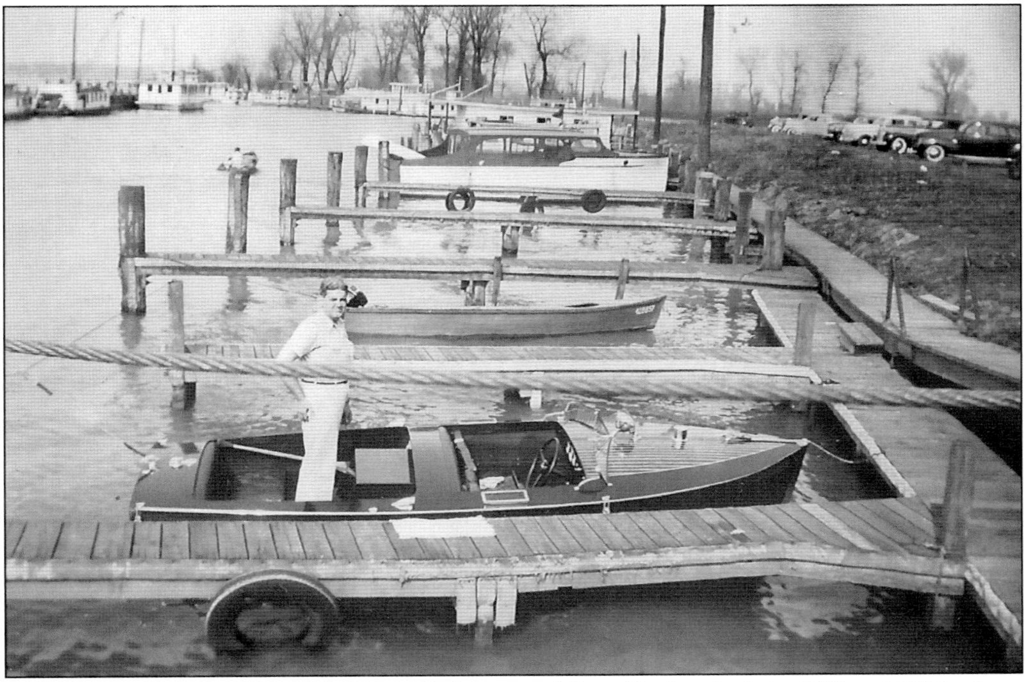

This undated picture shows the Louisville Municipal Boat Harbor, built in 1935 and 1936, where many Butchertown residents went during the summer months to fish or head out on the river in their boats. The harbor was built as a WPA (Works Progress Administration) project and was considered an engineering marvel. (Courtesy of the Kimpflein family.)

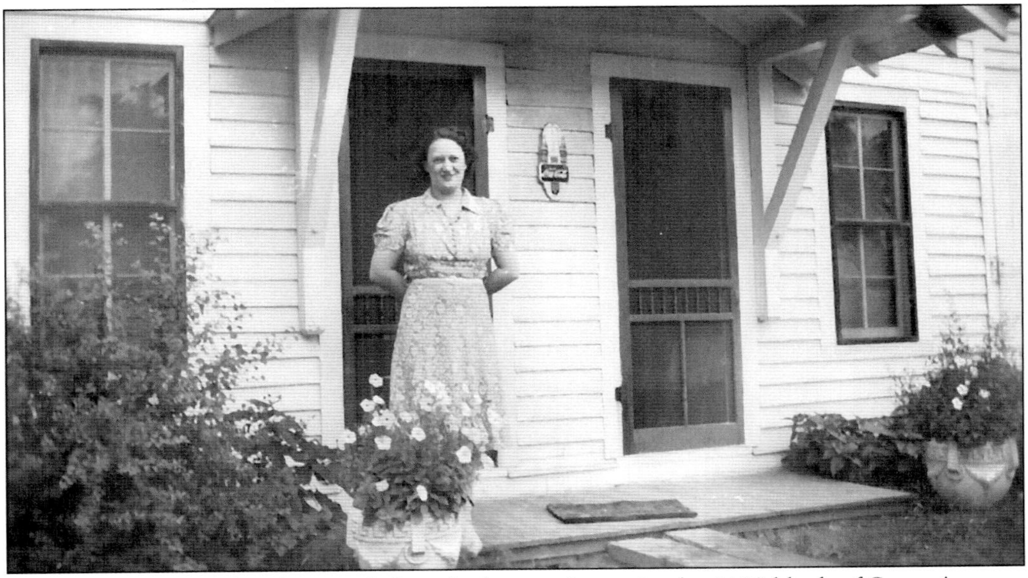

Beatrice Ottersbach lived in a side-by-side shotgun home in the 1400 block of Story Avenue, which has since been torn down. Duplexes such as these were a way for owners to economize by maximizing the buildable land and yard space and decrease building costs by sharing a common wall. Notice the matching screen doors with their delicate wood spindles in the center and the thick, wood boards used as a walkway to the house. (Courtesy of the Kimpflein family.)

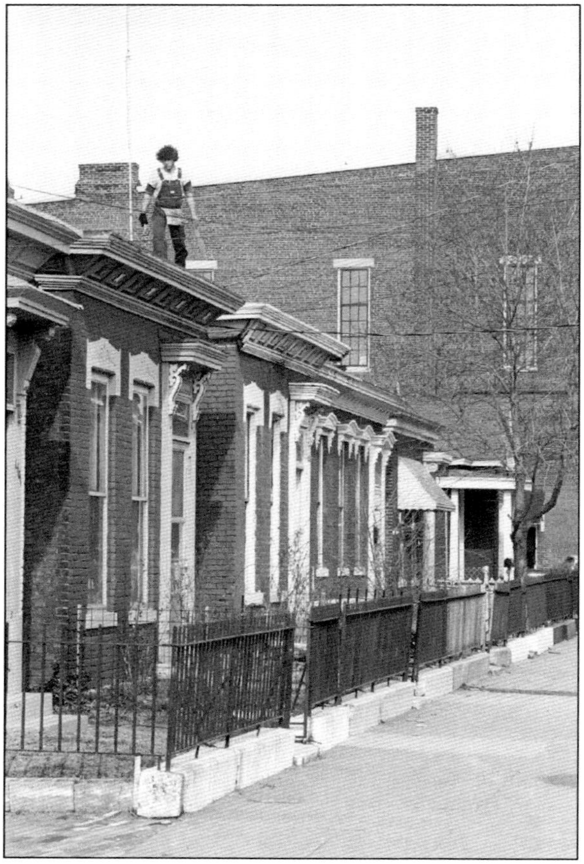

At left, a roofer stands on top of a house in the 1400 block of Washington Street looking east. These structures are typical of the camelback shotgun homes built throughout the neighborhood during the late 19th- and early-20th centuries. The houses share similar facade arrangements and basic floor plans but distinguish themselves with decorative details in different architectural styles, such as Italianate, Eastlake Victorian, or Queen Anne. The Letterle firehouse can be seen on the far right. Below is 1425 Washington Street, a brick shotgun home built next to the firehouse. The limestone alley to the right of the house runs between Washington and Quincy Streets. (Both, courtesy of John Beckman.)

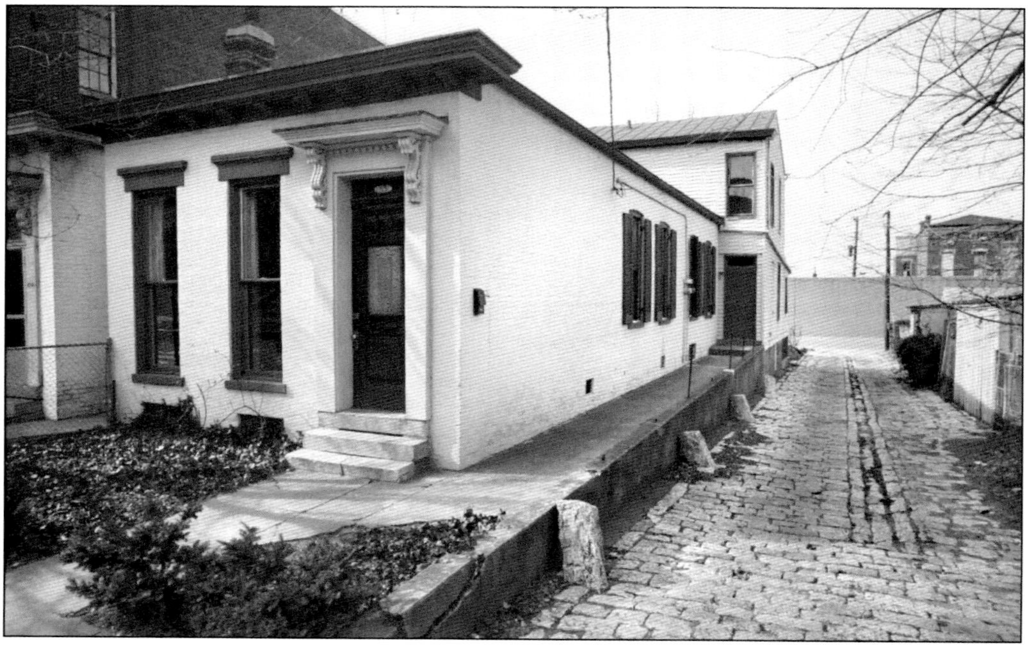

Above, looking west along the 1600 block of Story Avenue is the former East End Café in the distance on the right. When it was Min's East End Café in the 1950s and 1960s, the proprietor sat in the doorway snapping beans for the lunchtime crowd. The building is interesting because guests have to walk past the kitchen to the dining room in back. Below is a view of Story Avenue from the field behind Hadley Pottery. The influx of people, such as George and Mary Alice Hadley, to the neighborhood brought new business and home restorations. Mary Alice Hadley began making pottery in 1939 when she could not find any designs she liked for her houseboat, the *Mark Twain*. Her designs proved so popular, that in 1945, the Hadleys moved to Butchertown and opened a pottery business at 1570 Story Avenue. Her designs were exhibited at the Museum for Modern Art, the Good Design Institute in Chicago, and in New York's America House in the 1940s and 1950s. Well-known designs include a whimsical blue horse and a cereal bowl with "All Gone" written on the bottom. Hadley Pottery still produces her designs at 1570 Story Avenue. (Both, courtesy of John Beckman.)

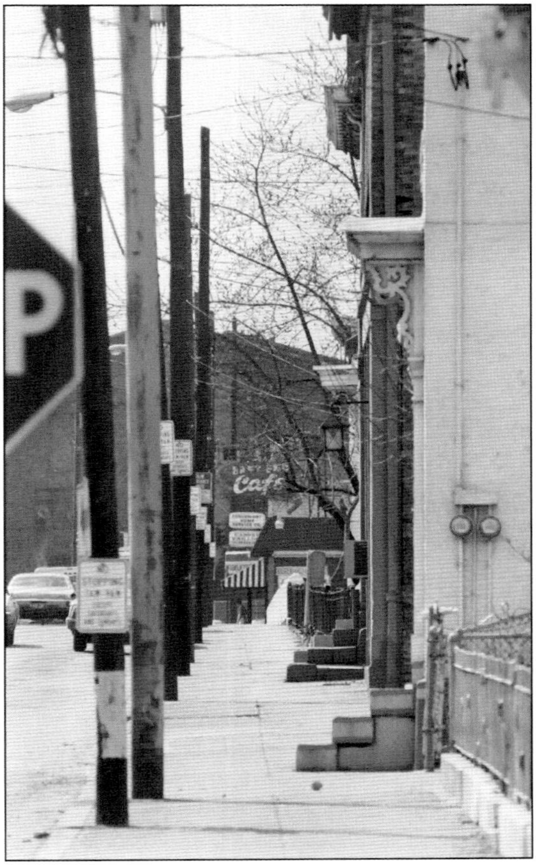

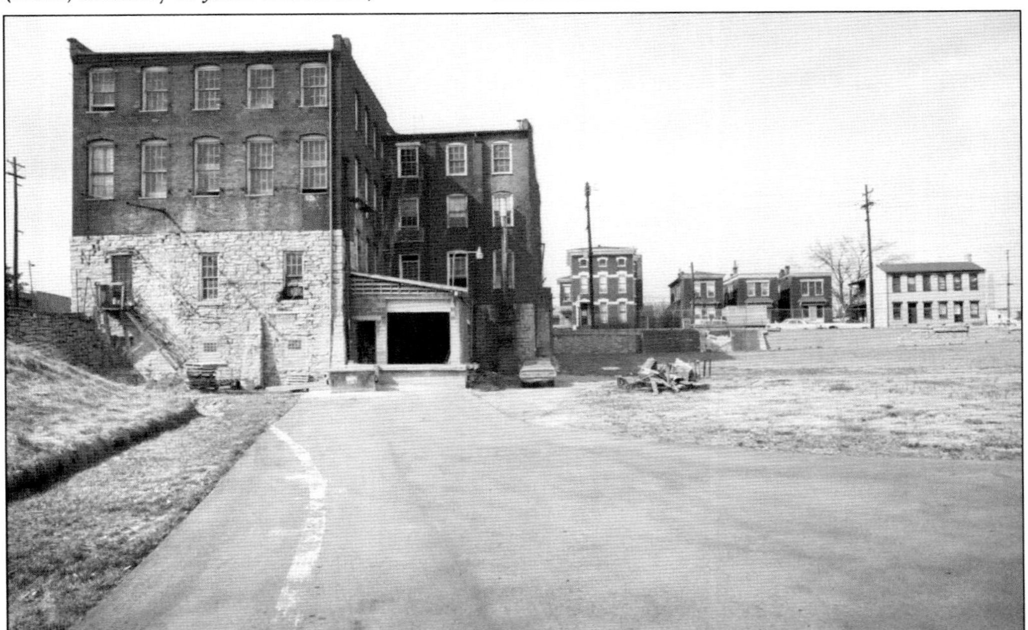

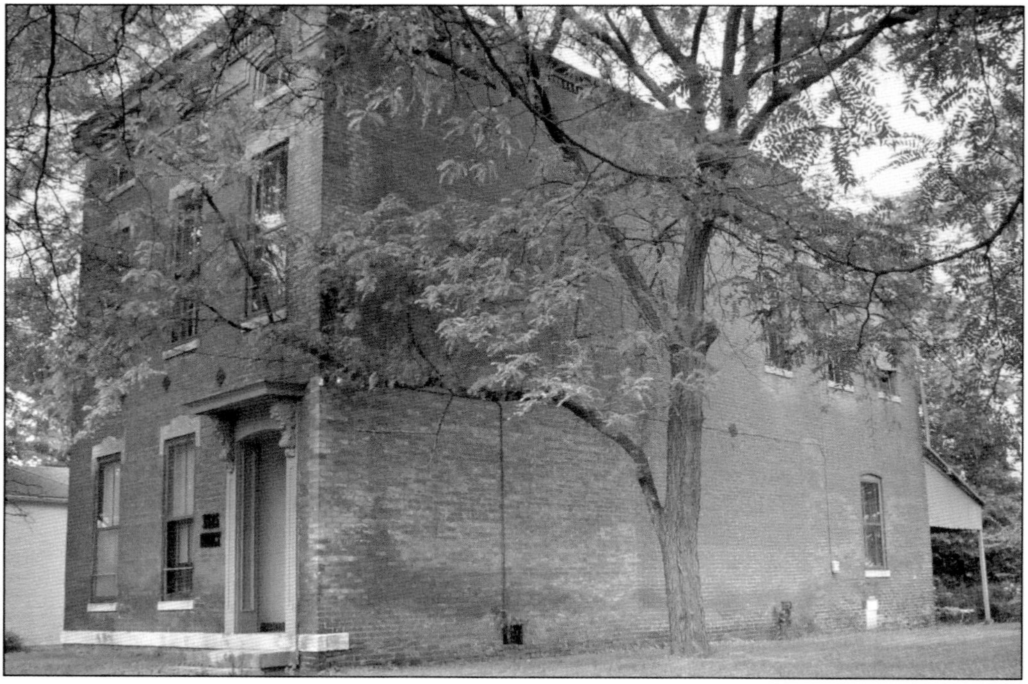

This fine two-story brick residence on Quincy Street may well have been the home of a local butcher. During the late 1800s, butchers operated in the rear and north side of Quincy Street with blood flowing to Beargrass Creek, which earned the nickname the "stinking mile," as it was little more than an open sewer. The butchers located on Quincy Streets between Adams and Webster Streets were Sam Hertel, John Beck, Jacob Koch, Ed Pfaffinger, Edwin Koch, Jake Henzel, George Koch Jr., John Koch, and George Koch Sr. (Courtesy of author's collection.)

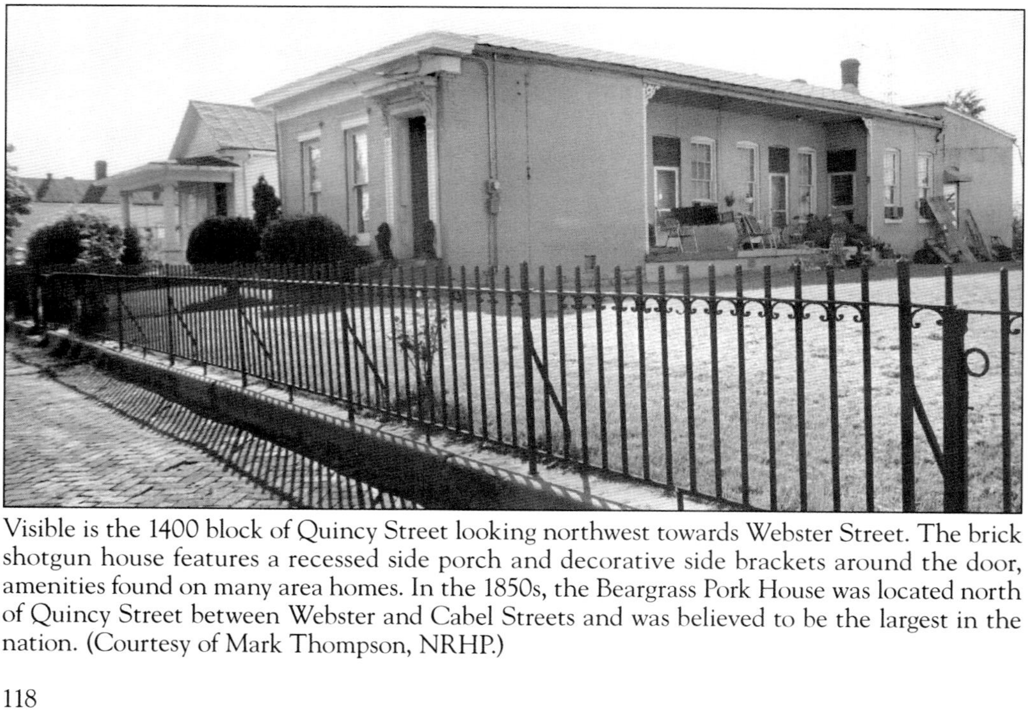

Visible is the 1400 block of Quincy Street looking northwest towards Webster Street. The brick shotgun house features a recessed side porch and decorative side brackets around the door, amenities found on many area homes. In the 1850s, the Beargrass Pork House was located north of Quincy Street between Webster and Cabel Streets and was believed to be the largest in the nation. (Courtesy of Mark Thompson, NRHP.)

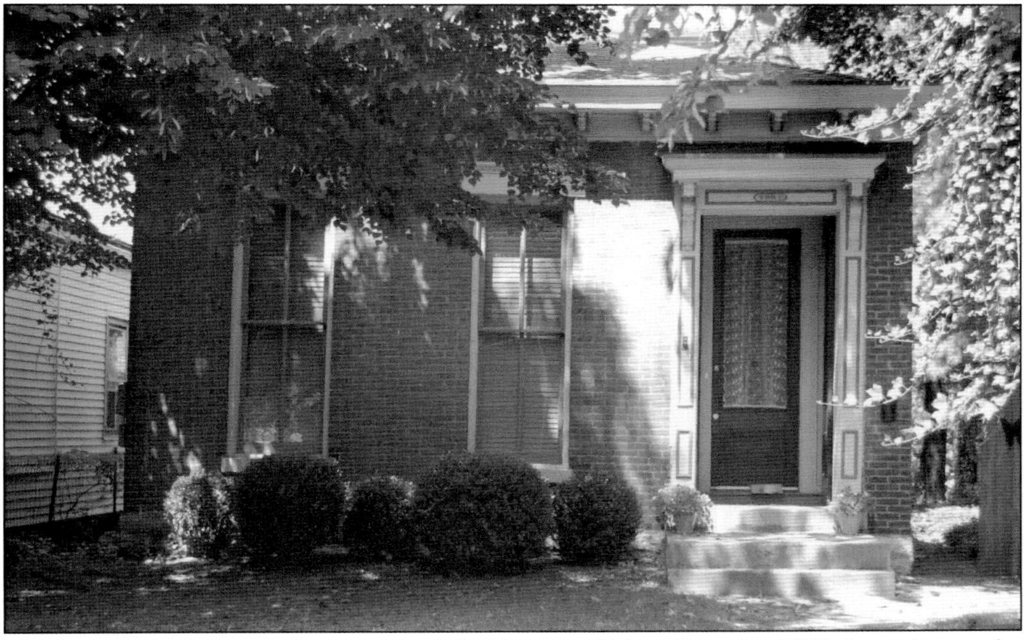

This home at 1411 Quincy Street was built by Henry and Mary Hensel in 1876. According to the research of Christine and James Romesburg, the Hensels lived there until their deaths in 1945 (one week apart) at the ages of 87 and 88. Henry worked as a driver for the firehouse on East Washington Street. (Courtesy of author's collection.)

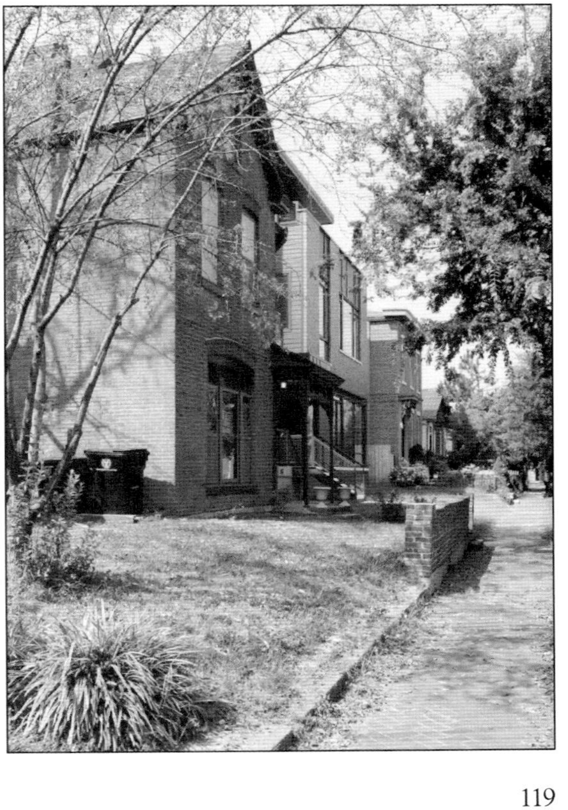

This is an example of how good design and sensitivity to the surrounding environment can make a modern home blend in with its historic counterparts. These condominiums on Franklin Street were built with the same setbacks, width, and height, and similar bricks as surrounding homes, thus seamlessly blending in with the neighborhood's character. (Courtesy of author's collection.)

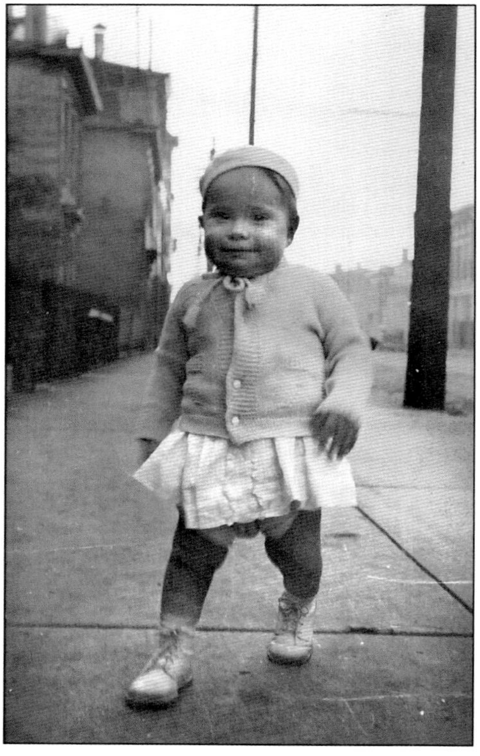

Marilyn Liebert is walking along Story Avenue in the 1920s. (Courtesy of the Kimpflein family.)

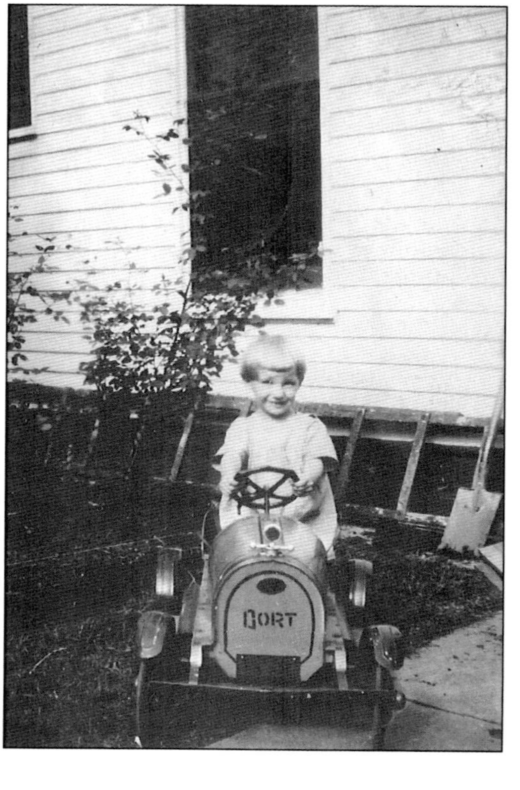

Bernice Wiggins is playing in front of her house in a metal push car in the 1920s. (Courtesy of the Kimpflein family.)

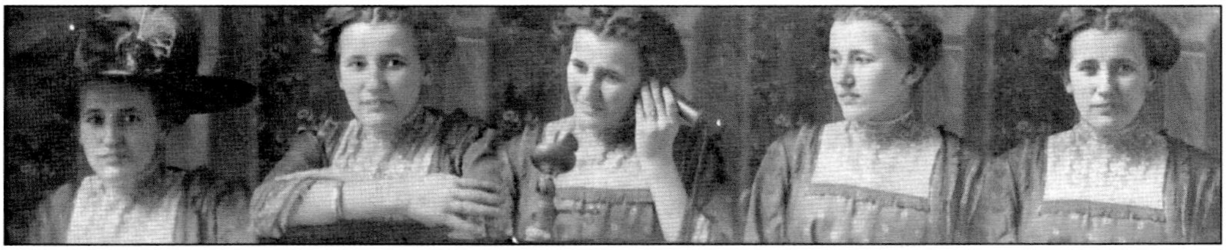

A series of five small pictures of Elizabeth Preher McClain, a Kimpflein family member, are seen here, showing her posing with a telephone handset. (Courtesy of the Kimpflein family.)

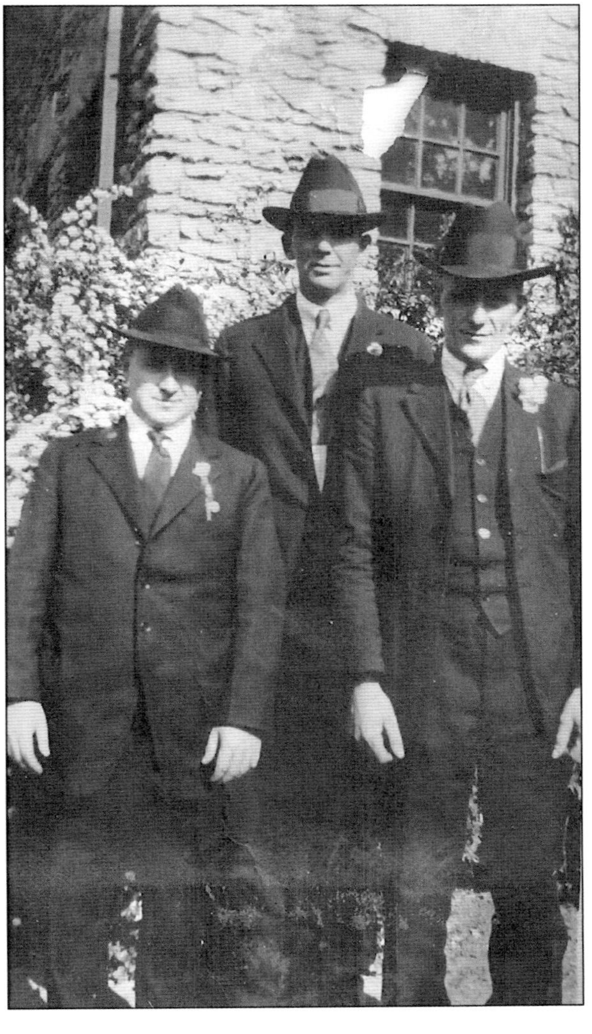

Members of the Kimpflein family, from left to right, Willy, Joe, and Zack, pose before an event in the early 1930s. (Courtesy of the Kimpflein family.)

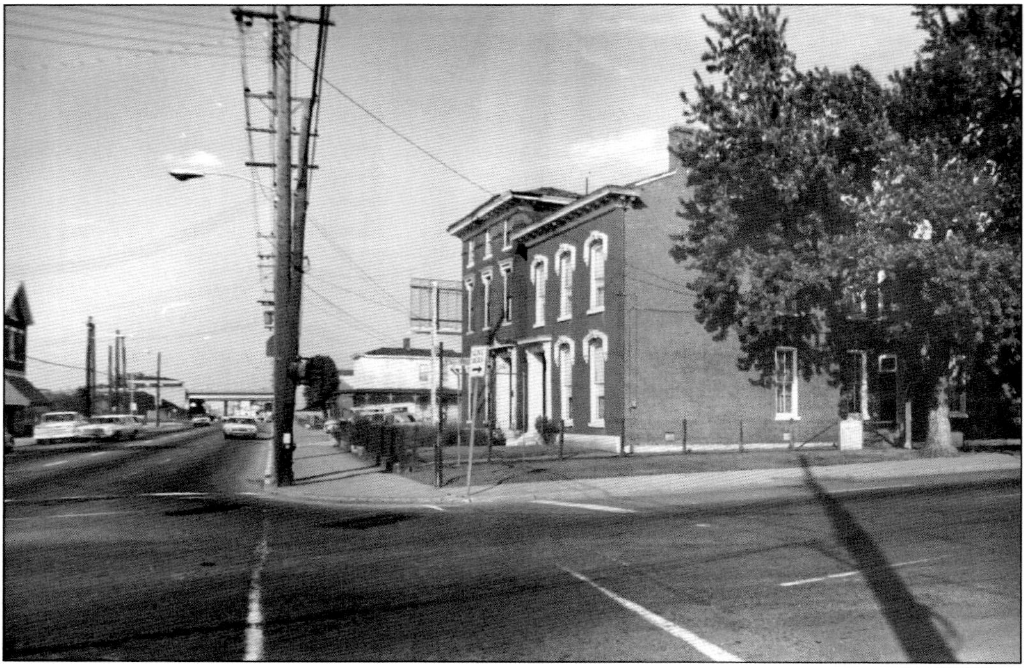

This view looks east on Story Avenue from the intersection of Adams Street. Interstate 64 can be seen in the background, the construction of which called for the demolition of many homes on the north side of Story Avenue. (Courtesy of Mark Thompson, NRHP.)

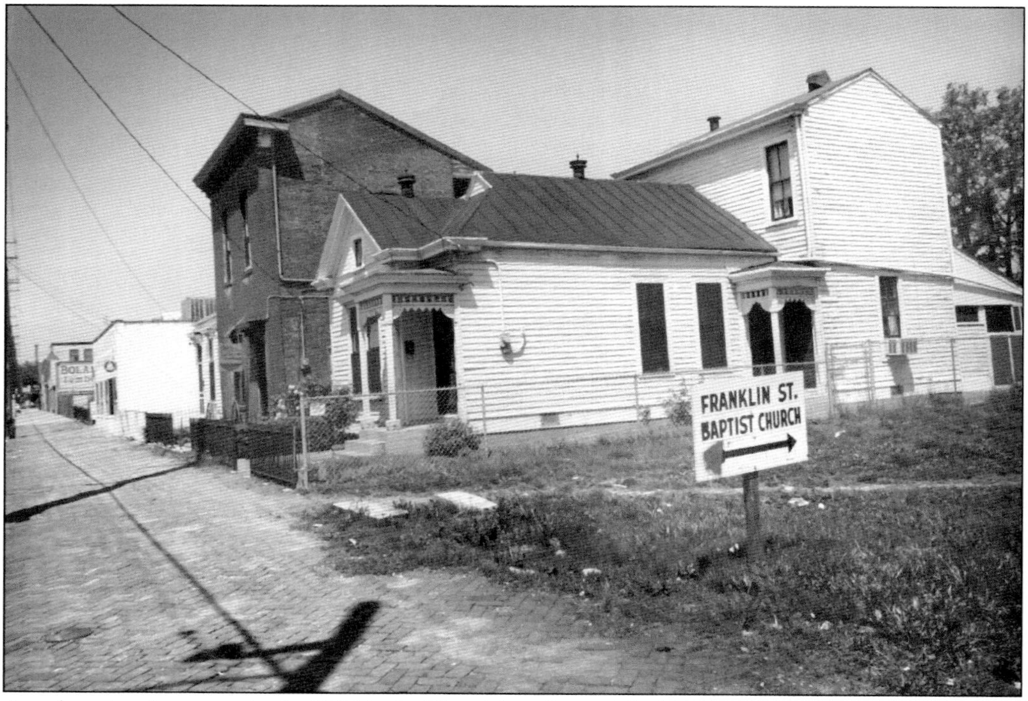

Another view faces west in the 900 block of East Main Street. The home in the foreground is a modified shotgun house with a built out two-story back. (Courtesy of Mark Thompson, NRHP.)

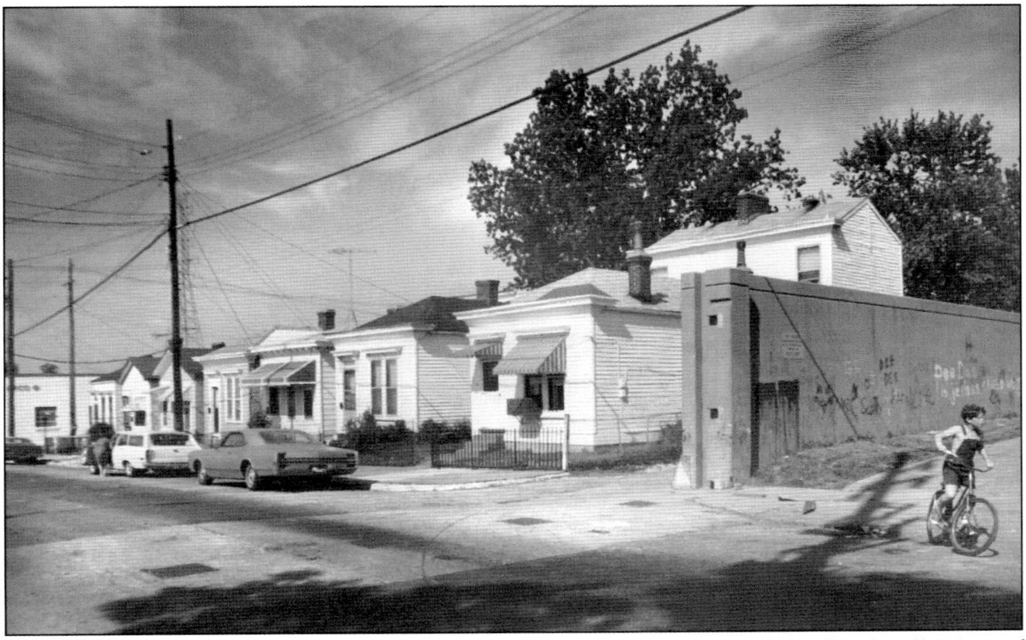

This picture looks north on the 100 block of Campbell Street north of the flood wall. Most of these homes have been demolished, and the remaining are deteriorating from years of neglect. This shows the relatively narrow lots in Butchertown, with small front and backyards. (Courtesy of Mark Thompson, NRHP.)

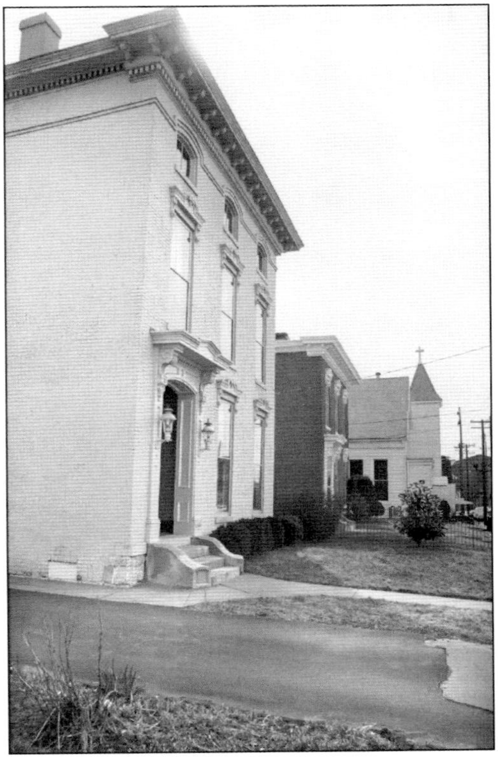

Looking west along the 1600 block of Story Avenue, Mary Alice Hadley's home is seen on the far left. The first year they moved to Story Avenue, the Hadleys threw a Halloween party for the neighborhood kids, with spiced apple cider, apple bobbing, and ceramic pieces from Hadley pottery as prizes. That year, Marilyn Rueff won first prize for the best costume. (Courtesy of John Beckman.)

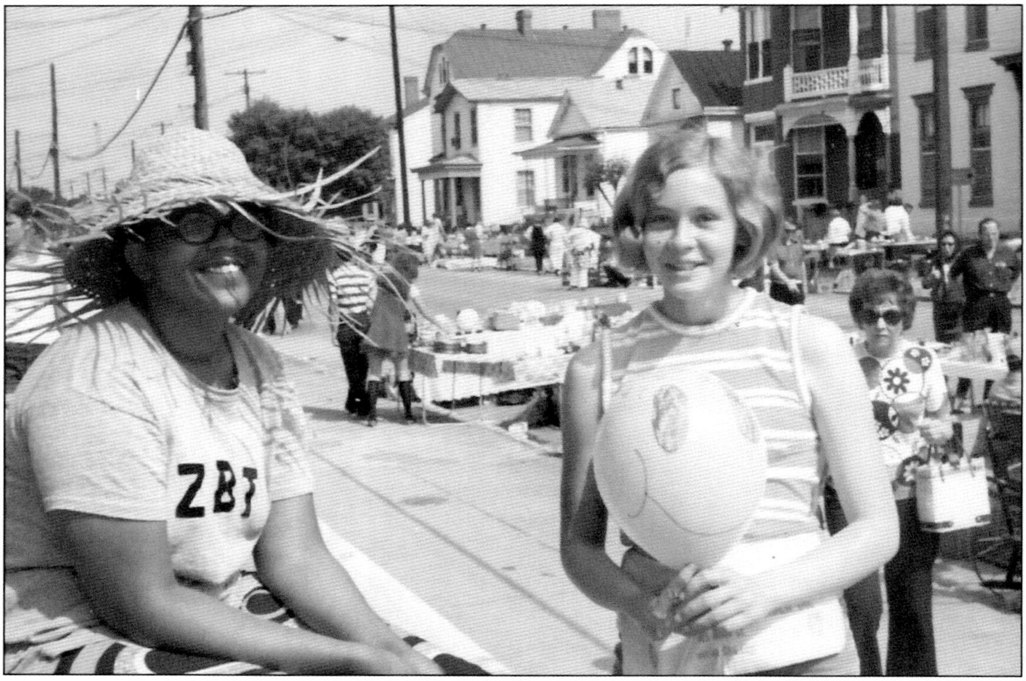

Here is a flea market in the 800 block of Washington Street around 1975, with Anne Stoke on the right. (Courtesy of Ethel and Ott Stoke.)

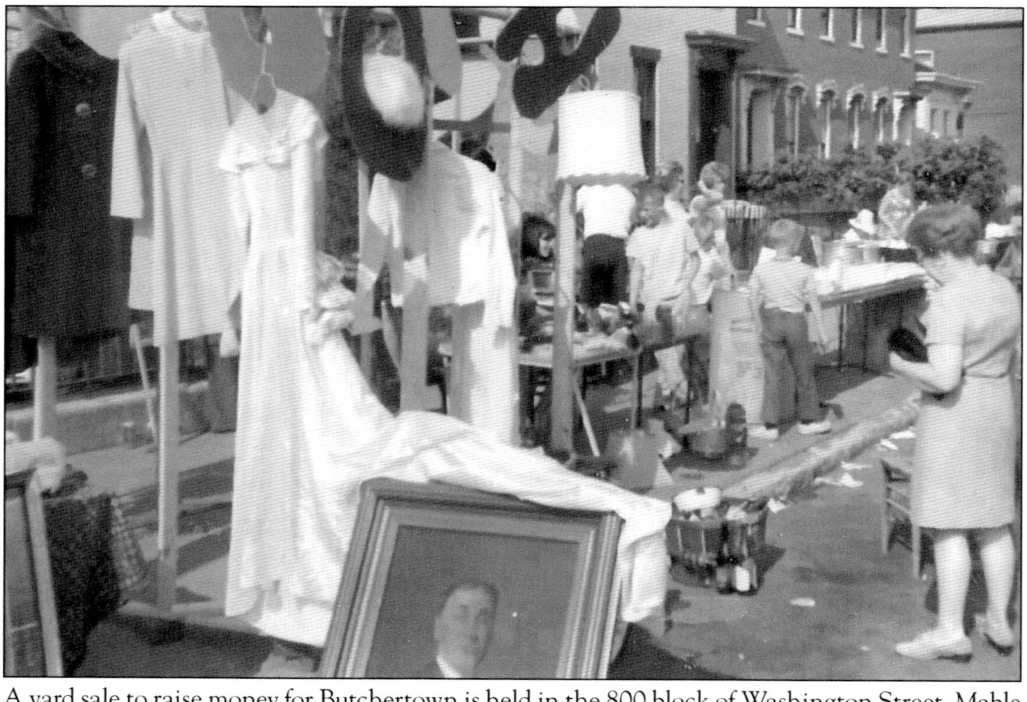

A yard sale to raise money for Butchertown is held in the 800 block of Washington Street. Mable Davidson Mills is on the right. The booth with the portrait in front is located in front of 825 East Washington Street. (Courtesy of Leslie Tichenor.)

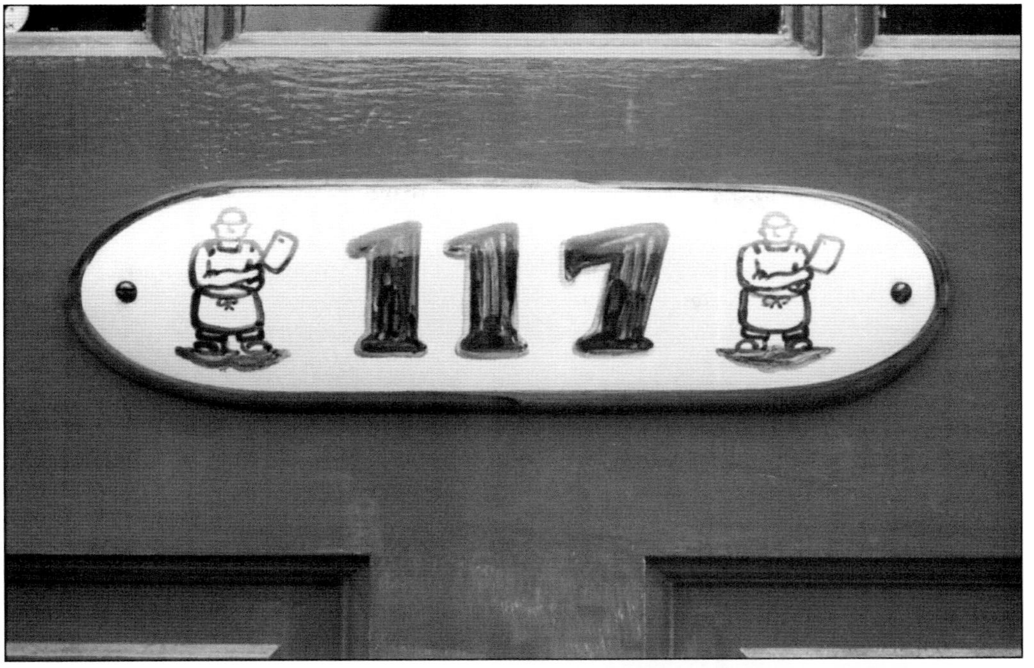

The caricature of the butcher was created by a member of the Louisville Metropolitan Planning Commission and was used as the logo for Butchertown, Inc. Several residents in Butchertown had the logo made into doorplates at Hadley Pottery. (Courtesy of John Beckman.)

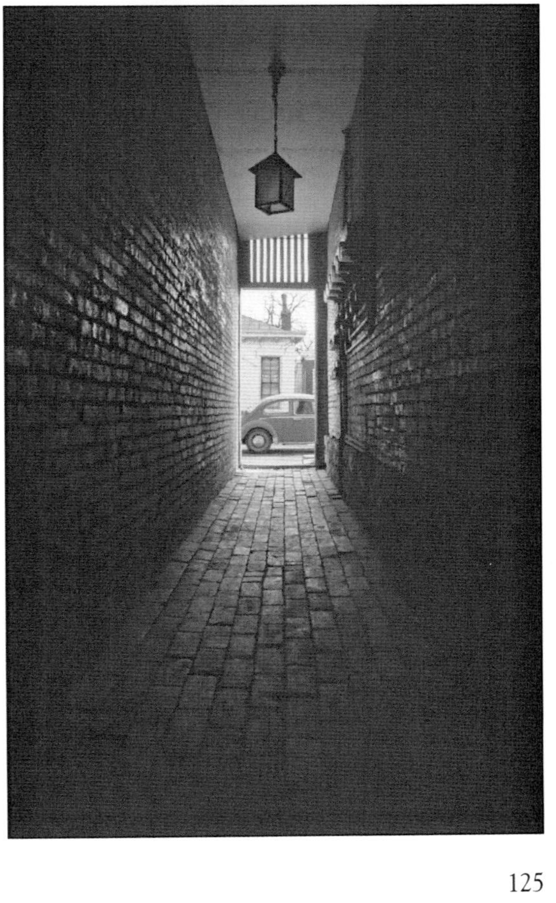

Here is an interesting passageway between two houses in the 1600 block of Story Avenue. (Courtesy of John Beckman.)

Bibliography

Butchertown. Louisville, KY: Louisville and Jefferson County Planning Commission.

Butchertown of Yesterday. Louisville, KY: Pohlkamp, Rogers Church Goods Company, 1946.

"Centennial Anniversary, St. Joseph's Parish." Louisville, KY: 1966.

Cullinane, John and Margaret Thomas. "Butchertown." The *Courier Journal*. May 18, 1974.

Ellis, Lana. "Louisville's Butchertown." The *Courier Journal and Times Magazine*. December 9, 1973.

Louisville Breweries: A History of the Brewing Industry in Louisville, Kentucky, New Albany, and Jeffersonville, Indiana. Guetig, Peter R. and Conrad D. Selle. Mark Skaggs Press, 1995.

National Register of Historic Places Nomination Form for the Butchertown Neighborhood, 1975

Rogers, John C. "The Story of Louisville Neighborhoods." The *Courier Journal and Louisville Times Company*. May 1955

Sladen, Gaby. "Cattle Baron Road Perks Up." The *Courier Journal*. April 1, 1962.

The Encyclopedia of Louisville. Lexington: The University Press of Kentucky, 2001.

The First 75 Years of St. Joseph's Parish. Louisville, 1941.

The Shotgun House. Preservation Alliance, 1980.

Vatter, Jonnie. "Butchertown Life Style." *Louisville Magazine*, 1972.

Yater, George. *Two Hundred Years at the Falls of the Ohio: History of Louisville and Jefferson County*. Pinaire Lithographing Corporation, 1987.

INDEX